enVision® Mathematics

Common Core

Volume 2 Topics 5–8

Authors

Robert Q. Berry, III
Professor of Mathematics Education, Department of Curriculum, Instruction and Special Education, University of Virginia, Charlottesville, Virginia

Zachary Champagne
Assistant in Research Florida Center for Research in Science, Technology, Engineering, and Mathematics (FCR-STEM) Jacksonville, Florida

Eric Milou
Professor of Mathematics Rowan University, Glassboro, New Jersey

Jane F. Schielack
Professor Emerita Department of Mathematics Texas A&M University, College Station, Texas

Jonathan A. Wray
Mathematics Supervisor, Howard County Public Schools, Ellicott City, Maryland

Randall I. Charles
Professor Emeritus Department of Mathematics San Jose State University San Jose, California

Francis (Skip) Fennell
Professor Emeritus of Education and Graduate and Professional Studies, McDaniel College Westminster, Maryland

SAVVAS
LEARNING COMPANY

Mathematician Reviewers

Gary Lippman, Ph.D.
Professor Emeritus
Mathematics and Computer Science
California State University, East Bay
Hayward, California

Karen Edwards, Ph.D.
Mathematics Lecturer
Arlington, MA

Additional Reviewers

Kristine Peterfeso
Teacher Middle School Math,
Palm Beach County School District

Tamala Ferguson
Math Curriculum Coach,
School District of Osceola County

Melissa Nelson
Math Coach and Assessment
Coordinator, St. Lucie Public Schools

ISBN-13: 978-1-4182-6950-0
ISBN-10: 1-4182-6950-6

CONTENTS

TOPICS

DIGITAL RESOURCES

Go Online

INTERACTIVE STUDENT EDITION
Access online or offline

VISUAL LEARNING
Interact with visual learning animations

ACTIVITY
Use with *Solve & Discuss It, Explore It,* and *Explain It* activities and Examples

VIDEOS
Watch clips to support *3-Act Mathematical Modeling* Lessons and *enVision*® STEM Projects

PRACTICE
Practice what you've learned and get immediate feedback

TUTORIALS
Get help from *Virtual Nerd* any time you need it

MATH TOOLS
Explore math with digital tools

GAMES
Play math games to help you learn

KEY CONCEPT
Review important lesson content

GLOSSARY
Read and listen to English and Spanish definitions

ASSESSMENT
Show what you've learned

realize™
Everything you need for math anytime, anywhere.

TOPIC 5

Solve Problems Using Equations and Inequalities

TOPIC 6 Use Sampling to Draw Inferences About Populations

TOPIC 7 Probability

TOPIC 8

Solve Problems Involving Geometry

Standards for Mathematical Content

RATIOS AND PROPORTIONAL RELATIONSHIPS

7.RP.A Analyze proportional relationships and use them to solve real-world and mathematical problems.

1. Compute unit rates associated with ratios of fractions, including ratios of lengths, areas and other quantities measured in like or different units. *For example, if a person walks $\frac{1}{2}$ mile in each $\frac{1}{4}$ hour, compute the unit rate as the complex fraction $\frac{\frac{1}{2}}{\frac{1}{4}}$ miles per hour, equivalently 2 miles per hour.*

2. Recognize and represent proportional relationships between quantities.

   a. Decide whether two quantities are in a proportional relationship, e.g., by testing for equivalent ratios in a table or graphing on a coordinate plane and observing whether the graph is a straight line through the origin.

   b. Identify the constant of proportionality (unit rate) in tables, graphs, equations, diagrams, and verbal descriptions of proportional relationships.

   c. Represent proportional relationships by equations. *For example, if total cost t is proportional to the number n of items purchased at a constant price p, the relationship between the total cost and the number of items can be expressed as $t = pn$.*

   d. Explain what a point (*x, y*) on the graph of a proportional relationship means in terms of the situation, with special attention to the points (0, 0) and (1, *r*) where *r* is the unit rate.

3. Use proportional relationships to solve multistep ratio and percent problems. *Examples: simple interest, tax, markups and markdowns, gratuities and commissions, fees, percent increase and decrease, percent error.*

THE NUMBER SYSTEM

7.NS.A Apply and extend previous understandings of operations with fractions to add, subtract, multiply, and divide rational numbers.

1. Apply and extend previous understandings of addition and subtraction to add and subtract rational numbers; represent addition and subtraction on a horizontal or vertical number line diagram.

   a. Describe situations in which opposite quantities combine to make 0. *For example, a hydrogen atom has 0 charge because its two constituents are oppositely charged.*

   b. Understand *p + q* as the number located a distance |*q*| from *p*, in the positive or negative direction depending on whether *q* is positive or negative. Show that a number and its opposite have a sum of 0 (are additive inverses). Interpret sums of rational numbers by describing real-world contexts.

   c. Understand subtraction of rational numbers as adding the additive inverse, $p - q = p + (-q)$. Show that the distance between two rational numbers on the number line is the absolute value of their difference, and apply this principle in real-world contexts.

   d. Apply properties of operations as strategies to add and subtract rational numbers.

Standards for Mathematical Content

2. Apply and extend previous understandings of multiplication and division and of fractions to multiply and divide rational numbers.

   a. Understand that multiplication is extended from fractions to rational numbers by requiring that operations continue to satisfy the properties of operations, particularly the distributive property, leading to products such as $(-1)(-1) = 1$ and the rules for multiplying signed numbers. Interpret products of rational numbers by describing real-world contexts.

   b. Understand that integers can be divided, provided that the divisor is not zero, and every quotient of integers (with non-zero divisor) is a rational number. If p and q are integers, then $-\left(\frac{p}{q}\right) = \frac{(-p)}{q} = \frac{p}{(-q)}$. Interpret quotients of rational numbers by describing real-world contexts.

   c. Apply properties of operations as strategies to multiply and divide rational numbers.

   d. Convert a rational number to a decimal using long division; know that the decimal form of a rational number terminates in 0s or eventually repeats.

3. Solve real-world and mathematical problems involving the four operations with rational numbers.[1]

EXPRESSIONS AND EQUATIONS

7.EE.A Use properties of operations to generate equivalent expressions.

1. Apply properties of operations as strategies to add, subtract, factor, and expand linear expressions with rational coefficients.

2. Understand that rewriting an expression in different forms in a problem context can shed light on the problem and how the quantities in it are related. *For example, $a + 0.05a = 1.05a$ means that "increase by 5%" is the same as "multiply by 1.05."*

7.EE.B Solve real-life and mathematical problems using numerical and algebraic expressions and equations.

3. Solve multi-step real-life and mathematical problems posed with positive and negative rational numbers in any form (whole numbers, fractions, and decimals), using tools strategically. Apply properties of operations to calculate with numbers in any form; convert between forms as appropriate; and assess the reasonableness of answers using mental computation and estimation strategies. *For example: If a woman making $25 an hour gets a 10% raise, she will make an additional $\frac{1}{10}$ of her salary an hour, or $2.50, for a new salary of $27.50. If you want to place a towel bar $9\frac{3}{4}$ inches long in the center of a door that is $27\frac{1}{2}$ inches wide, you will need to place the bar about 9 inches from each edge; this estimate can be used as a check on the exact computation.*

4. Use variables to represent quantities in a real-world or mathematical problem, and construct simple equations and inequalities to solve problems by reasoning about the quantities.

   a. Solve word problems leading to equations of the form $px + q = r$ and $p(x + q) = r$, where p, q, and r are specific rational numbers. Solve equations of these forms fluently. Compare an algebraic solution to an arithmetic solution, identifying the sequence of the operations used in each approach. *For example, the perimeter of a rectangle is 54 cm. Its length is 6 cm. What is its width?*

   b. Solve word problems leading to inequalities of the form $px + q > r$ or $px + q < r$, where p, q, and r are specific rational numbers. Graph the solution set of the inequality and interpret it in the context of the problem. *For example: As a salesperson, you are paid $50 per week plus $3 per sale. This week you want your pay to be at least $100. Write an inequality for the number of sales you need to make, and describe the solutions.*

Standards for Mathematical Content

GEOMETRY

7.G.A **Draw, construct, and describe geometrical figures and describe the relationships between them.**

1. Solve problems involving scale drawings of geometric figures, including computing actual lengths and areas from a scale drawing and reproducing a scale drawing at a different scale.

2. Draw (freehand, with ruler and protractor, and with technology) geometric shapes with given conditions. Focus on constructing triangles from three measures of angles or sides, noticing when the conditions determine a unique triangle, more than one triangle, or no triangle.

3. Describe the two-dimensional figures that result from slicing three-dimensional figures, as in plane sections of right rectangular prisms and right rectangular pyramids.

7.G.B **Solve real-life and mathematical problems involving angle measure, area, surface area, and volume.**

4. Know the formulas for the area and circumference of a circle and use them to solve problems; give an informal derivation of the relationship between the circumference and area of a circle.

5. Use facts about supplementary, complementary, vertical, and adjacent angles in a multi-step problem to write and solve simple equations for an unknown angle in a figure.

6. Solve real-world and mathematical problems involving area, volume, and surface area of two- and three-dimensional objects composed of triangles, quadrilaterals, polygons, cubes, and right prisms.

STATISTICS AND PROBABILITY

7.SP.A **Use random sampling to draw inferences about a population.**

1. Understand that statistics can be used to gain information about a population by examining a sample of the population; generalizations about a population from a sample are valid only if the sample is representative of that population. Understand that random sampling tends to produce representative samples and support valid inferences.

2. Use data from a random sample to draw inferences about a population with an unknown characteristic of interest. Generate multiple samples (or simulated samples) of the same size to gauge the variation in estimates or predictions. *For example, estimate the mean word length in a book by randomly sampling words from the book; predict the winner of a school election based on randomly sampled survey data. Gauge how far off the estimate or prediction might be.*

7.SP.B **Draw informal comparative inferences about two populations.**

3. Informally assess the degree of visual overlap of two numerical data distributions with similar variabilities, measuring the difference between the centers by expressing it as a multiple of a measure of variability. *For example, the mean height of players on the basketball team is 10 cm greater than the mean height of players on the soccer team, about twice the variability (mean absolute deviation) on either team; on a dot plot, the separation between the two distributions of heights is noticeable.*

4. Use measures of center and measures of variability for numerical data from random samples to draw informal comparative inferences about two populations. *For example, decide whether the words in a chapter of a seventh-grade science book are generally longer than the words in a chapter of a fourth-grade science book.*

Standards for Mathematical Content

7.SP.C Investigate chance processes and develop, use, and evaluate probability models.

5. Understand that the probability of a chance event is a number between 0 and 1 that expresses the likelihood of the event occurring. Larger numbers indicate greater likelihood. A probability near 0 indicates an unlikely event, a probability around $\frac{1}{2}$ indicates an event that is neither unlikely nor likely, and a probability near 1 indicates a likely event.

6. Approximate the probability of a chance event by collecting data on the chance process that produces it and observing its long-run relative frequency, and predict the approximate relative frequency given the probability. *For example, when rolling a number cube 600 times, predict that a 3 or 6 would be rolled roughly 200 times, but probably not exactly 200 times.*

7. Develop a probability model and use it to find probabilities of events. Compare probabilities from a model to observed frequencies; if the agreement is not good, explain possible sources of the discrepancy.

   a. Develop a uniform probability model by assigning equal probability to all outcomes, and use the model to determine probabilities of events. *For example, if a student is selected at random from a class, find the probability that Jane will be selected and the probability that a girl will be selected.*

   b. Develop a probability model (which may not be uniform) by observing frequencies in data generated from a chance process. *For example, find the approximate probability that a spinning penny will land heads up or that a tossed paper cup will land open-end down. Do the outcomes for the spinning penny appear to be equally likely based on the observed frequencies?*

8. Find probabilities of compound events using organized lists, tables, tree diagrams, and simulation.

   a. Understand that, just as with simple events, the probability of a compound event is the fraction of outcomes in the sample space for which the compound event occurs.

   b. Represent sample spaces for compound events using methods such as organized lists, tables and tree diagrams. For an event described in everyday language (e.g., "rolling double sixes"), identify the outcomes in the sample space which compose the event.

   c. Design and use a simulation to generate frequencies for compound events. *For example, use random digits as a simulation tool to approximate the answer to the question: If 40% of donors have type A blood, what is the probability that it will take at least 4 donors to find one with type A blood?*

---

[1]Computations with rational numbers extend the rules for manipulating fractions to complex fractions.

Math Practices and Problem Solving Handbook

The **Math Practices and Problem Solving Handbook** is available online.

MP.1 Make sense of problems and persevere in solving them.

MP.2 Reason abstractly and quantitatively.

MP.3 Construct viable arguments and critique the reasoning of others.

MP.4 Model with mathematics.

MP.5 Use appropriate tools strategically.

MP.6 Attend to precision.

MP.7 Look for and make use of structure.

MP.8 Look for and express regularity in repeated reasoning.

Jordan helps his uncle set up for an event. Jordan's uncle drew a diagram to show Jordan how he wants the tables set up. Jordan needs to set up enough tables for 42 guests. How can Jordan figure out how many tables to set up?

Enough tables for 42 Guests

Can I see a pattern or structure in the problem or solution strategy?
I can see that each end table has 5 seats and each middle table has 4 seats. Each additional table increases the number of seats by 4.

How can I use the pattern or structure I see to help me solve the problem?
I can write an equation that includes a term for the two end tables and a term for the middle tables.

Do I notice any repeated calculations or steps? Each additional table adds 4 seats.

Are there general methods that I can use to solve the problem? I can multiply the number of middle tables by 4 and then add the seats on the two end tables.

Other questions to consider:
• Are there attributes in common that help me?
• Can I see the expression or equation as a single object? Or as a composition of several objects?

Other questions to consider:
• What can I generalize from one problem to another?
• Can I derive an equation from a series of data points?
• How reasonable are the results that I am getting?

Math Practices and Problem Solving Handbook

Common Core State Standards
Standards for Mathematical Practice

MP.1 ▸ Make sense of problems and persevere in solving them.

Mathematically proficient students:
- can explain the meaning of a problem
- look for entry points to begin solving a problem
- analyze givens, constraints, relationships, and goals
- make conjectures about the solution
- plan a solution pathway
- think of similar problems, and try simpler forms of the problem
- evaluate their progress toward a solution and change pathways if necessary
- can explain similarities and differences between different representations
- check their solutions to problems.

MP.2 ▸ Reason abstractly and quantitatively.

Mathematically proficient students:
- make sense of quantities and their relationships in problem situations:
  - They *decontextualize*—create a coherent representation of a problem situation using numbers, variables, and symbols; and
  - They *contextualize* – attend to the meaning of numbers, variables, and symbols in the problem situation
- know and use different properties of operations to solve problems.

MP.3 ▸ Construct viable arguments and critique the reasoning of others.

Mathematically proficient students:
- use definitions and problem solutions when constructing arguments
- make conjectures about the solutions to problems
- build a logical progression of statements to support their conjectures and justify their conclusions
- analyze situations and recognize and use counterexamples
- reason inductively about data, making plausible arguments that take into account the context from which the data arose
- listen or read the arguments of others, and decide whether they make sense
- respond to the arguments of others
- compare the effectiveness of two plausible arguments
- distinguish correct logic or reasoning from flawed, and—if there is a flaw in an argument—explain what it is
- ask useful questions to clarify or improve arguments of others.

MP.4 Model with mathematics.

Mathematically proficient students:

- can develop a representation—drawing, diagram, table, graph, expression, equation–to model a problem situation
- make assumptions and approximations to simplify a complicated situation
- identify important quantities in a practical situation and map their relationships using a range of tools
- analyze relationships mathematically to draw conclusions
- interpret mathematical results in the context of the situation and propose improvements to the model as needed.

MP.5 Use appropriate tools strategically.

Mathematically proficient students:

- consider appropriate tools when solving a mathematical problem
- make sound decisions about when each of these tools might be helpful
- identify relevant mathematical resources, and use them to pose or solve problems
- use tools and technology to explore and deepen their understanding of concepts.

MP.6 Attend to precision.

Mathematically proficient students:

- communicate precisely to others
- use clear definitions in discussions with others and in their own reasoning
- state the meaning of the symbols they use
- specify units of measure, and label axes to clarify their correspondence with quantities in a problem
- calculate accurately and efficiently
- express numerical answers with a degree of precision appropriate for the problem context.

MP.7 Look for and make use of structure.

Mathematically proficient students:

- look closely at a problem situation to identify a pattern or structure
- can step back from a solution pathway and shift perspective
- can see complex representations, such as some algebraic expressions, as single objects or as being composed of several objects.

MP.8 Look for and express regularity in repeated reasoning.

Mathematically proficient students:

- notice if calculations are repeated, and look both for general methods and for shortcuts
- maintain oversight of the process as they work to solve a problem, while also attending to the details
- continually evaluate the reasonableness of their intermediate results.

TOPIC 5

SOLVE PROBLEMS USING EQUATIONS AND INEQUALITIES

? Topic Essential Question

How can you solve real-world and mathematical problems with numerical and algebraic equations and inequalities?

Topic Overview

5-1 Write Two-Step Equations

5-2 Solve Two-Step Equations

5-3 Solve Equations Using the Distributive Property

5-4 Solve Inequalities Using Addition or Subtraction

5-5 Solve Inequalities Using Multiplication or Division

3-Act Mathematical Modeling: Digital Downloads

5-6 Solve Two-Step Inequalities

5-7 Solve Multi-Step Inequalities

Topic Vocabulary

• isolate the variable

Lesson Digital Resources

 **INTERACTIVE STUDENT EDITION**
Access online or offline.

 VISUAL LEARNING ANIMATION
Interact with visual learning animations.

 ACTIVITY Use with *Solve & Discuss It, Explore*
and *Explain It* activities, and to explore Exampl

 VIDEOS Watch clips to support *3-Act Mathematical Modeling Lessons* and *STEM Pr*

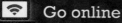 Go online

Digital
Downloads

▶ Digital Downloads

Experts estimate that almost a billion dollars' worth of gift cards go unused every year! However, gift cards may still be your preference. They prevent waste, and you can choose the exact items you want. Plus, if you know you won't use the gift card, it's easy to regift it to someone who can use it.

There are a number of clever ways to get the most out of your gift card. Think about this during the 3-Act Mathematical Modeling lesson.

$25
Gift Card

PRACTICE Practice what you've learned.

TUTORIALS Get help from *Virtual Nerd*, right when you need it.

MATH TOOLS Explore math with digital tools.

GAMES Play Math Games to help you learn.

KEY CONCEPT Review important lesson content.

GLOSSARY Read and listen to English/Spanish definitions.

ASSESSMENT Show what you've learned.

Did You Know?

Total world population in 2015
7.4 billion

According to the World Health Organization, **2.6 billion people have gained access to safe drinking water** since 1990.

A 2015 WHO report states that **663 million people do not have access to clean, safe water. 8 out of 10 of these people live in rural areas.**

80% of all illness and death in developing countries is a result of water-related disease.

Water filtration systems purify water by removing contaminates. In developing countries, water filters need to be affordable and easy to use.

Three common water filters used in developing countries are:

Ceramic Water Filters

Sand Filters

Hollow Fiber Microfiltration System

Your Task: Water is Life!

You have water to drink, to use to brush your teeth, and to bathe. You and your classmates will research the need for safe, clean water in developing countries. Based on your research, you will determine the type, size, and cost of a water filtration system needed to provide clean, safe water to a community. You will also develop a plan to raise money to purchase the needed filtration system.

Review What You Know!

Vocabulary

Choose the best term from the box to complete each definition.

inverse relationship
like terms
inequality
properties of equality

1. A statement that contains the symbols $<$, $>$, $\leq$, or $\geq$ is called a(n)

   _____ .

2. Properties that state that performing the same operation on both sides of

   an equation will keep the equation true are called _____ .

3. Addition and subtraction have a(n) _____ because they can "undo" each other.

4. Terms that have the same variable are called _____ .

Properties of Equality

Use properties to solve each equation for *x*.

5. $x + 9.8 = 14.2$

6. $14x = 91$

7. $\frac{1}{3}x = 24$

Like Terms

Combine like terms in each expression.

8. $\frac{1}{4}k + \frac{1}{4}m - \frac{2}{3}k + \frac{5}{9}m$

9. $-4b + 2w + (-4b) + 8w$

10. $6 - 5z + 8 - 4z + 1$

Inequalities

11. Write an inequality that represents the situation: *A large box of golf balls has more than 12 balls*. Describe how your inequality represents the situation.

Language Development

Fill in the Venn diagram to compare and contrast equations and inequalities.

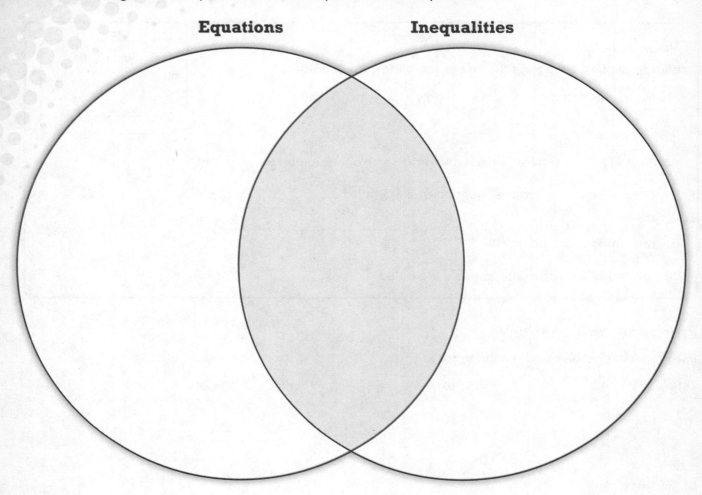

Equations   **Inequalities**

In the box below, draw pictures to represent the terms and phrases in the overlap section of your diagram.

PROJECT 5A

How many different ways could you sort a basket of vegetables?

PROJECT: COMPARING WITH A VENN DIAGRAM

PROJECT 5B

Which character would you be from your favorite play? Why?

PROJECT: WRITE A PLAY

PROJECT 5C

If you could live in another country, where would you live, and why?

PROJECT: EXCHANGE SOUVENIRS

PROJECT 5D

How would you prepare for being on a game show?

PROJECT: SOLVE RANDOMIZED EQUATIONS AND INEQUALITIES

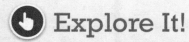 **Explore It!**

 ACTIVITY

Marley collects golf balls. His neighbor Tucker collects 3 more than twice as many golf balls as Marley.

Marley

Tucker

I can...
represent a problem with a two-step equation.

© **Common Core Content Standards**
7.EE.B.4
Mathematical Practices
MP.2, MP.4, MP.7

A. How can you use a table to represent the number of golf balls in Marley's collection, *m*, and the number of golf balls in Tucker's collection?

B. How can you use an algebraic expression to represent the number of golf balls in Tucker's collection?

Focus on math practices

Look for Relationships How do the terms of the expression you wrote in Part B relate to the values in the table?

Essential Question How does an equation show the relationship between variables and other quantities in a situation?

 VISUAL LEARNING   ASSESS

EXAMPLE 1 Write a Two-Step Equation to Represent a Situation

Scan for Multimedia

What equation can be used to represent the numbers of golf balls in Marley's and Tucker's collections?

Model with Math
How can an equation represent a given situation?

159 golf balls

Marley's Collection

Tucker's Collection

Tucker has 3 more than twice Marley's golf ball collection.

Use a bar diagram to represent the situation.

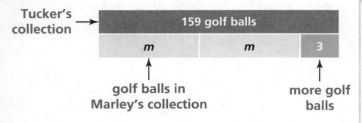

Tucker's collection → | 159 golf balls |
| m | m | 3 |

golf balls in Marley's collection

more golf balls

Use the bar diagram to write an equation.

| Tucker's collection | = | twice Marley's collection | + | more golf balls |
| 159 | = | 2m | + | 3 |

The equation $159 = 2m + 3$ can be used to represent Marley's and Tucker's golf ball collections.

✅ Try It!

Cole buys a new laptop for $335. He makes a down payment of $50 and pays the rest in 6 equal monthly payments, p. What equation represents the relationship between the cost of the laptop and Cole's payments?

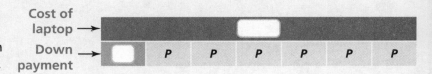

Cost of laptop →
Down payment →
P P P P P P

cost = [ ] + [ ] × monthly payment

[ ] = [ ] + [ ] × [ ]

[ ] = [ ]

Convince Me! Why are both multiplication and addition used in the equation that represents Cole's monthly payments?

EXAMPLE **2** Write More Two-Step Equations   ACTIVITY ASSESS

A baseball weighs 25.75 ounces less than a bat. Write an equation that represents the relationship between the weights of a baseball and a bat in terms of the weight of the box, *w*.

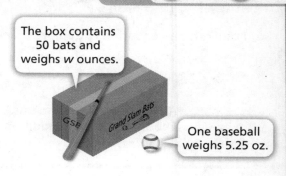

The box contains 50 bats and weighs *w* ounces.

One baseball weighs 5.25 oz.

weight of one baseball	=	weight of one bat	−	difference in weight
5.25	=	$\dfrac{\text{weight of box}}{\text{number of bats in box}}$	−	25.75
5.25	=	$\dfrac{w}{50}$	−	25.75

The equation $5.25 = \dfrac{w}{50} - 25.75$ can be used to represent the relationship between the weights of a baseball and a bat.

Try It!

Marcia and Tamara are running a race. Marcia has run 4 kilometers. Tamara has completed $\frac{3}{4}$ of the race and is 2.5 kilometers ahead of Marcia. Write an equation that represents the relationship between the distances each girl has run. Let *k* represent the total length of the race in kilometers.

EXAMPLE **3** **Interpret Quantities and Operations in Equations**

Claire bought 8 tickets for a total cost of $104. She had used a coupon code to get $3 off each ticket. Let *x* be the original cost of each ticket. Which of the following equations correctly represents the situation?

$3(x - 8) = 104$ ← Total cost

$3 discount times the difference of 8 tickets and the cost per ticket

$8x - 3 = 104$ ← Total cost

8 tickets times the cost per ticket minus a total discount of $3

$8(x - 3) = 104$ ← Total cost

8 tickets times the difference of the cost per ticket and $3.

The equation $8(x - 3) = 104$ represents this situation.

Try It!

At the mall, Claire buys a hat that is 60% off and socks that are reduced to $5.49. She spends a total of $9.49. Let *x* represent the cost of the hat. Which of the following equations correctly represents Claire's shopping trip?

$0.4x + 5.49 = 5.09$ $\qquad$ $0.4x + 5.49 = 9.49$ $\qquad$ $0.6x + 9.49 = 5.49$

You can write an equation with more than one operation to represent a situation.

$$3(x + 5) = 24$$

$$\frac{x}{4} - 15 = 18$$

This two-step equation uses multiplication and addition.

This two-step equation uses division and subtraction.

Do You Understand?

1. **? Essential Question** How does an equation show the relationship between variables and other quantities in a situation?

2. **Use Structure** Do the equations $\frac{1}{5}x + 2 = 6$ and $\frac{1}{5}(x + 2) = 6$ represent the same situation? Explain.

3. How do you decide which operations to use when writing an equation?

Do You Know How?

4. Rita started the day with r apps. Then she deleted 5 apps and still had twice as many apps as Cora has. Write an equation that represents the number of apps each girl has.

5. Write a problem that could be represented by the equation $5n - 6 = 19$.

6. Kayleigh babysat for 11 hours this week. That was 5 fewer than $\frac{2}{3}$ as many hours as she babysat last week, h. Write an equation to represent the number of hours she babysat each week.

Practice & Problem Solving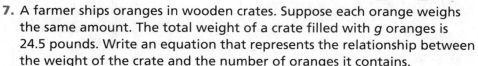

7. A farmer ships oranges in wooden crates. Suppose each orange weighs the same amount. The total weight of a crate filled with g oranges is 24.5 pounds. Write an equation that represents the relationship between the weight of the crate and the number of oranges it contains.

empty crate: 15 lb

$$24.5 = \boxed{} + \boxed{} \times \boxed{}$$

0.38 lb

8. Jordan wrote the following description: Three fewer than one fourth of x is 12. Write an equation to represent the description.

9. At a graduation dinner, an equal number of guests were seated at each of 3 large tables, and 7 late-arriving guests were seated at a smaller table. There were 37 guests in all. If n represents the number of people seated at each of the large tables, what equation represents the situation?

10. Last night, 4 friends went out to dinner at a restaurant. They split the bill evenly. Each friend paid $12.75 for his or her meal and each left the same amount for a tip, t. The total dinner bill including the tip was $61. What equation could you use to describe the situation?

11. Mia buys $4\frac{1}{5}$ pounds of plums. The total cost after using a coupon for 55¢ off her entire purchase was $3.23. If c represents the cost of the plums in dollars per pound, what equation could represent the situation?

For 12 and 13, use the equation shown at the right.

12. Describe a situation that the equation could represent.

$$\frac{g + 3}{6} = 15$$

13. Reasoning Would the situation you wrote for Problem 12 work if the denominator in the equation were doubled? Explain why or why not.

14. You want to buy a pet iguana. You already have $12 and plan to save $9 per week.

Iguana $48

a. Model with Math If w represents the number of weeks until you have enough money to buy the iguana, what equation represents your plan to afford the iguana?

b. Explain how you could set up an equation to find the amount of money you should save each week to buy the iguana in 6 weeks.

15. In a certain country, the life expectancy of a woman born in 1995 was 80.2 years. Between 1995 and 2005, the life expectancy increased 0.4 year every 5 years.

a. If L represents the life expectancy of a woman born in 2005, what equation could you use to represent the situation?

b. Reasoning Could two different equations be used to find the value of L? Explain.

16. Higher Order Thinking Use the equation $5x - 13 = 12$.

a. Write a description that represents the equation.

b. Of the numbers 1, 2, 3, 4, and 5, which are solutions to the equation?

Assessment Practice

17. A garden contains 135 flowers, each of which is either red or yellow. There are 3 beds of yellow flowers and 3 beds of red flowers. There are 30 yellow flowers in each yellow flower bed.

PART A

If r represents the number of red flowers in each red flower bed, what equation could you use to represent the number of red and yellow flowers?

PART B

Write another real-world situation that your equation from Part A could represent.

Solve & Discuss It! 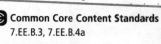 ACTIVITY

Elizabeth wrote the following clues. What is the relationship between the shapes?

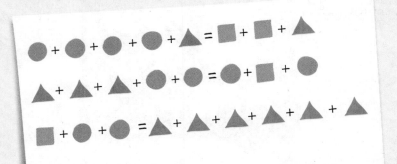

Use Structure How can you use properties of equality to reason about these equations?

I can...
solve a problem with a two-step equation.

© **Common Core Content Standards**
7.EE.B.3, 7.EE.B.4a

Mathematical Practices
MP.1, MP.7

Focus on math practices

Look for Relationships Complete the equation with only triangles using the relationships from the clues shown above.

? **Essential Question** How is solving a two-step equation similar to solving a one-step equation?

  VISUAL LEARNING ASSESS

EXAMPLE 1 **Solve Two-Step Equations Using Models**

Scan for Multimedia

Nala and two friends spent $21 on movie tickets and a box of popcorn. How could they figure out how much each movie ticket costs?

> **Use Structure** Two-step equations can be solved in two steps by using two different properties of equality.

Use a bar diagram and an equation to represent the situation.

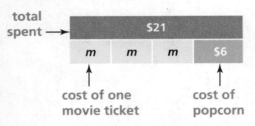

total spent → $21

| m | m | m | $6 |

cost of one movie ticket ↑   cost of popcorn ↑

Total spent = 3 • Cost of one movie ticket + Cost of popcorn

21 = 3 • m + 6

Use the Subtraction Property of Equality to isolate the term containing the variable.

| $15 | | | $6 |
| m | m | m | $6 |

$$21 = 3m + 6$$
$$21 - 6 = 3m + 6 - 6$$
$$15 = 3m$$

Use the Division Property of Equality to **isolate the variable**, or get the variable by itself on one side of the equation.

| $5 | $5 | $5 | $6 |
| m | m | m | $6 |

$$15 = 3m$$
$$\frac{15}{3} = \frac{3m}{3}$$
$$5 = m$$

So, each movie ticket costs $5.

✓ **Try It!**

Andrew rents bowling shoes for $4. He bowls 2 games. Andrew spent a total of $22. How much was the cost of each game, b?

Complete the bar diagrams, and then solve the problem.

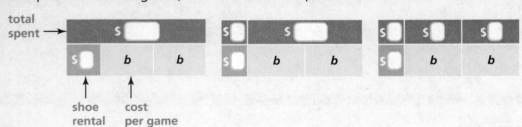

total spent →

| $ [   ] | | |
| $[ ] | b | b |

| $[ ] | $ [   ] | |
| $[ ] | b | b |

| $[ ] | $[ ] | $[ ] |
| $[ ] | b | b |

shoe rental ↑   cost per game ↑

Each game cost [   ].

Convince Me! What were the two steps you used to solve this equation?

EXAMPLE 2   Solve Two-Step Equations Algebraically

Jon has a $21.61 balance on a gift card that can be used to purchase online music. He bought some songs that each cost $1.29. Now he has $10 left. How many songs did Jon purchase?

Write and solve a two-step equation.

Let d represent the number of songs Jon purchased.

Balance on gift card	−	Cost of one song	•	Number of songs	=	$10 balance
21.61	−	1.29	•	d	=	10

$$21.61 - 1.29d = 10$$

> Use inverse operations and the Subtraction Property of Equality to isolate the term with the variable.

$$21.61 - 1.29d - 21.61 = 10 - 21.61$$

$$-1.29d = -11.61$$

> Use the inverse operations and the Division Property of Equality to isolate the variable.

$$\frac{-1.29d}{-1.29} = \frac{-11.61}{-1.29}$$

$$d = 9$$

Jon purchased 9 songs.

EXAMPLE 3   Compare Algebraic and Arithmetic Solutions

The number of trumpet players is 2 more than $\frac{1}{4}$ of the entire band. How many students are in the band?

An algebraic and an arithmetic solution are shown to find b, the total number of students in the band.

> 18 students play the trumpet in the band.

Algebraic Solution

$$\frac{1}{4}b + 2 = 18$$

$$\frac{1}{4}b + 2 - 2 = 18 - 2$$

$$\frac{1}{4}b = 16$$

$$\frac{4}{1} \cdot \frac{1}{4}b = \frac{4}{1} \cdot 16$$

$$b = 64$$

Arithmetic Solution

> Subtract 2.

$$4 \cdot (18 - 2)$$

> Multiply by 4.

$$4 \cdot (16)$$

$$64$$

So, there are 64 students in the band.

Try It!

Kirsty ran 24 laps in a charity run and then walked 0.2 kilometer to the presentation table. The total distance Kirsty traveled was 29.6 kilometers. What was the distance of each lap? Explain how you solved the problem.

The properties of equality can be applied the same way when solving two-step equations as when solving one-step equations.

$$5x + 27 = 122$$

> The inverse relationship between operations determines the property of equality needed to "undo" the operations in the equation.

$$5x + 27 - 27 = 122 - 27$$

$$\frac{5x}{5} = \frac{95}{5}$$

$$x = 19$$

Do You Understand?

1. **? Essential Question** How is solving a two-step equation similar to solving a one-step equation?

2. **Use Structure** Preston uses the bar diagram below to represent $4x - 3 = 13$. How would you use the bar diagram to solve for x?

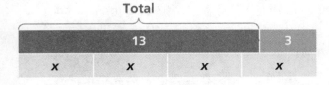

Total

| 13 | 3 |
| x | x | x | x |

3. Clara has solved the problem $6p - 12 = 72$ and says that $p = 14$. How can you check to see if Clara is correct?

Do You Know How?

4. Clyde is baking, and the recipe requires $1\frac{1}{3}$ cups of flour. Clyde has 2 cups of flour, but he is doubling the recipe to make twice as much. How much more flour does Clyde need?

Recipe

$1\frac{1}{3}$ cups flour
eggs
vanilla

2 Cups

1 Cup

a. Write an equation to represent the problem. Let c represent the amount of flour Clyde needs.

b. Solve the equation.

5. Four times a number, n, added to 3 is 47.

a. Write an equation that you can use to find the number.

b. What is the number represented by n?

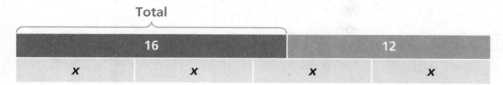

Practice & Problem Solving

6. Use the bar diagram to help you solve the equation $4x - 12 = 16$.

Total

16	12

x	x	x	x

7. Complete the steps to solve the equation.

$$\frac{1}{5}t + 2 - \boxed{} = 17 - \boxed{}$$

$$\frac{1}{5}t = \boxed{}$$

$$\boxed{} \cdot \frac{1}{5}t = \boxed{}$$

$$t = \boxed{}$$

8. Use the bar diagram to write an equation. Then solve for x.

Total

7	5

x	x	x

9. While shopping for clothes, Tracy spent $38 less than 3 times what Daniel spent. Write and solve an equation to find how much Daniel spent. Let x represent how much Daniel spent.

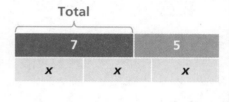

**Tracy spent
$10.**

10. Solve the equation $0.5p - 3.45 = -1.2$.

11. Solve the equation $\frac{n}{10} + 7 = 10$.

12. A group of 4 friends went to the movies. In addition to their tickets, they bought a large bag of popcorn to share for $6.25. The total was $44.25.

    a. Write and solve an equation to find the cost of one movie ticket, *m*.

    b. Draw a model to represent the equation.

13. Oliver incorrectly solved the equation $2x + 4 = 10$. He says the solution is $x = 7$.

    a. What is the correct solution?

    b. What mistake might Oliver have made?

14. Use the equation $4.9x - 1.9 = 27.5$.

    a. Make Sense and Persevere What two properties of equality do you need to use to solve the equation?

    b. The solution is $x = \boxed{}$.

15. Higher Order Thinking At a party, the number of people who ate meatballs was 11 fewer than $\frac{1}{3}$ of the total number of people. Five people ate meatballs.

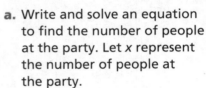

    a. Write and solve an equation to find the number of people at the party. Let *x* represent the number of people at the party.

    b. Write a one-step equation that has the same solution.

☑ Assessment Practice

16. In a week, Tracy earns $12.45 less than twice the amount Kayla earns. Tracy earns $102.45. How much does Kayla earn?

17. Solve the equation $2x + 4\frac{1}{5} = 9$. Explain the steps and properties you used.

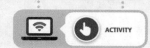
Lesson 5-3
Solve Equations
Using the
Distributive
Property

 Go Online

Explain It! 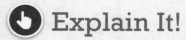 ACTIVITY

Six friends go jet skiing. The total cost for the adventure
is $683.88, including a $12 fee per person to rent
flotation vests. Marcella says they can use the equation
$6r + 12 = 683.88$ to find the jet ski rental cost, r, per person.
Julia says they need to use the equation $6(r + 12) = 683.88$.

I can...
use the Distributive Property to
solve equations.

© **Common Core Content Standards**
7.EE.B.3, 7.EE.B.4a

Mathematical Practices
MP.1, MP.2, MP.3, MP.4, MP.7

A. Construct Arguments Whose equation
accurately represents the situation?
Construct an argument to support your
response.

B. What error in thinking might explain
the inaccurate equation?

Focus on math practices

Use Structure How can you use the correct equation to determine the
jet ski rental cost per person?

? **Essential Question** How does the Distributive Property help you solve equations?

EXAMPLE **1** **Solve Equations Using the Distributive Property**

Each of the graphic novels in Chen's collection increased in value by $3.50 in the last few years. If each graphic novel has the same value, what was the original value of one graphic novel?

10 graphic novels

Current total value: $75

Model with Math How can you write an equation in the form $p(x + q) = r$ to relate the quantities in the problem?

Use an area model to represent the situation and write an equation.

Let g represent the original value of a graphic novel.

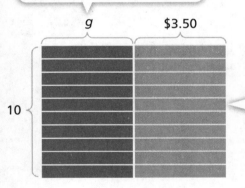

g $3.50

10

Total value: $75

$10(g + 3.50) = 75$

Solve for g to find the original cost of each graphic novel.

$$10(g + 3.50) = 75$$
$$(10 \cdot g) + (10 \cdot 3.50) = 75$$ Use the Distributive Property.
$$10g + 35 = 75$$
$$10g + 35 - 35 = 75 - 35$$
$$\frac{10g}{10} = \frac{40}{10}$$
$$g = 4$$

Use mental math to check that the solution is reasonable.
Think: $10(4 + 3.50)$ is $10(7.5)$, or 75.

The original value of one graphic novel was $4.00.

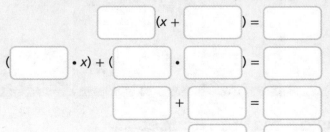

☑ Try It!

A collector has a box of 32 figurines. The value of each figurine increased by $2.32 over the past year. The box of figurines is now worth $114.24. What was the original cost, x, of one figurine?

The original cost of one figurine was [   ].

$\boxed{}(x + \boxed{}) = \boxed{}$

$(\boxed{} \cdot x) + (\boxed{} \cdot \boxed{}) = \boxed{}$

$\boxed{} + \boxed{} = \boxed{}$

$\boxed{} = \boxed{} - \boxed{}$

$x = \boxed{} \div \boxed{}$

$x = \boxed{}$

Convince Me! Can the equation $32x + 2.32 = 114.24$ be used to find the original cost of each figurine in the problem above? Explain.

EXAMPLE 2 Solve Equations by Distributing a Negative Number

  ACTIVITY ASSESS

Solve the equation $-5(s + 30) = -17$.

$$-5(s + 30) = -17$$

$$-5s + (-5)(30) = -17$$

> Use the Distributive Property to distribute the negative number.

$$-5s - 150 = -17$$

> Remember the rules for multiplying negative integers.

$$-5s - 150 + 150 = -17 + 150$$

$$-5s = 133$$

$$\frac{-5s}{-5} = \frac{133}{-5}$$

$$s = -26\frac{3}{5}$$

 EXAMPLE 3 Solve Equations by Distributing a Rational Number

The cheerleading squad received $\frac{1}{4}$ of the total sales of foam fingers and pom-poms at a pep rally. The squad received a total of **$136.75**. What was the value of the pom-poms sales, p?

> $258 in sales of foam fingers

Write and solve an equation.

$$\frac{1}{4} \text{ of } \left(\begin{matrix}\text{pom-pom} \\ \text{sales}\end{matrix} + \begin{matrix}\text{foam finger} \\ \text{sales}\end{matrix}\right) = \begin{matrix}\text{total amount} \\ \text{squad received}\end{matrix}$$

$$\frac{1}{4}(p + 258) = 136.75$$

$$\frac{1}{4}p + \frac{1}{4}(258) = 136.75$$

> Use the Distributive Property.

$$\frac{1}{4}p + 64.5 = 136.75$$

$$\frac{1}{4}p + 64.5 - 64.5 = 136.75 - 64.5$$

$$\frac{1}{4}p = 72.25$$

$$\left(\frac{4}{1}\right)\frac{1}{4}p = 72.25\left(\frac{4}{1}\right)$$

$$p = 289$$

The total received from pom-pom sales was $289.

✅ Try It!

Use the Distributive Property to solve each equation.

a. $-\frac{1}{2}(b - 6) = 5$ b. $0.4(x - 0.45) = 9.2$ c. $-4(p - 212) = 44$

When solving equations written in the form $p(x + q) = r$, you can use the Distributive Property to multiply the two terms in the parentheses by the term outside the parentheses.

$$6(x + 8.5) = 123$$
$$6x + 51 = 123$$
$$6x = 72$$
$$x = 12$$

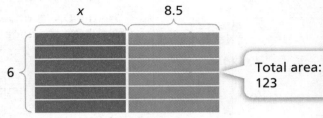

Total area: 123

Do You Understand?

1. **Essential Question** How does the Distributive Property help you solve equations?

2. **Make Sense and Persevere** How are the terms in parentheses affected when multiplied by a negative coefficient when the Distributive Property is applied?

3. **Reasoning** How can an area model help you set up an equation for a problem situation?

Do You Know How?

4. A family of 7 bought tickets to the circus. Each family member also bought a souvenir that cost $6. The total amount they spent was $147. How much did one ticket cost?

5. David reads the problem:

   Ally bought a T-shirt and a pair of shorts on sale, which reduced prices by $\frac{1}{4}$. The total savings on the two garments was $10.25. Find the original price for the pair of shorts.

   ORIGINAL PRICE $18.00

   David says that the original price of the shorts was $41. Does his answer seem reasonable? Defend your answer by writing and solving an equation that represents the situation.

6. Which of the following shows the correct use of the Distributive Property when solving $\frac{1}{3}(33 - x) = 135.2$?

   Ⓐ $(33 - x) = 1 \_- 3 \cdot 135.2$

   Ⓑ $\frac{1}{3} \cdot 33 - \frac{1}{3}x = \frac{1}{3} \cdot 135.2$

   Ⓒ $\frac{1}{3} \cdot 33 + \frac{1}{3}x = 135.2$

   Ⓓ $\frac{1}{3} \cdot 33 - \frac{1}{3}x = 135.2$

Name: _____

Practice & Problem Solving

Leveled Practice For **7–10**, use the Distributive Property to solve the equations.

7. $-2(x + 5) = 4$

$(\boxed{} \cdot x) + (\boxed{} \cdot 5) = 4$

$\boxed{} + \boxed{} = 4$

$\boxed{} = 4 + \boxed{}$

$x = \dfrac{14}{\boxed{}}$

$x = \boxed{}$

8. $3.2 = \frac{4}{5}(b - 5)$

$3.2 = (\frac{4}{5} \cdot \boxed{}) + (\frac{4}{5} \cdot \boxed{})$

$3.2 = \boxed{} - 4$

$3.2 + \boxed{} = \boxed{}$

$\frac{5}{4} \cdot \boxed{} = \boxed{}$

$9 = b$

9. $\frac{1}{8}(p + 24) = 9$

$(\boxed{}) + (\boxed{}) = \boxed{}$

$p = \boxed{}$

10. $\frac{2}{3}(6a + 9) = 20.4$

$(\boxed{}) + (\boxed{}) = \boxed{}$

$a = \boxed{}$

---

11. Use the equation at the right.

   a. Make Sense and Persevere If you apply the Distributive Property first to solve the equation, what operation will you need to use last?

   b. If instead you divide first to solve the equation, what operation would you need to use last?

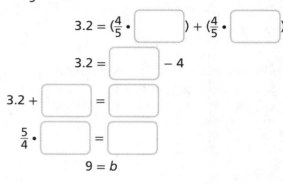

$$6\left(\frac{d}{3} - 5\right) = 34$$

---

12. A family buys 4 airline tickets online. The family buys travel insurance that costs $19 per ticket. The total cost is $752. Let x represent the price of one ticket.

   a. Write an equation to represent this situation.

   b. What is the price of one ticket?

13. A local charity receives $\frac{1}{3}$ of funds raised during a craft fair and a bake sale. The total amount given to charity was $137.45. How much did the bake sale raise?

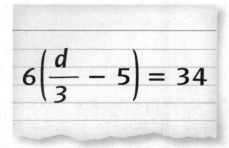

Craft Fair	Bake Sale
Funds raised.	Funds raised.
$252.60	$?

14. The solution shown for the equation is incorrect.

    a. What is the correct solution?

    b. What was the likely error?

$$-3(6 - r) = 6$$
$$-18 - 3r = 6$$
$$-3r = 24$$
$$r = -8$$

15. Vita wants to center a towel bar on her door that is $27\frac{1}{2}$ inches wide. She determines that the distance from each end of the towel bar to the end of the door is 9 inches. Write and solve an equation to find the length of the towel bar.

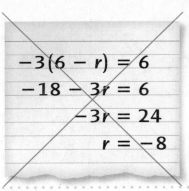

16. Higher Order Thinking A cell phone plan is shown at the right. The rates, which include an unlimited data plan, are the same each month for 7 months. The total cost for all 7 months is $180.39. Let m represent the average number of minutes that exceeds 700 minutes each month.

    a. Write an equation to represent the given situation.

    b. Solve the equation to determine how many additional minutes, on average, you use each month.

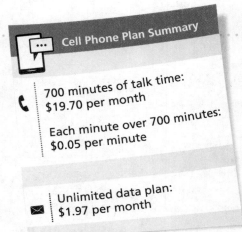

Cell Phone Plan Summary

700 minutes of talk time:
$19.70 per month

Each minute over 700 minutes:
$0.05 per minute

Unlimited data plan:
$1.97 per month

✅ Assessment Practice

17. Fidel earns a fixed amount, m, for each television he sells, and an additional $15 if the buyer gets an extended warranty. Fidel sells 12 televisions with extended warranties, earning $900. Write an equation to represent the situation. Then solve the equation to find the amount earned for each television sold.

1. **Vocabulary** Explain how to *isolate the variable* in the equation $-\frac{2}{3}n + 7 = 15$. *Lesson 5-2*

2. Jake paid $13.50 for admission to the county fair and bought 9 tickets to play games. If he spent a total of $36, what is the cost, c, of one ticket? Write and solve an equation. *Lessons 5-1 and 5-2*

3. Select all the equations that are equivalent to $\frac{1}{2}(4 + 8x) = 17$. *Lesson 5-3*

   ☐ $2 + 4x = 8.5$ ☐ $4x = 15$ ☐ $4 + 8x = 8.5$

   ☐ $4 + 8x = 34$ ☐ $2 = 17 - 8x$

4. Clara has 9 pounds of apples. She needs $1\frac{1}{4}$ pounds to make one apple pie. If she sets aside 1.5 pounds of apples to make applesauce, how many pies, p, can she make? Write and solve an equation. *Lessons 5-1 and 5-2*

5. Solve the equation $-4(1.75 + x) = 18$. Show your work. *Lesson 5-3*

6. Four friends attend a school play and pay $6.75 per ticket. Each also buys a Healthy Snack Bag sold by the Theater Club. If the friends spent a total of $37.00, how much did each Healthy Snack Bag cost, b? Write and solve an equation. *Lessons 5-1, 5-2, 5-3*

How well did you do on the mid-topic checkpoint? Fill in the stars.

MID-TOPIC PERFORMANCE TASK

Marven and three friends are renting a car for a trip. Rental prices are shown in the table.

Item	Price
Small car rental fee – seats 4 passengers	$39/day
Full-size car rental fee – seats 4 passengers	$49/day
Insurance	$21/day

PART A

Marven has a coupon that discounts the rental of a full-size car by $25. They decide to buy insurance for each day. If the cost is $465, how many days, *d*, will they rent the car? Write and solve an equation.

PART B

If they still use the coupon, how many days could they rent the small car with insurance if they have $465 to spend?

PART C

They rent a car with insurance for 5 days but lost their coupon. If Marven and the three friends spend $75 each, which car did they rent? Write and solve an equation to justify your answer.

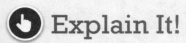

Explain It! ACTIVITY

Selena and Martin are waiting at the bus stop. The number lines show the possible wait times in minutes, *t*, for Selena and Martin.

Bus every 15 minutes

Next Arrivals

Blue Bus Line

DELAYED

Trip From ▸   Trip To ▸

Blue Bus Station

Lesson 5-4
Solve Inequalities Using Addition or Subtraction

Go Online

I can...
solve inequalities using addition or subtraction.

Ⓒ **Common Core Content Standards**
7.EE.B.4b

Mathematical Practices
MP.2, MP.4

Selena's Possible Wait Time

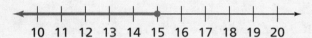

Martin's Possible Wait Time

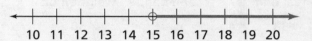

A. Construct Arguments Who anticipates a longer wait? Justify your response with a mathematical explanation.

B. If Selena and Martin both wait 10 minutes for the bus, whose possible wait time was closer to his or her actual wait time? Explain.

Focus on math practices

Be Precise If Selena and Martin both wait exactly 15 minutes for the bus, whose possible wait time was closer to his or her actual wait time? Explain.

? Essential Question How is solving inequalities with addition and subtraction similar to and different from solving equations with addition and subtraction?

EXAMPLE 1 👁 **Solve Inequalities That Involve Addition**

Scan for Multimedia

On the airline that Raul is using, the weight limit for both suitcases combined is 50 pounds. How much can Raul's second bag weigh without going over the limit?

Reasoning Is there more than one possible weight for Raul's second bag?

38 lbs

Write an inequality to represent the situation. Then solve the inequality to find the weight of the second bag, *p*.

Weight of first bag	+	Weight of second bag	≤	Baggage weight limit
38	+	*p*	≤	50

Solve the inequality as you would an equation.

$$38 + p \leq 50$$
$$38 + p - 38 \leq 50 - 38$$
$$p \leq 12$$

Use the inverse relationship between addition and subtraction to isolate the variable.

The *Subtraction Property of Inequality* is like the Subtraction Property of Equality: subtracting the same number from both sides maintains the inequality.

Use a number line to show all of the possible solutions to $p \leq 12$

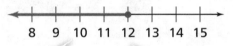

8 9 10 11 12 13 14 15

If the second bag weighs 10 pounds, the total weight is 38 + 10 = 48, which is ≤ 50.

The second bag can weigh at most 12 pounds.

Raul's second bag must weigh 12 pounds or less to avoid going over the weight limit for both suitcases combined.

✓ **Try It!**

Kyoko has completed 26 hours of community service. Her goal is to complete at least 90 hours this semester. Write and solve an inequality to show how many more hours, *h*, Kyoko needs to complete to meet her goal. Use the number line to graph the solutions.

Convince Me! Is there more than one solution to the problem about Kyoko? Explain. Give one value that is a solution and one value that is not a solution.

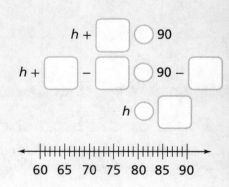

$h +$ ⬜ ◯ 90

$h +$ ⬜ − ⬜ ◯ 90 − ⬜

h ◯ ⬜

60 65 70 75 80 85 90

EXAMPLE **2** Solve Inequalities That Involve Subtraction

ACTIVITY   ASSESS

The weather forecast predicted that the evening temperature could get as low as −12.5°F. Between afternoon and evening, the temperature dropped by 7.5°F, which was consistent with the forecast. What could the afternoon temperature, t, have been?

MONDAY EVENING

Low of −12.5°F

Tue	Wed	Thu	Fri	Sat
−12°	−14°	−15°	−11°	−10°

Write an inequality to represent the situation. Then solve as you would an equation.

$$t - 7.5 \geq -12.5$$
$$t - 7.5 + 7.5 \geq -12.5 + 7.5$$
$$t \geq -5$$

> The *Addition Property of Inequality* is like the Addition Property of Equality: adding the same number to both sides maintains the inequality.

Look for Relationships How is the Addition Property of Inequality similar to the Subtraction Property of Inequality?

The afternoon temperature could have been −5°F or warmer.

 Try It!

The speed limit on a road drops down to 15 miles per hour around a curve. Mr. Gerard slows down by 10 miles per hour as he drives around the curve. He never drives above the speed limit. At what speed was Mr. Gerard driving before the curve? Graph the solution.

EXAMPLE **3**  **Solve More Inequalities**

Solve the inequality $x - \frac{1}{2} < -\frac{2}{3}$. Then graph the solution.

$$x - \frac{1}{2} < -\frac{2}{3}$$
$$x - \frac{1}{2} + \frac{1}{2} < -\frac{2}{3} + \frac{1}{2}$$
$$x < -\frac{1}{6}$$

> Remember to isolate the variable.

 Try It!

Solve the inequality $n - 1\frac{3}{4} \leq -\frac{5}{8}$. Then graph the solution.

Solving inequalities with addition and subtraction is the same as solving equations with addition and subtraction. Use the inverse relationship between addition and subtraction to isolate the variable.

$$x + 15.76 > 26.05$$
$$x + 15.76 - 15.76 > 26.05 - 15.76$$
$$x > 10.29$$

Remember: The Addition and Subtraction Properties of Inequality are like the Addition and Subtraction Properties of Equality.

$$-6\frac{4}{5} + y \le 3\frac{1}{10}$$
$$-6\frac{4}{5} + y + 6\frac{4}{5} \le 3\frac{1}{10} + 6\frac{4}{5}$$
$$y \le 9\frac{9}{10}$$

Do You Understand?

1. **Essential Question** How is solving inequalities with addition and subtraction similar to and different from solving equations with addition and subtraction?

2. **Be Precise** How do the solutions of the two inequalities differ? Are any of the solutions the same? Explain.

   a. $x + 5 < 8$ and $x + 5 > 8$

   b. $x + 5 \le 8$ and $x + 5 \ge 8$

3. **Reasoning** Write two different inequalities in which one of the solutions is the same as the solution to $x - 23 = 191$.

Do You Know How?

4. Solve each inequality. Then graph the solution.

   a. $x + 5 > 3$

   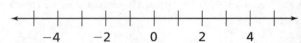

   b. $x + 5 \le 3$

   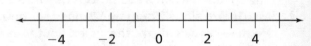

   c. $x - \frac{3}{2} < -3$

   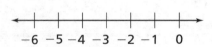

5. Elanor is driving below the speed limit on a highway.

   a. Write the inequality to show how much faster Elanor can drive without going over the speed limit.

   b. Solve the inequality you wrote. By how much can Elanor increase her speed?

Name: _____

Practice & Problem Solving

Leveled Practice In **6** and **7**, fill in the boxes to solve each inequality. Then graph the solutions.

6. $x + 5 < 7$

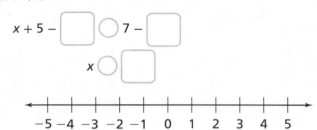

$x + 5 - \boxed{} \bigcirc 7 - \boxed{}$

$x \bigcirc \boxed{}$

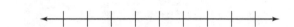

$$-5 \quad -4 \quad -3 \quad -2 \quad -1 \quad 0 \quad 1 \quad 2 \quad 3 \quad 4 \quad 5$$

7. $x - 4 \geq 12$

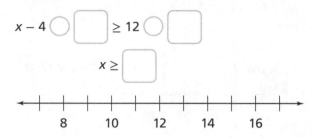

$x - 4 \bigcirc \boxed{} \geq 12 \bigcirc \boxed{}$

$x \geq \boxed{}$

$$8 \quad 10 \quad 12 \quad 14 \quad 16$$

8. Solve $x + 10 \geq 14$. Then graph the solution.

9. Solve $x - 20 \leq -11$. Then graph the solution.

10. The maximum number of students in a classroom is 26. If there are 16 students signed up for the art class, how many more students can join the class without exceeding the maximum?

11. Higher Order Thinking The inequality $x + c > -2.55$ has the solution $x > 4.85$ What is the value of c? How do you know?

12. Rina is climbing a mountain. She has not yet reached base camp. Write an inequality to show the remaining distance, d, in feet she must climb to reach the peak.

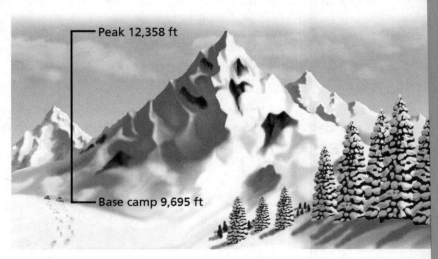

Peak 12,358 ft

Base camp 9,695 ft

13. On a math test, students must solve the inequality $x - 5 < 11$ and then graph the solution. Mason said the solution is $x < 6$ and graphed the solution as shown below.

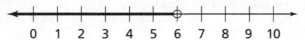

a. What error did Mason make?

b. Show the correct solution on the number line.

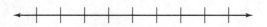

14. Model with Math Dani's neighbors paid her to take care of their bird during their vacation. Dani spent $4 of her earnings on an afternoon snack and $16 on a new book. Afterward, she had at least $8 left. Write an inequality to represent how much Dani's neighbors paid her.

15. Reasoning The temperature in a greenhouse should be 67°F or higher. One morning, the heater stopped working. The temperature dropped 4 degrees before someone fixed the heater. The temperature was still at least 67°F when the heater started working again. How can you best describe the temperature in the greenhouse before the heater stopped working?

Keep at least
67°F
or higher

Assessment Practice

16. Ramiro has $21. He wants to buy a skateboard that costs $47. How much more money does he need to have at least $47? Write an inequality that represents the situation. Solve the inequality and graph your solution.

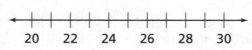

17. Kendra has $7.35 in her purse. She needs at least $2.87 more to buy a special bead. What is the total amount, x, she needs for the bead? Which inequalities can be used to represent the situation? Select all that apply.

☐ $x + 7.35 \leq 2.87$

☐ $x - 7.35 \leq 2.87$

☐ $x + 7.35 \geq 2.87$

☐ $x - 7.35 \geq 2.87$

☐ $x \geq 10.22$

☐ $x \leq 2.87$

☐ $x \leq 10.22$

☐ $x \leq 4.48$

Solve & Discuss It!

Alex and Hope were trying to solve $-6x > 24$.

Whose inequality shows the solution? Show your work.

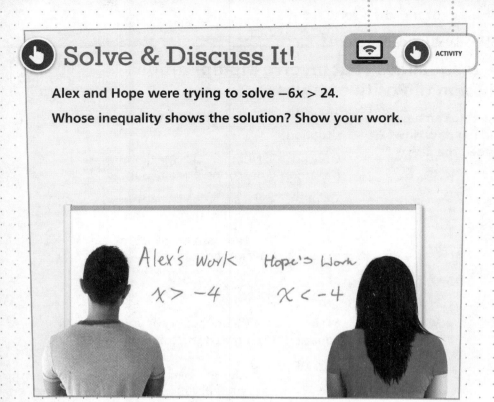

Alex's Work
$x > -4$

Hope's Work
$x < -4$

I can...
solve inequalities using multiplication or division.

© **Common Core Content Standards**
7.EE.B.4b

Mathematical Practices
MP.2, MP.3, MP.6, MP.7

Construct Arguments Why does more than one value of x make the inequality true?

Focus on math practices

Be Precise What do you notice about the inequality symbols used in the original inequality and in the correct solution?

? **Essential Question** How is solving inequalities with multiplication and division similar to and different from solving equations with multiplication and division?

  VISUAL LEARNING ASSESS

EXAMPLE 1 **Solve Inequalities That Involve Multiplication or Division of Positive Values**

Scan for Multimedia

Gina's pet pot-bellied pig is on a diet. He can have no more than 18 ounces of pig food per day. How many scoops of pig food can Gina feed the pig without going over 18 ounces?

STEP 1 Write an inequality to represent the situation.

$$\text{Ounces per scoop} \cdot \text{Number of scoops} \leq \text{Maximum daily ounces}$$

$$4 \cdot s \leq 18$$

The total can be equal to but not more than 18.

STEP 2 Solve the inequality as you would an equation. Then graph the solution.

$$4s \leq 18$$
$$\frac{4s}{4} \leq \frac{18}{4}$$
$$s \leq 4.5$$

Use the inverse relationship between multiplication and division and the *Division Property of Inequality* to isolate the variable.

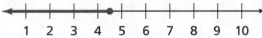

Gina can feed her pig up to $4\frac{1}{2}$ scoops of food.

Look for Relationships How can the Multiplication Property of Equality help you solve this problem?

✓ **Try It!**

Solve the inequality $\frac{d}{7} > 15$. Then graph the solution.

$$\frac{d}{7} > 15$$

$$\boxed{} \cdot \frac{d}{7} \bigcirc 15 \cdot \boxed{}$$

$$d \bigcirc \boxed{}$$

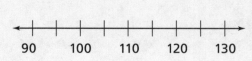

Convince Me! Frances solved the inequality $5g \geq 35$. She says that 7 is a solution to the inequality. Is Frances correct? Explain.

EXAMPLE 2

Solve Inequalities Using Division by a Negative Value

  ACTIVITY ASSESS

Solve the inequality $-3.4m \le 17$. **Then graph the solution.**

$-3.4m \le 17$

$\dfrac{-3.4m}{-3.4} \ge \dfrac{17}{-3.4}$

> Use the inverse relationship between multiplication and division and the *Division Property of Inequality* to isolate the variable.

$m \ge -5$

> Dividing by a negative value reverses the inequality symbol.

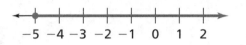

Try It!

Solve each inequality. Then graph the solution.

a. $149.76 > -19.2x$

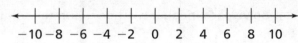

b. $-3.25y < -61.75$

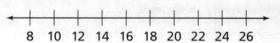

EXAMPLE 3

Solve Inequalities Using Multiplication by a Negative Value

Solve the inequality $\dfrac{r}{-2.25} \ge 7$. **Then graph the solution.**

$\dfrac{r}{-2.25} \ge 7$

$-2.25 \cdot \dfrac{r}{-2.25} \le 7 \cdot -2.25$

> Use the inverse relationship between multiplication and division and the *Multiplication Property of Inequality* to isolate the variable.

$r \le -15.75$

> Multiplying by a negative value reverses the inequality symbol.

Try It!

Solve each inequality. Then graph the solution.

a. $\dfrac{k}{-0.5} < 12$

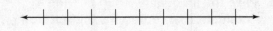

b. $-\dfrac{5}{4}h \ge 25$

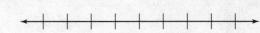

Solving inequalities with multiplication and division is the same as solving equations with multiplication and division when the values are positive. Use the inverse relationship between multiplication and division to isolate the variable.

$2.5x \geq 15$

$\dfrac{2.5x}{2.5} \geq \dfrac{15}{2.5}$ — Use inverse relationships and properties of inequality to isolate the variable.

$x \geq 6$

When multiplying or dividing by negative values, the inequality symbol is reversed.

$-2.5x \geq 15$

$\dfrac{-2.5x}{-2.5} \leq \dfrac{15}{-2.5}$ — Multiplying or dividing by a negative value reverses the inequality.

$x \leq -6$

Do You Understand?

1. **? Essential Question** How is solving inequalities with multiplication and division similar to and different from solving equations with multiplication and division?

2. Construct Arguments Why is $-x < 3$ equivalent to $x > -3$? Provide a convincing argument.

3. If *a, b,* and *c* are rational numbers and $a > b$, is $ac > bc$ always true? Justify your answer.

Do You Know How?

4. Solve each inequality. Then graph the solution.

a. $4x > 12$

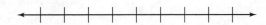

b. $\dfrac{x}{4} \leq -12$

c. $-4x > 12$

5. Vanna is saving for a trip. The hotel room will be $298.17 for 3 nights, and there will be additional fees. What is her daily cost?

$298.17 for 3 nights

a. Write an inequality for the situation.

b. Solve the inequality. Then provide a statement that represents the solution of the problem.

Practice & Problem Solving

Scan for Multimedia

Leveled Practice In 6–9, fill in the boxes to solve the inequality. Then graph the solution.

6.
$$8m \le 56$$

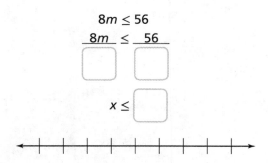

7.
$$-\frac{4}{3}x < -8$$

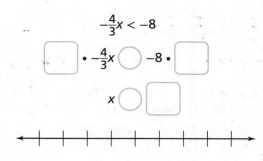

8.
$$-7x > 56$$

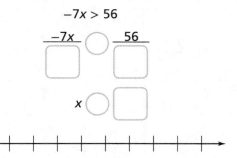

9.
$$\frac{m}{-5} \ge 2$$

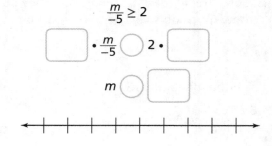

10. Kyra and five friends shared a bag of fruit snacks. Each person got no more than 3 fruit snacks. The inequality $x \div 6 \le 3$ represents this situation. Solve the inequality to find the possible numbers of fruit snacks that were in the bag.

11. Over the next 17 months, Eli needs to read more than 102 e-books. The inequality $17x > 102$ represents the number of e-books he needs to read per month. Solve the inequality to find the number of e-books Eli needs to read per month.

12. Brittney can spend no more than $15 for new fish in her aquarium.

a. Let *f* be the number of fish she can buy. What inequality represents the problem?

b. How many fish can Brittney buy?

$3.00 each

13. Isaac has a bag of n peanuts. He shares the peanuts with 5 of his friends. Each person gets at least 18 peanuts. The inequality $18 \leq n \div 6$ represents this situation. Graph the solution of this inequality.

14. a. Solve the inequality $-3x < 12$.

b. Reasoning Describe how you know the direction of the inequality sign without solving the inequality.

15. Higher Order Thinking Renata and her family go through an average of more than 15 cans of sparkling water each day. They buy cases of 24 cans at $3.50 a case.

Sparkling water $3.⁵⁰ PER CASE

a. Write an inequality for the number of cases they go through in 30 days.

b. Solve the inequality in part **a**. If they buy only full cases, how much do they spend on sparkling water in 30 days?

16. Solve the inequality. Graph the solution on the number line.

$$-6.25x > -38\tfrac{3}{4}$$

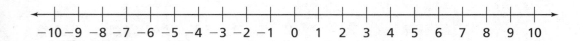

Assessment Practice

17. Cynthia plans to build a tree house that is $\frac{1}{3}$ the size of Andrew's tree house. Cynthia plans to make the area of her tree house at least 13 square feet.

PART A

Write and solve an inequality to find the area of Andrew's tree house. Let x be the area of Andrew's tree house.

PART B

Describe how you know which tree house is larger without solving the inequality.

3-ACT MATH ▶ ▶ ▶

3-Act Mathematical Modeling: Digital Downloads

📶 Go Online

© **Common Core Content Standards**
7.EE.B.3, 7.EE.B.4

Mathematical Practices
MP.4, MP.1, MP.2, MP.3, MP.5, MP.7, MP.8

ACT 1

1. After watching the video, what is the first question that comes to mind?

2. Write the Main Question you will answer.

3. Construct Arguments Make a prediction to answer this Main Question. Explain your prediction.

4. On the number line below, write a number that is too small to be the answer. Write a number that is too large.

Too small   Too large

←————————————————————————————————→

5. Plot your prediction on the same number line.

6. What information in this situation would be helpful to know? How would you use that information?

7. Use Appropriate Tools What tools can you use to solve the problem? Explain how you would use them strategically.

8. Model with Math Represent the situation using mathematics. Use your representation to answer the Main Question.

9. What is your answer to the Main Question? Is it higher or lower than your initial prediction? Explain why.

10. Write the answer you saw in the video.

11. Reasoning Does your answer match the answer in the video? If not, what are some reasons that would explain the difference?

12. Make Sense and Persevere Would you change your model now that you know the answer? Explain.

Reflect

13. Model with Math Explain how you used a mathematical model to represent the situation. How did the model help you answer the Main Question?

14. Reasoning If all single tracks were on sale for 10% off, how would your model change? How would the answer to the Main Question change?

15. Make Sense and Persevere Suppose you have a $50 gift card to the same site. You want to buy an album with 16 tracks for $12.99 and then use the rest of the gift card for single tracks. How many songs can you buy with the gift card?

👆 Solve & Discuss It!

 ACTIVITY

Rico and Halima are shopping for craft sticks, glue, and electrical tape for a science project. Together, they have $30 to spend on supplies. How should they spend their $30 if they need at least 1,000 craft sticks?

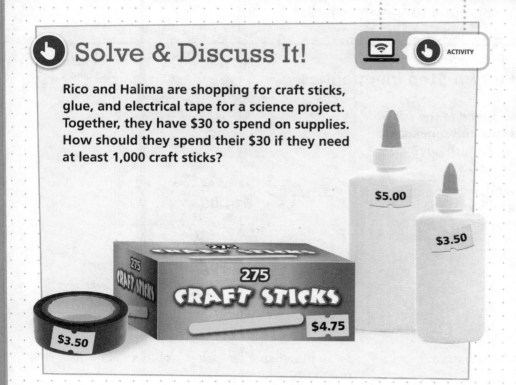

$5.00

$3.50

275 CRAFT STICKS

$4.75

$3.50

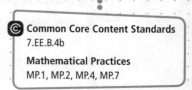

Go Online

I can...
write and solve two-step inequalities.

© **Common Core Content Standards**
7.EE.B.4b

Mathematical Practices
MP.1, MP.2, MP.4, MP.7

Focus on math practices

Make Sense and Persevere At the store, Rico and Halima find boxes of 500 craft sticks for $7.50. Which boxes of craft sticks should they buy?

Essential Question How is solving a two-step inequality similar to and different from solving a two-step equation?

| EXAMPLE 1 | ⊙ Solve Two-Step Inequalities |

Hamish has $25.97 in his pocket to spend at the craft store. He wants to buy a paint canvas and some paint pens. How many paint pens, *p*, can Hamish buy?

> **Use Structure** How are inverse relationships and properties used to solve equations and inequalities?

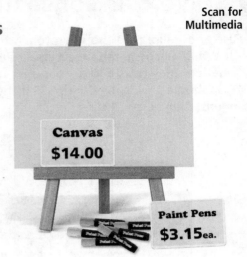

Scan for Multimedia

Canvas **$14.00**

Paint Pens **$3.15**ea.

Write an inequality to represent the situation.

Cost of the canvas	+	Cost of one pen	•	Number of pens	≤	Money available
14	+	3.15	•	*p*	≤	25.97

> The total cost can be equal to but not more than $25.97.

Solve the inequality as you would an equation. Then graph the solution.

$$14 - 14 + 3.15p \leq 25.97 - 14$$

> Use the Subtraction Property of Inequality.

$$\frac{3.15p}{3.15} \leq \frac{11.97}{3.15}$$

> Use the Division Property of Inequality.

$$p \leq 3.80$$

> Only whole numbers are solutions.

```
←———┼———┼———┼———┼———●———┼———┼———→
    0   1   2   3   4   5   6
```

Hamish can purchase only a whole number of paint pens. So, Hamish can buy 3 or fewer paint pens.

☑ Try It!

Erin has $52 to spend at the florist. She wants to buy a vase for $11.75 and several roses for $3.50 each. What are the possible numbers of roses Erin can buy?

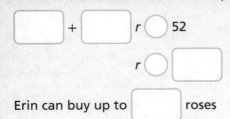

[ ] + [ ] *r* ◯ 52

r ◯ [ ]

Erin can buy up to [ ] roses

Convince Me! What properties did you use to solve the inequality?

EXAMPLE 2 Solve More Two-Step Inequalities

Members of the science club are selling coupon booklets for $17.95 as a fundraiser. They hope to exceed the amount of money they raised last year. How many more coupon booklets, b, must the club members sell to achieve their goal?

Write an inequality to represent the situation. Then solve.

Current funds raised	+	Cost of one booklet	·	Number of booklets	>	Last year's total funds raised
498.75	+	17.95	·	b	>	658.35

> The amount raised this year should exceed last year's amount.

$$498.75 + 17.95b > 658.35$$

$$498.75 + 17.95b - 498.75 > 658.35 - 498.75$$

$$17.95b > 159.6$$

$$\frac{17.95b}{17.95} > \frac{159.6}{17.95}$$

$$b > 8.89$$

> **Make Sense and Persevere** What values for b make sense in the context of the problem?

The members of the science club must sell at least 9 booklets to exceed last year's total fundraising amount.

 Try It!

The Jazz Band needs to raise at least $600 to travel to an upcoming competition. The members of the band have already raised $350. If they sell calendars for $8 each, how many calendars would they need to sell to exceed their goal?

EXAMPLE 3 Solve Inequalities with Negative Values

Solve the inequality $-10 - \frac{9}{2}x < 80$.

$$-10 + 10 - \frac{9}{2}x < 80 + 10$$

$$-\frac{2}{9} \cdot -\frac{9}{2}x > -\frac{2}{9} \cdot 90$$

> Remember: When you multiply or divide by a negative value, the inequality symbol is reversed.

$$x > -20$$

 Try It!

Solve the inequality $5 - \frac{1}{2}x > 30$.

Like two-step equations, solving two-step inequalities involves carrying out two different operations—addition or subtraction, and multiplication or division. Unlike two-step equations, which have a single solution, two-step inequalities have multiple solutions.

Do You Understand?

1. **Essential Question** How is solving a two-step inequality similar to and different from solving a two-step equation?

2. **Reasoning** What is the difference between the number of solutions for a two-step equation and for a two-step inequality?

3. Why are inverse relationships between operations used to solve two-step inequalities?

Do You Know How?

4. Joe ran 3 miles yesterday and wants to run at least 12 miles this week. Write an inequality that can be used to determine the additional number of days Joe must run this week if each run is 3 miles. Then solve the inequality.

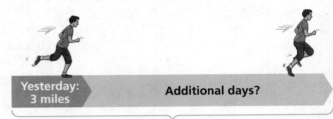

Joe's goal this week: Run at least 12 miles

5. Solve $4 + 6.5x < 36.5$.

6. Tomas has $1,000 to spend on a vacation. His plane ticket costs $348.25. If he stays 5.5 days at his destination, how much can he spend each day? Write an inequality and then solve.

7. Solve $12 - \frac{3}{5}x > 39$.

Practice & Problem Solving

Scan for
Multimedia

Leveled Practice For 8 and 9, fill in the boxes to write and solve each inequality.

8. Eight less than the product of a number n and $\frac{1}{5}$ is no more than 95.

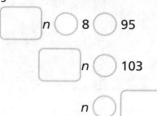

9. Seven more than the quotient of a number b and 45 is greater than 5.

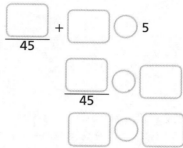

---

10. Solve the inequalities and compare.

    a. Solve $2x + 6 < 10$.

    b. Solve $-2x + 22 < 18$.

    c. Which is the correct comparison of solutions for $2x + 6 < 10$ and $-2x + 22 < 18$?

    Ⓐ The inequalities have some common solutions.

    Ⓑ The inequalities have one common solution.

    Ⓒ The inequalities have no common solutions.

    Ⓓ The inequalities have the same solutions.

---

11. **Make Sense and Persevere** Talia has a daily budget of $94 for a car rental. Write and solve an inequality to find the greatest distance Talia can drive each day while staying within her budget.

Car Rental
$30 per day
plus $0.20 per mile

---

12. **Model with Math** A manager needs to rope off a rectangular section for a private party. The length of the section must be 7.6 meters. The manager can use no more than 28 meters of rope. What inequality could you use to find the possible width, w, of the roped-off section?

13. **Higher Order Thinking** Andrea went to the store to buy a sweater that was on sale for 40% off the original price. It was then put on clearance at an additional 25% off the sale price. She also used a coupon that saved her an additional $5. Andrea did not spend more than $7.60 for the sweater. What are the possible values for the original price of the sweater?

14. A pool can hold 850 gallons. It now has 598 gallons of water and is being filled at the rate shown. How many more minutes, m, can water continue to flow into the pool before it overflows? Write and solve an inequality.

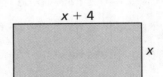
filling rate of 15.75 gallons per minute

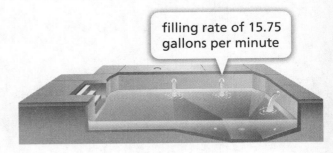

Assessment Practice

15. Use the rectangle diagram at the right.

    PART A

    Write and solve an inequality to find the values of x for which the perimeter of the rectangle is less than 120.

    $x + 4$

    x

    PART B

    Based on your answer to Part A, are there any values that can be eliminated from the solution set? Explain.

16. Kari is building a rectangular garden bed. The length is 6 feet. She has 20 feet of boards to make the sides. Write and solve an inequality to find the possible width of her garden bed.

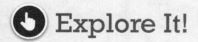

Explore It!

 ACTIVITY

Charlene has 2 flash drives of the same size that she uses to store pictures and videos. Each drive is holding the same number of GB of data, *d*. She wants to move everything to a memory card that can hold up to 8 GB.

I can...
solve inequalities that require multiple steps.

© **Common Core Content Standards**
7.EE.B.4b

Mathematical Practices
MP.2, MP.3, MP.4, MP.7

A. Charlene is going to delete 1 GB of data from each flash drive. How can the total amount of data left on the two flash drives be represented as an expression?

B. How can the expression you wrote be used to write an inequality that shows the maximum amount of data each flash drive can have on it in order to have all the data transfer to the 8 GB memory card?

Focus on math practices

Reasoning If each flash drive has 5 GB of memory, can all of the data be transferred to the memory card? Explain.

? Essential Question How is solving a multi-step inequality similar to and different from solving a multi-step equation

EXAMPLE 1 **Write and Solve Multi-Step Inequalities**

Gabriela likes to make people guess her age. She gives them this clue:

Add 13 to the product of 3 and the sum of my age and 2, and you get a number greater than my height in inches.

What are possible ages for Gabriela? Graph the solution.

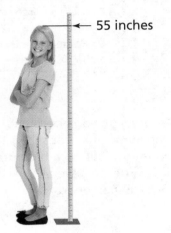

← 55 inches

STEP 1 Write an inequality to represent Gabriela's age, x.

Multiply by 3	The sum of Gabriela's age and 2	Add 13	>	Gabriela's height
3 $\cdot$	$(x + 2)$	+ 13	>	55

STEP 2 Solve the inequality. Then graph the solution.

$$3(x + 2) + 13 > 55$$

$$3x + 6 + 13 > 55 \quad \text{Use the Distributive Property.}$$

$$3x + 19 > 55$$

$$3x + 19 - 19 > 55 - 19$$

Use the Subtraction and Division Properties of Inequality to isolate the variable.

$$\frac{3x}{3} > \frac{36}{3}$$

$$x > 12$$

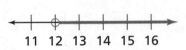

11 12 13 14 15 16

Gabriela is more than 12 years old.

☑ Try It!

Twice the difference of Felipe's age, f, and 4 is at least 2.
What are possible values for Felipe's age? Graph the solution.

Write the inequality.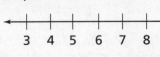

Use the Distributive Property to rewrite the inequality as $2f - \boxed{} \geq 2$.

Solve the inequality.   Graph the solution.

$2f \geq \boxed{}$

3 4 5 6 7 8

$f \geq \boxed{}$

Convince Me! Describe the similarity between the process of solving an inequality with two steps and solving an inequality with more than two steps.

EXAMPLE **2**

Solve More Multi-Step Inequalities

ACTIVITY   ASSESS

Solve the inequality −3(x + 4) + 3 ≥ 9. **Then graph the solution.**

$$-3(x + 4) + 3 \geq 9$$

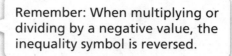
Remember to use the Distributive Property.

$$-3x - 12 + 3 \geq 9$$

$$-3x - 9 \geq 9$$

$$-3x \geq 18$$

$$\frac{-3x}{-3} \leq \frac{18}{-3}$$

Remember: When multiplying or dividing by a negative value, the inequality symbol is reversed.

$$x \leq -6$$

−10 −9 −8 −7 −6 −5

EXAMPLE **3**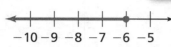

Solve Multi-Step Inequalities by Combining Like Terms

Solve the inequality 2(3.5t − 2) + 6t ≥ −2. **Then graph the solution.**

$$2(3.5t - 2) + 6t \geq -2$$

Distribute and then combine like terms.

$$7t - 4 + 6t \geq -2$$

$$13t - 4 \geq -2$$

$$13t - 4 + 4 \geq -2 + 4$$

$$13t \geq 2$$

Use the Division Property of Inequality.

$$t \geq \frac{2}{13}$$

0    $\frac{2}{13}$ 1

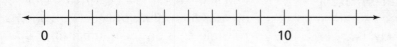 **Try It!**

Solve the inequality −1−6(6 + 2x) < 11. Then graph the solution.

−5   0   5

Solve the inequality 3(4 − 6) + 2 ≥ 2(−t + 3) + 4. Then graph the solution.

0   10

Solving multi-step inequalities is similar to solving multi-step equations.
You may need to use the Distributive Property, combine like terms, and use
inverse relationships and properties to solve them.

$4(y - 4) + 8 \leq 20$

$4y - 16 + 8 \leq 20$

$4y - 8 \leq 20$

$4y - 8 + 8 \leq 20 + 8$

$4y \leq 28$

$\dfrac{4y}{4} \leq \dfrac{28}{4}$

$y \leq 7$

Do You Understand?

1. **❓ Essential Question** How is solving a multi-step inequality similar to and different from solving a multi-step equation?

2. **Be Precise** Explain how you would combine like terms and use properties of operations to solve the inequality $5(2t + 3) - 3t < 16$.

3. **Critique Reasoning** Gloria's solution to a multi-step inequality is $r > 7$. She states that the graph will have an open dot at 7 and extend with an arrow to the right indefinitely. Is she correct? Explain.

Do You Know How?

4. Solve the inequality $2(n + 3) - 4 < 6$. Then graph the solution.

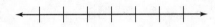

5. Solve the inequality $-2(x + 3) + 2 \geq 6$. Then graph the solution.

6. Three times the difference of Federico's age and 4, increased by 7, is greater than 37. What are possible values of Federico's age? Graph his possible ages on the number line.

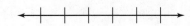

Practice & Problem Solving

7. Use the inequality $18 < -3(4x - 2)$.

   a. Solve the inequality for x.

   b. Which graph shows the solution to the inequality?

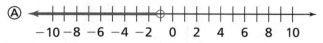

Ⓐ
−10 −8 −6 −4 −2 0 2 4 6 8 10

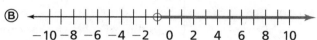

Ⓑ
−10 −8 −6 −4 −2 0 2 4 6 8 10

Ⓒ
−10 −8 −6 −4 −2 0 2 4 6 8 10

Ⓓ
−10 −8 −6 −4 −2 0 2 4 6 8 10

8. Michelle says that the solution to the inequality $2(4y - 3) > -22$ is $y > -3.5$. Her work is shown.

$$2(4y - 3) > -22$$
$$8y > -28$$
$$y > -3.5$$

   a. What was Michelle's mistake?

   b. What is the solution to the inequality?

9. Model with Math The length of a picture frame is 7 inches more than the width. For what values of x is the perimeter of the picture frame greater than 154 inches?

10. Critique Reasoning Sierra says that she can simplify the left side of the inequality $2(-3 + 5) + 2 \geq -4(x - 2) - 3$ by combining the terms within the parentheses, but that she can't do the same on the right side. Is Sierra correct? Explain.

11. a. Solve the inequality $30 \geq 6\left(\frac{2}{3}z + \frac{1}{3}\right)$.

b. Solve the inequality $15.6 < 2.7(z - 1) - 0.6$.

c. Are there any values of z that solve both inequalities? Use a number line to support your answer.

---

12. Mr. Lin baked banana bread for a bake sale to raise money for the math team. He said that he added a spoonful of walnuts for each of the students in his three classes, and that he added more than 250 walnuts. He used the inequality $16w + 24w + 10w > 250$ to represent the situation, where w represents the number of walnuts in each spoonful. How many walnuts could be in each spoonful?

13. Use both the Addition and Multiplication Properties of Inequality to solve the inequality. Graph the solutions on a number line.

$2(3y - 5) < -16$

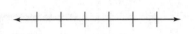

---

14. Higher Order Thinking Solve each of the given inequalities for z. Which of the inequalities has 5 as a solution?

Inequality 1
$4(2.8z + 1.75) > -26.6$

Inequality 2
$2(1.9z + 1.5) \leq 18.2$

✓ Assessment Practice

15. The school band needs $500 to buy new hats. They already have $200. They are selling bumper stickers for $1.50 each. How many bumper stickers do they need to sell to have at least $500? Write and solve an inequality that represents the situation.

? Topic Essential Question

How can you solve real-world and mathematical problems with numerical and algebraic equations and inequalities?

Vocabulary Review

Complete each definition and then provide an example of each vocabulary word used.

Vocabulary isolate the variable equation
Distributive Property inequality

Definition	Example
1. You _____ when you divide both sides of the equation $3n = 12$ by 3.	
2. A statement that contains $>$, $<$, $\geq$, $\leq$, or $\neq$ to compare two expressions is a(n) _____.	
3. You can use the _____ to remove parentheses in the process of solving the equation $-10(x + 5) = 40$.	

Use Vocabulary in Writing

Write an equation or inequality to represent the following situation: *17 is at least 5 more than 3 times x*. Explain how you wrote your equation or inequality. Use vocabulary from Topic 5 in your explanation.

Concepts and Skills Review

Quick Review

Equations can be used to represent situations. Two-step equations have two different operations. The properties of equality can be applied the same way when solving two-step equations as when solving one-step equations.

Example

There are red and yellow flowers in a city park. The number of yellow flowers is 3 more than $\frac{1}{3}$ of the number of red flowers. There are 21 yellow flowers. Write an equation to find the number of red flowers. Let r represent the number of red flowers. Then solve for r.

$$\frac{1}{3}r + 3 = 21$$
$$\frac{1}{3}r + 3 - 3 = 21 - 3$$
$$\frac{1}{3}r = 18$$
$$(3)\frac{1}{3}r = 18(3)$$
$$r = 54$$

The garden has 54 red flowers.

Practice

1. The total number of students in the seventh grade is 9 more than 4 times as many students as are in the art class. There are 101 students in the seventh grade. Write and solve an equation to find the number of students in the art class. Let x represent the number of students in the art class.

2. List the steps to solve the following equation: $5x - 6 = 44$. Then solve for x.

3. Solve for the given variable.
   a. $4y + 3 = 19$
   b. $\frac{1}{2}n - 3 = 5$

LESSON **5-3** Solve Equations Using the Distributive Property

Quick Review

Use the Distributive Property to solve problems of the form $p(x + q) = r$.

Example

Solve the equation $2(4.3 + n) = 17.63$.

$$8.6 + 2n = 17.63$$
$$2n = 9.03$$
$$n = 4.515$$

Practice

1. There are 450 seats in the lower level of a concert hall with b balcony seats in the upper level. So far, 170 tickets have been sold, which is $\frac{1}{5}$ of the total number of seats in the concert hall. How many tickets sold are balcony seats?

2. Solve the equation $-4(8 + y) = 90$.

LESSON 5-4 › Solve Inequalities Using Addition or Subtraction

Quick Review

When you add or subtract the same number on both sides of an inequality, the relationship between the sides stays the same. Solutions to inequalities can be graphed on number lines.

Example

Solve $x + 13 \geq 43$. Then graph the solution.

$x + 13 - 13 \geq 43 - 13$

$\qquad x \geq 30$

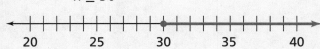

Practice

1. Carson's wheelbarrow can hold 345 pounds. If he has 121 pounds of rock in the wheelbarrow, what number of pounds, p, can he put in the wheelbarrow without going over the weight limit?

2. Solve $x - 19 < 81$. Then graph the solution.

LESSON 5-5 › Solve Inequalities Using Multiplication or Division

Quick Review

When you multiply or divide both sides of an inequality by the same positive number, the inequality remains true. When you multiply or divide both sides of an inequality by the same negative number, you need to reverse the inequality symbol, but the inequality remains true.

Example

Solve $-15n > 75$. Then graph the solution.

$-15n > 75$

$\dfrac{-15n}{-15} < \dfrac{75}{-15}$

$\qquad n < -5$

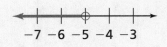

Practice

1. Travis has 3 months to save money for a trip. An airplane ticket costs more than $300. If he saves the same amount of money, a, each month, how much does he need to save each month to pay for the ticket?

2. Solve $-\frac{1}{8}y \leq 34$. Then graph the solution.

Solve Two-Step Inequalities

Quick Review

Inverse relationships and properties can be used to isolate the variable and solve two-step inequalities in the form $px + q < r$ or $px + q > r$ in the same way that they are used to solve two-step equations.

Example

Write and solve the inequality.

9 less than the product of 6 and x is greater than 54.

$6x - 9 > 54$

$6x - 9 + 9 > 54 + 9$

$6x > 63$

$\frac{6x}{6} > \frac{63}{6}$

$x > 10\frac{1}{2}$

Practice

1. The school band gets $5 for each T-shirt they sell at a fundraiser. They have a goal of raising $150. If $45 has been raised so far, how many more T-shirts do they have to sell to reach or exceed the goal?

2. Solve the inequality $-8 - \frac{1}{3}n \le -25$.

Solve Multi-Step Inequalities

Quick Review

Solving a multi-step inequality is similar to solving a multi-step equation. All of the rules and properties for solving one- and two-step inequalities apply to solving multi-step inequalities.

Example

Solve the inequality $7(x + 8) - 4 < 143$. Then graph the solution.

$7(x + 8) - 4 < 143$

$7x + 56 - 4 < 143$

$7x + 52 < 143$

$7x < 91$

$x < 13$

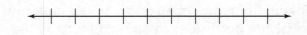

Practice

1. Solve $1.9(2.3n + 6) + 10.45 > 43.7$. Then graph the solution.

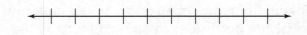

2. Solve $4(-2n + 2.5) - 8 \le 50$. Then graph the solution.

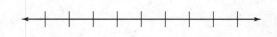

Crisscrossed

Solve each problem. Write your answers in the cross-number puzzle below. Each digit, decimal point, dollar sign, and percent symbol of your answer goes in its own box. Round money amounts to the nearest cent as needed.

I can...
use the percent equation to solve problems. © 7.RP.A.3

ACROSS

A Antonia buys 0.75 yard of fabric at $12.00 per yard. If she pays 5% sales tax, what is the total cost of the fabric?

B Five friends plan to split a restaurant bill evenly. The total cost of the meal is $89.75, and they want to leave a 20% tip. What amount should each friend pay?

E Kaylie buys a sweater on sale for $40.11. If the discount is 20% off and she pays $1.91 in sales tax, what is the original price of the sweater?

F Randy buys a pair of shoes that were originally priced at $147. He receives a 35% discount and pays 8.5% sales tax. How much does Randy pay?

G A basketball player makes 8 of 22 shots in Game 1, 6 of 15 shots in Game 2, and 10 of 23 shots in Game 3. What percent of the shots did the player make in the three games?

DOWN

A Jack buys a tablet that costs $99 and a memory card that costs $15. He has a coupon for a 15% discount. What is the amount of the discount on the two items?

B Tara buys two pairs of socks for $4.99 each and three T-shirts for $11.45 each. If she pays 6% sales tax, what is the total amount of her purchase?

C Sunil receives a 20% discount on a concert ticket that costs $75. If Sunil pays $3.30 in sales tax on the discounted ticket, what is the sales tax rate?

D Dylan works for 4 hours and is paid $17.50 per hour. He must pay 15% in income taxes. What amount does he earn after taxes?

E Miles earns a 6% commission on each vehicle he sells. Today he sold a truck for $18,500 and a car for $9,600. What is the total amount of his commission for these vehicles?

TOPIC 6

USE SAMPLING TO DRAW INFERENCES ABOUT POPULATIONS

? Topic Essential Question

How can sampling be used to draw inferences about one or more populations?

Topic Overview

6-1 Populations and Samples

6-2 Draw Inferences from Data

6-3 Make Comparative Inferences About Populations

6-4 Make More Comparative Inferences About Populations

3-Act Mathematical Modeling: Raising Money

Topic Vocabulary

- inference
- population
- random sample
- representative sample
- sample
- valid inference

Lesson Digital Resources

INTERACTIVE STUDENT EDITION
Access online or offline.

VISUAL LEARNING ANIMATION
Interact with visual learning animations.

ACTIVITY Use with *Solve & Discuss It, Explore* and *Explain It* activities, and to explore Examp

VIDEOS Watch clips to support *3-Act Mathematical Modeling Lessons* and *STEM Pro*

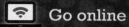 Go online

▶ Raising Money

What was the last fundraiser your school hosted? How much money was your school trying to raise? Fundraisers can help your school finance improvements and special events. However, if you have too many fundraisers, people might stop participating.

You can start planning a fundraiser once you know how you will use the money and how much money you will need. Think about this during your 3-Act Mathematical Modeling lesson.

PRACTICE Practice what you've learned.

TUTORIALS Get help from *Virtual Nerd*, right when you need it.

MATH TOOLS Explore math with digital tools.

GAMES Play Math Games to help you learn.

KEY CONCEPT Review important lesson content.

GLOSSARY Read and listen to English/Spanish definitions.

ASSESSMENT Show what you've learned.

enVision® STEM Project

 VIDEO

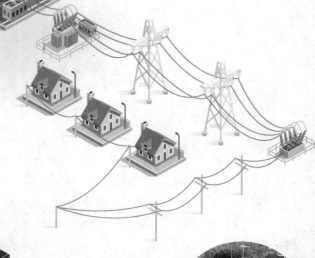

Did You Know?

Federal and local governments provide their citizens with the basic equipment and structures needed for the region to function properly. This **infrastructure** includes water, electricity, waste removal, and communication networks.

Roads and public **transportation** are the most visible elements of infrastructure.

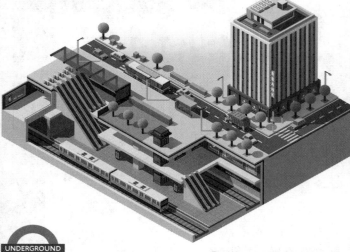

Motorists in cities like Los Angeles, Moscow, and Istanbul experience some of the worst **traffic congestion**.

London's Metropolitan Railway began operating as the world's first rapid public transportation system in 1863. Boston's Tremont Street Subway, opened in 1897, was the first **subway system** in the United States.

Residents of large cities like New York, Amsterdam, and Tel Aviv enjoy a **bike-sharing** service. City governments provide this infrastructure to **reduce traffic congestion** and promote fitness.

Your Task: Golden Path

Walking trails and paths and bikeways provide important recreational opportunities and commuting alternatives. They also promote the preservation of green spaces and eco-friendly, energy-efficient transportation. The appropriate design of walking trails and paths and bikeway facilities affects the experience, enjoyment, safety, and comfort of walkers and bicyclists. You and your classmates will develop a survey to understand the needs of walkers and bicyclists and to examine the current and potential uses of existing and planned paths or bikeways.

Review What You Know!

Vocabulary

Choose the best term from the box to complete each definition.

center
data distribution
statistical question
variability

1. A _____ is how data values are arranged.

2. The part of a data set where the middle values are concentrated is called

   the _____ of the data.

3. A _____ anticipates that there will be different
   answers when gathering information.

4. _____ is a measure that describes the spread of values in a data set.

Statistical Measures

Use the following data to determine each statistical measure.
9, 9, 14, 7, 12, 8, 11, 19, 15, 11

5. mean   **6.** median   **7.** range

8. mode   **9.** interquartile range (IQR)   **10.** mean absolute deviation (MAD)

Data Representations

Make each data display using the data from Problems 5–7.

11. Box plot

12. Dot plot

Statistical Questions

13. Which is *NOT* a statistical question that might be used to gather data
   from a certain group?

   Ⓐ In what state were you born?   Ⓒ What is the capital of the United States?

   Ⓑ How many pets do you have?   Ⓓ Do you like strawberry yogurt?

Language Development

Fill in the graphic organizer. Write each definition in your own words. Illustrate or cite supporting examples.

Vocabulary Word	Definition	Illustration or Example
inference		
population		
random sample		
representative sample		
sample		
valid inference		

PROJECT 6A

What types of changes would you like to see in your community?

PROJECT: WRITE TO YOUR REPRESENTATIVE

PROJECT 6B

How could you combine physical activity and a fundraiser?

PROJECT: ANALYZE AN ACTIVITY

PROJECT 6C

If you could study an animal population in depth, which animal would you choose, and why?

PROJECT: SIMULATE A POPULATION STUDY

PROJECT 6D

If you were to design a piece of art that moved, how would you make it move?

PROJECT: BUILD A MOBILE

Lesson 6-1
Populations and Samples

 Go Online

The table shows the lunch items sold on one day at the middle school cafeteria. Use the given information to help the cafeteria manager complete his food supply order for next week.

Lunch Item	Number Sold
Turkey Sandwich	43
Hot Dog	51
Veggie Burger	14
Fish Taco	27

Generalize What conclusions can you draw from the lunch data?

I can...
determine if a sample is representative of a population.

© **Common Core Content Standards**
7. SP.A.1

Mathematical Practices
MP.1, MP.2, MP.3, MP.6, MP.8

Focus on math practices

Construct Arguments Why might it be helpful for the cafeteria manager to look at the items ordered on more than one day?

? Essential Question How can you determine a representative sample of a population?

VISUAL LEARNING

ASSESS

EXAMPLE 1 — Understand Populations and Samples

Scan for Multimedia

The 2,468 registered voters in Morgan's town are voting on whether to build a new stadium. Morgan and her friends really want the town to vote in favor of the new stadium. How can they determine how the voters will vote before the day of the vote?

Model with Math
How can you represent the problem situation?

Morgan and her friends could ask every registered voter, or the entire **population** of voters in town, how they plan to vote.

However, surveying 2,468 people takes a long time. Morgan and her friends may not be able to survey the entire population of voters.

Morgan and her friends could ask a subset, or a **sample**, of the registered voters in town how they plan to vote.

Surveying a sample of voters does not take as long and is more reasonable to do. Morgan and her friends would be able to ask 100 or 200 people.

☑ Try It!

Miguel thinks the science teachers in his school give more homework than the math teachers. He is researching the number of hours middle school students in his school spend doing math and science homework each night.

The [ ] includes all of the students in Miguel's middle school.

A possible [ ] is some students from each of the grades in the middle school.

Convince Me! Why is it more efficient to study a sample rather than an entire population?

EXAMPLE 2 ▶ Describe a Representative Sample

Morgan decides to survey a sample of the town's voting population. How can she know that the survey results from the sample of voters represent the position of the entire town's population?

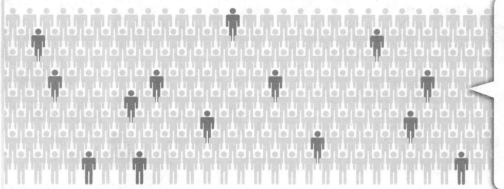

A **representative sample** accurately reflects the characteristics of the entire population.

In a **random sample**, each member of the population has an equal chance of being included. A random sample tends to be a representative sample.

Morgan can survey a random sample, or a randomly selected group of voters, to make sure her results represent the position of the entire town.

☑ Try It!

A produce manager is deciding whether there is customer demand for expanding the organic food section of her store. How could she obtain the information she needs?

EXAMPLE 3 ▶ Generate a Random Sample

How can Morgan generate a random sample of the town's voting population?

Morgan can follow these steps:

STEP 1 Define the population.
The population consists of the registered voters in the town.

STEP 2 Choose the sample size.
Morgan plans to survey 100 registered voters.

> The larger the sample, the more confident Morgan can be that the results represent the position of the population.

STEP 3 Make or acquire a list of all members of the population.

STEP 4 Assign a number to each member of the population.

STEP 5 Generate a list of random numbers to select sample members.

☑ Try It!

Ravi is running against two other candidates for student council president. All of the 750 students in Ravi's school will vote for student council president. How can Ravi generate a representative sample that will help him determine whether he will win the election?

EXAMPLE **4** **Generate Multiple Random Samples**

Morgan and Maddy will each generate a random sample of the 138 students in 7th grade at their school. They each write the numbers from 1 to 138 on small pieces of paper and put them in different hats. Then they draw 20 numbers randomly from their hats. What do you notice about the two random samples taken from the same population? What does this tell you about the sampling technique?

Morgan's Sample			
55	49	28	79
114	(106)	18	130
97	50	83	109
(38)	91	36	46
87	96	15	93

Maddy's Sample			
(38)	(106)	21	102
25	35	94	126
100	119	27	51
135	103	13	72
67	7	74	54

- There are 20 members in each sample.
- The only numbers common to both samples are 38 and 106.
- The numbers are distributed differently in each sample.

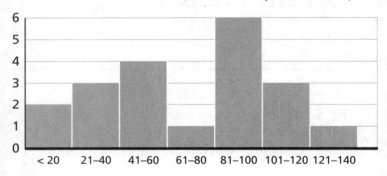

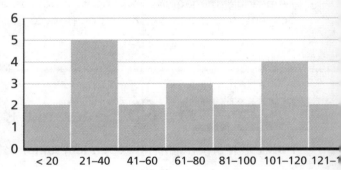

The sampling method produces random samples that have mostly different members, but that are each likely to be representative of the population.

☑ Try It!

The table at the right shows the random sample that Jeremy generated from the same population as Morgan's and Maddy's samples. Compare Jeremy's sample to Morgan's and Maddy's.

Jeremy's Sample			
77	8	32	17
34	95	81	57
125	116	30	126
92	61	22	36
111	68	110	69

A *population* is an entire group of objects—people, animals, plants—from which data can be collected. A *sample* is a subset of the population. When you ask a statistical question about a population, it is often more efficient to gather data from a sample of the population.

A *representative sample* of a population has the same characteristics as the population. Generating a *random sample* is one reliable way to produce a representative sample of a population.

You can generate multiple random samples that are different but that are each representative of the population.

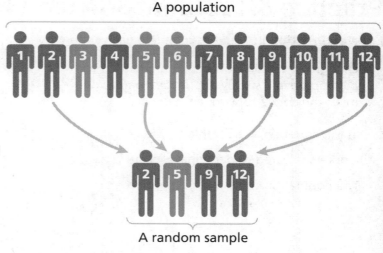

A population

A random sample

Do You Understand?

1. **Essential Question** How can you determine a representative sample of a population?

2. **Construct Arguments** Why does a sample need to be representative of a population?

3. **Be Precise** The quality control manager of a peanut butter manufacturing plant wants to ensure the quality of the peanut butter in the jars coming down the assembly line. Describe a representative sampling method she could use.

Do You Know How?

4. A health club manager wants to determine whether the members would prefer a new sauna or a new steam room. The club surveys 50 of its 600 members. What is the population of this study?

5. A journalism teacher wants to determine whether his students would prefer to attend a national writing convention or tour of a local newspaper press. The journalism teacher has a total of 120 students in 4 different classes. What would be a representative sample in this situation?

6. Garret wants to find out which restaurant people think serves the best beef brisket in town.

   a. What is the population from which Garret should find a sample?

   b. What might be a sample that is not representative of the population?

Practice & Problem Solving

Multimedia

Leveled Practice In **7** and **8**, complete each statement with the correct number.

7. Of a group of 200 workers, 15 are chosen to participate in a survey about the number of miles they drive to work each week.

In this situation, the sample consists of the ☐ workers selected to participate in the survey.

The population consists of ☐ workers.

8. The ticket manager for a minor league baseball team awarded prizes by drawing four numbers corresponding to the ticket stub numbers of four fans in attendance.

In this situation, the sample consists of the ☐ people selected to win a prize. The population consists of ☐ the spectators who purchased tickets to attend the game.

9. A supermarket conducts a survey to find the approximate number of its customers who like apple juice. What is the population of the survey?

10. A national appliance store chain is reviewing the performances of its 400 sales associate trainees. How can the store choose a representative sample of the trainees?

11. Of the 652 passengers on a cruise ship, 30 attended the magic show on board.

a. What is the sample?

b. What is the population?

12. **Make Sense and Persevere** The owner of a landscaping company is investigating whether his 120 employees would prefer a water cooler or bottled water. Determine the population and a representative sample for this situation.

13. **Higher Order Thinking** A bag contains 6 yellow marbles and 18 red marbles. If a representative sample contains 2 yellow marbles, then how many red marbles would you expect it to contain? Explain.

14. Chung wants to determine the favorite hobbies among the teachers at his school. How could he generate a representative sample? Why would it be helpful to generate multiple samples?

15. The table shows the results of a survey conducted to choose a new mascot. Yolanda said that the sample consists of all 237 students at Tichenor Middle School.

   a. What was Yolanda's error?

   b. What is the sample size? Explain.

Tichenor M.S. Mascot Survey Results

Mascot	Number of Students
Panthers	24
Lions	6
Cyclones	2
Comets	8

16. **Reasoning** To predict the outcome of the vote for the town budget, the town manager assigned random numbers and selected 125 registered voters. He then called these voters and asked how they planned to vote. Is the town manager's sample representative of the population? Explain.

17. David wants to determine the number of students in his school who like Brussels sprouts. What is the population of David's study?

18. Researchers want to determine the percentage of Americans who have visited The Florida Everglades National Park in Florida. The diagram shows the population of this study, as well as the sample used by the researchers. After their study, the researchers conclude that nearly 75% of Americans have visited the park.

   a. What error was likely made by the researchers?

Population

Sample

The Florida Everglades National Park

   b. Give an example of steps researchers might take to improve their study.

19. An art teacher asks a sample of students if they would be interested in studying art next year. Of the 30 students he surveys, 81% are already enrolled in one of his art classes this year. Only 11% of the school's students are studying art this year. Did the teacher survey a representative sample of the students in the school? Explain.

20. Make Sense and Persevere A supermarket wants to conduct a survey of its customers to find whether they enjoy oatmeal for breakfast. Describe how the supermarket could generate a representative sample for the survey.

21. Critique Reasoning Gwen is the manager of a clothing store. To measure customer satisfaction, she asks each shopper who makes big purchases for a rating of his or her overall shopping experience. Explain why Gwen's sampling method may not generate a representative sample.

☑ Assessment Practice

22. Sheila wants to research the colors of houses on a highly populated street. Which of the following methods could Sheila use to generate a representative sample? Select all that apply.

☐ Assign each house a number and use a random number generator to produce a list of houses for the sample.

☐ Choose every house that has at least 3 trees in the front yard.

☐ Choose only the houses of the people you know.

☐ List the house numbers on slips of paper and draw at least 20% of the numbers out of a box.

☐ Choose all of the houses on the street that have shutters.

23. A national survey of middle school students asks how many hours a day they spend doing homework. Which sample best represents the population?

PART A

Ⓐ A group of 941 students in eighth grade in a certain town

Ⓑ A group of 886 students in sixth grade in a certain county

Ⓒ A group of 795 students in seventh grade in different states

Ⓓ A group of 739 students in different middle school grade levels from various states

PART B

Explain the reasoning for your answer in Part A.

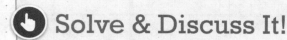

Solve & Discuss It!   ACTIVITY

The students in Ms. Miller's class cast their votes in the school-wide vote for which color to paint the cafeteria walls. Based on the data, what might you conclude about how the rest of the school will vote?

I can...
make inferences about a population from a sample data set.

© **Common Core Content Standards**
7.SP.A.1, 7.SP.A.2, 7.RP.A.2c, 7.EE.B.3
Mathematical Practices
MP.1, MP.2, MP.3, MP.4

Make Sense and Persevere
How many students are in Ms. Miller's class? How many students voted for each color?

Focus on math practices

Reasoning How can you determine whether a sample is representative of a population?

Essential Question How can inferences be drawn about a population from data gathered from samples?

Scan for Multimedia

EXAMPLE 1 Draw Qualitative Inferences from Data

Sasha is trying to convince her mother to change her bedtime on school nights. She gathers data on the average number of hours of sleep that a random sample of seventh-grade students in her school get each night. Will Sasha be able to convince her mother to let her go to bed later?

Model with Math How can you represent the data?

On School Days

My bedtime: **9:00 p.m.**

My wake-up time: **6:30 a.m.**

Hours of sleep: $9\frac{1}{2}$

STEP 1 Sasha displays the data she collected in a dot plot. She describes the data.

About half of the dots are clustered between 9 and $9\frac{1}{2}$ hours.

$9\frac{1}{2}$ hours has the most dots.

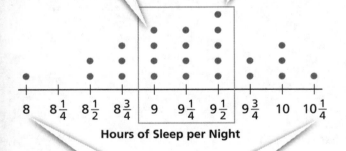

Hours of Sleep per Night

The range is $10\frac{1}{4} - 8 = 2\frac{1}{4}$ hours.

STEP 2 Sasha concludes that about half of the students in her sample get between 9 and $9\frac{1}{2}$ hours of sleep each night, the same number she gets.

You can draw a curve to see the distribution or shape of the data.

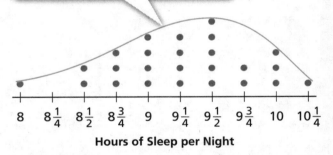

Hours of Sleep per Night

An **inference** is a conclusion made by interpreting data. Sasha infers that about half of the seventh graders in her school get between 9 and $9\frac{1}{2}$ hours of sleep each night. Sasha will probably not be able to convince her mother to let her go to bed later.

☑ **Try It!**

Dash collects data on the hair lengths of a random sample of seventh-grade boys in his school.

The data are clustered between ☐ and ☐ inches and between ☐ and ☐ inches. Dash can infer from the data that seventh-grade boys in his school have both short and long hair.

Hair Length (in.)

Convince Me! How does a dot plot help you make inferences from data?

EXAMPLE 2 Draw Quantitative Inferences from Data

Sasha's friend Margo suggests that Sasha calculate the mean and median of the data set to determine whether they support her previous inferences about the population.

Mean: about 9 hours, 16 minutes

Median: $9\frac{1}{4}$ hours (or 9 hours, 15 minutes)

> An inference is valid if it is based on a representative sample, and there are enough data to support it.
>
> A **valid inference** is one that is very likely to be true about the population.

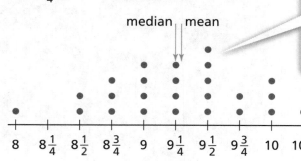

median mean

Hours of Sleep per Night

The mean and median support Sasha's inference that seventh graders get an average of 9 to $9\frac{1}{2}$ hours of sleep each night.

EXAMPLE 3 **Compare Inferences Based on Different Samples**

Margo and Ravi are also trying to get their parents to let them stay up later. They collect data about the number of hours of sleep a random sample of seventh graders get each night. The two box plots show their data. Do Margo's and Ravi's data support Sasha's inference about the number of hours of sleep that seventh graders get?

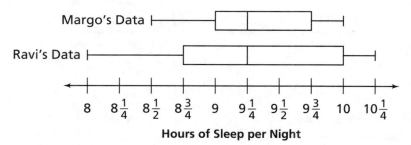

Margo's Data

Ravi's Data

Hours of Sleep per Night

The median time is $9\frac{1}{4}$ hours in each random sample. However, based on the box plots, Margo and Ravi can infer that less than half of seventh graders get between 9 and $9\frac{1}{2}$ hours of sleep each night. So, these data do not support Sasha's inference.

✓ **Try It!**

Alexis surveys three different samples of 20 students selected randomly from the population of 492 students in the seventh grade about their choice for class president. In each sample, Elijah receives the fewest votes. Alexis infers that Elijah will not win the election. Is her inference valid? Explain.

EXAMPLE 4  **Make an Estimate from Sample Data**

Derek is writing a report on cell phone usage. He collects data from a random sample of seventh graders in his school, and finds that 16 out of 20 seventh graders have cell phones. If there are 290 seventh graders in his school, estimate the number of seventh graders who have cell phones.

Write and solve a proportion to estimate the number of seventh graders, c, who have cell phones.

$$\frac{\text{7th graders with cell phones in sample}}{\text{number of 7th graders in sample}} = \frac{\text{7th graders with cell phones in school}}{\text{number of 7th graders in school}}$$

$$\frac{16}{20} = \frac{c}{290}$$

$$\frac{16}{20} \cdot 290 = \frac{c}{290} \cdot 290$$

$$232 = c$$

Based on the sample, about 232 seventh graders in Derek's school have cell phones.

 Try It!

For his report, Derek also collects data from a random sample of eighth graders in his school, and finds that 18 out of 20 eighth graders have cell phones. If there are 310 eighth graders in his school, estimate the number of eighth graders who have cell phones.

KEY CONCEPT

You can analyze numerical data from a random sample to draw inferences about the population. Measures of center, like mean and median, and measures of variability, like range, can be used to analyze the data in a sample.

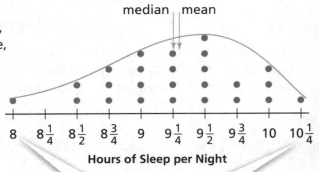

The range is $10\frac{1}{4} - 8 = 2\frac{1}{4}$ hours.

Do You Understand?

1. **? Essential Question** How can inferences be drawn about a population from data gathered from samples?

2. Reasoning Why can you use a random sample to make an inference?

3. Critique Reasoning Darrin surveyed a random sample of 10 students from his science class about their favorite types of TV shows. Five students like detective shows, 4 like comedy shows, and 1 likes game shows. Darrin concluded that the most popular type of TV show among students in his school is likely detective shows. Explain why Darrin's inference is not valid.

4. Reasoning How can you use proportional reasoning to make an estimate about a population using data from a sample?

Do You Know How?

5. In a carnival game, players get 5 chances to throw a basketball through a hoop. The dot plot shows the number of baskets made by 20 different players.

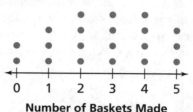

Number of Baskets Made

a. Make an inference by looking at the shape of the data.

b. What is the median of the data? What is the mean? Do these measures of center support the inference you made in part (a)?

6. In the dot plot above, 3 of 20 players made all 5 baskets. Based on this data, about how many players out of 300 players will make all 5 baskets?

7. The manager of a box office gathered data from two different ticket windows where tickets to a music concert were being sold. Does the data shown in the box plots below support the inference that most of the tickets sold were about $40? Explain.

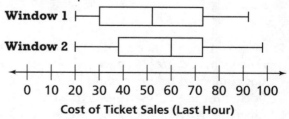

Cost of Ticket Sales (Last Hour)

Practice & Problem Solving

Leveled Practice In 8–10, use the sample data to answer the questions.

Alicia and Thea are in charge of determining the number of T-shirts to order to sell in the school store. Each student collected sample data from the population of 300 students. Alicia surveyed 50 students in the cafeteria. Thea surveyed the first 60 students who arrived at school one morning.

Results of Alicia's Survey	Results of Thea's Survey
$\dfrac{30}{50}$ said they would like a T-shirt.	$\dfrac{51}{60}$ said they would like a T-shirt.

8. Use Alicia's data to estimate the number of T-shirts they should order.

$$\frac{\boxed{}}{\boxed{}} = \frac{x}{\boxed{}}$$

$$\boxed{} = x$$

They should order about $\boxed{}$ T-shirts.

9. Use Thea's data to estimate the number of T-shirts they should order.

$$\frac{\boxed{}}{\boxed{}} = \frac{x}{\boxed{}}$$

$$\boxed{} = x$$

They should order about $\boxed{}$ T-shirts.

10. Construct Arguments Can Alicia or Thea make a valid inference? Explain.

11. Three of the five medical doctors surveyed by a biochemist prefer his newly approved Brand X as compared to the leading medicine. The biochemist used these results to write the TV advertisement shown. Is the inference valid? Explain your answer.

3 out of 5 doctors prefer
Brand X
medicine

Brand X
50 CAPSULES

12. Aaron conducted a survey of the type of shoes worn by a random sample of students in his school. The results of his survey are shown at the right.

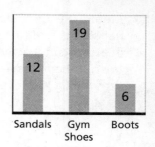

a. Make a valid inference that compares the number of students who are likely to wear gym shoes and those likely to wear boots.

b. Make a valid inference that compares the number of students who are likely to wear boots and those likely to wear sandals.

---

13. Shantel and Syrus are researching the types of novels that people read. Shantel asks every ninth person at the entrance of a mall. She infers that about 26% of the population prefers fantasy novels. Syrus asks every person in only one store. He infers that about 47% of the population prefers fantasy novels.

a. Construct Arguments Whose inference is more likely to be valid? Explain.

b. What mistake might Syrus have made?

14. Higher Order Thinking A national TV news show conducted an online poll to find the nation's favorite comedian. The website showed the pictures of 5 comedians and asked visitors of the site to vote. The news show inferred that the comedian with the most votes was the funniest comedian in the nation.

a. Is the inference valid? Explain.

b. How could you improve the poll? Explain.

In **15** and **16**, use the table of survey results from a random sample of people about the way they prefer to view movies.

15. Lindsay infers that out of 400 people, 300 would prefer to watch movies in a theater. Is her inference valid? Explain.

Preferred Ways to View Movies

Method	Number of People
Theater	30
Streaming	62
DVD	8

16. Which inferences are valid? Select all that apply.

☐ Going to a theater is the most popular way to watch a movie.

☐ About twice as many people would prefer to stream movies instead of watching in a theater.

☐ About 3 times as many people would prefer to watch a movie on DVD instead of watching in a theater.

☐ About 8 times as many people would prefer to watch a movie on DVD instead of streaming.

☐ Most people would prefer streaming over any other method.

17. Monique collects data from a random sample of seventh graders in her school and finds that 10 out of 25 seventh graders participate in after-school activities. Write and solve a proportion to estimate the number of seventh graders, *n*, who participate in after-school activities if 190 seventh graders attend Monique's school.

18. Each of the 65 participants at a basketball camp attempted 20 free throws. Mitchell collected data for the first 10 participants, most of whom were first-time campers. Lydia collected data for the next 10 participants, most of whom had attended the camp for at least one week.

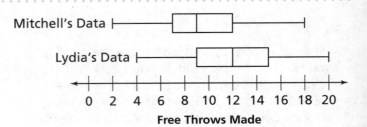

a. Using only his own data, what inference might Mitchell make about the median number of free throws made by the 65 participants?

b. Using only her own data, what inference might Lydia make about the median number of free throws made by the 65 participants?

c. Who made a valid inference? Explain.

Assessment Practice

19. June wants to know how many times most people have their hair cut each year. She asks two of her friends from Redville and Greenburg, respectively, to conduct a random survey. The results of the surveys are shown below.

Redville: 50 people surveyed

Median number of haircuts: 7

Mean number of haircuts: 7.3

Greenburg: 60 people surveyed

Median number of haircuts: 6.5

Mean number of haircuts: 7.6

June infers that most people get 7 haircuts per year. Based on the survey results, is this a valid inference? Explain.

Name: _____

1. **Vocabulary** Krista says that her chickens lay the most eggs of any chickens in the county. To prove her claim, she could survey chicken farms to see how many eggs each of their chickens laid that day. In this scenario, what is the *population* and what is a possible *representative sample*? *Lesson 6-1*

2. Marcy wants to know which type of book is most commonly checked out by visitors of her local public library. She surveys people in the children's reading room between 1:00 and 2:00 on Saturday afternoon. Select all the statements about Marcy's survey that are true. *Lesson 6-1*

    ☐ Marcy's sample is not representative because not all of the library's visitors go to the children's reading room.

    ☐ Marcy's sample is a representative sample of the population.

    ☐ Marcy will get a random sample by surveying as many people in the children's reading room as possible.

    ☐ The population of Marcy's study consists of all visitors of the public library.

    ☐ The results of Marcy's survey include a mode, but neither a mean nor a median.

For Problems 3–5, use the data from the table.

3. Michael surveyed a random sample of students in his school about the number of sports they play. There are 300 students in Michael's school. Use the results of the survey to estimate the number of students in Michael's school who play exactly one sport. Explain your answer. *Lesson 6-2*

Number of Sports Students Play

Number of Sports	Number of Students
None	13
Exactly 1	15
More than 1	32

4. What inference can you draw about the number of students who play more than one sport? *Lesson 6-2*

5. Avi says that Michael's sample was not random because he did not survey students from other schools. Is Avi's statement correct? Explain. *Lesson 6-1*

How well did you do on the mid-topic checkpoint? Fill in the stars.

Topic 6 Use Sampling to Draw Inferences About Populations   **339**

MID-TOPIC PERFORMANCE TASK

Sunil is the ticket manager at a local soccer field. He wants to conduct a survey to determine how many games most spectators attend during the soccer season.

PART A

What is the population for Sunil's survey? Give an example of a way that Sunil could collect a representative sample of this population.

PART B

Sunil conducts the survey and obtains the results shown in the table below. What can Sunil infer from the results of the survey?

Soccer Game Attendance

Number of Games	Number of Spectators
1–2	57
3–4	43
5 or more	50

PART C

Suppose 2,400 spectators attend at least one game this soccer season. Use the survey data to estimate the number of spectators who attended 5 or more games this season. Explain how you made your estimate.

Explore It!

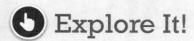

ACTIVITY

Ella surveys a random sample of 20 seventh graders about the number of siblings they have.

Lesson 6-3
Make Comparative Inferences About Populations

📶 Go Online

I can...
draw comparative inferences about two populations using median and interquartile range (IQR).

Ⓒ **Common Core Content Standards**
7.SP.B.3, 7.SP.B.4

Mathematical Practices
MP.1, MP.2, MP.4, MP.7, MP.8

The table shows the results of her survey.

Student	A	B	C	D	E	F	G	H	I	J	K	L	M	N	O	P	Q	R	S	T
Number of Siblings	1	1	2	0	2	1	3	1	1	6	1	2	3	2	1	3	2	0	2	1

A. Model with Math Draw a model to show how Ella can best display her data.

B. Explain why you chose that model.

Focus on math practices
Reasoning Using your data display, what can you infer about the number of siblings that most seventh graders have? Explain.

341

? **Essential Question** ▶ How can data displays be used to compare populations?

VISUAL LEARNING   ASSE

EXAMPLE 1 ▶ 👁 Use Box Plots to Compare Populations

Scan for Multimedia

Finn and Jonah attend different middle schools. They compare the number of hours students at each school spend on homework each week. Finn and Jonah each conduct a random sample of 20 students who attend their schools, and then list the data in order from least to greatest. What can Finn notice about the time spent on homework?

Hours That 20 Students Spend on Homework Each Week

Finn's School	1	1	2	3	3	4	4	4	4	5	5	5	5	6	6	7	7	8	9	11
Jonah's School	1	5	5	5	5	6	6	6	6	8	8	8	8	8	8	9	9	10	11	

STEP 1 Display the two data sets in box plots.

This box is between $3\frac{1}{2}$ and $6\frac{1}{2}$. The median is 5.

This box is between $5\frac{1}{2}$ and 8. The median is 7.

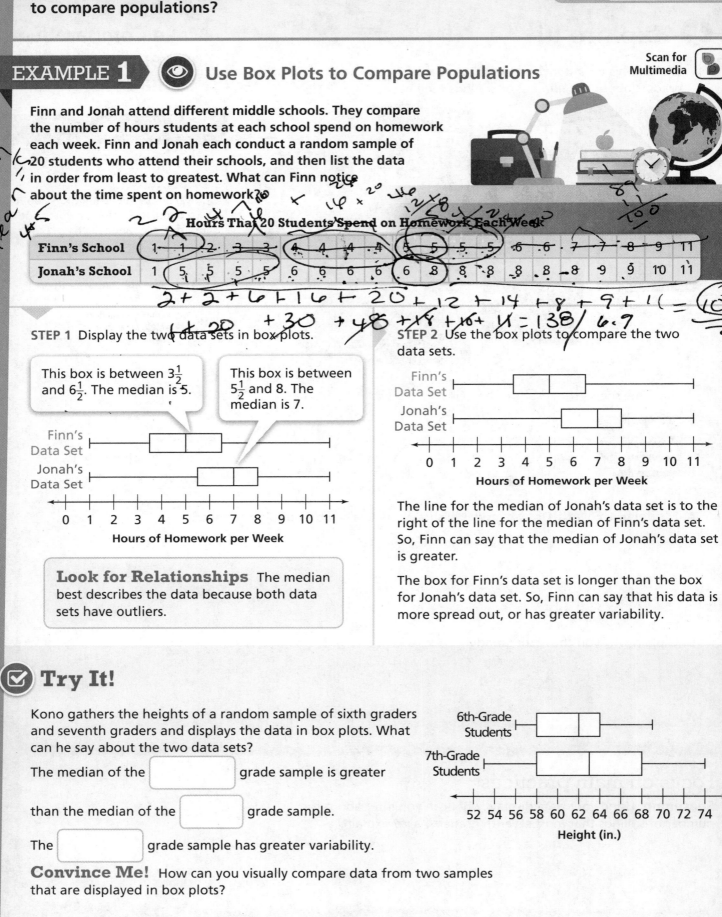

Finn's Data Set
Jonah's Data Set

Hours of Homework per Week
0 1 2 3 4 5 6 7 8 9 10 11

Look for Relationships The median best describes the data because both data sets have outliers.

STEP 2 Use the box plots to compare the two data sets.

Finn's Data Set
Jonah's Data Set

0 1 2 3 4 5 6 7 8 9 10 11
Hours of Homework per Week

The line for the median of Jonah's data set is to the right of the line for the median of Finn's data set. So, Finn can say that the median of Jonah's data set is greater.

The box for Finn's data set is longer than the box for Jonah's data set. So, Finn can say that his data is more spread out, or has greater variability.

☑ Try It!

Kono gathers the heights of a random sample of sixth graders and seventh graders and displays the data in box plots. What can he say about the two data sets?

The median of the [ ] grade sample is greater

than the median of the [ ] grade sample.

The [ ] grade sample has greater variability.

6th-Grade Students

7th-Grade Students

52 54 56 58 60 62 64 66 68 70 72 74
Height (in.)

Convince Me! How can you visually compare data from two samples that are displayed in box plots?

EXAMPLE 2

Draw Inferences Using Median and Interquartile Range

Finn and Jonah analyze the measures of center and variability of the data they collected. Do these measures support Finn's assessment of the two data sets in Example 1?

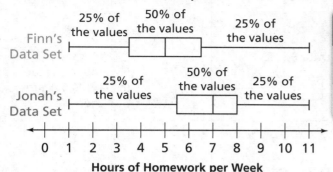

	First Quartile	Median	Third Quartile	Interquartile Range
Finn's Data Set	$3\frac{1}{2}$	5	$6\frac{1}{2}$	3
Jonah's Data Set	$5\frac{1}{2}$	7	8	$2\frac{1}{2}$

The median of Jonah's data set is greater. So the students at Jonah's school generally spend more hours on homework each week than the students at Finn's school.

The interquartile range of Finn's data set is greater. So there is greater variability, or spread, in the number of hours students in Finn's school spend on homework.

EXAMPLE 3

Draw More Inferences Using Measures of Center and Variability

Mr. Bunsen had students grow the same type of plant in two different rooms to test the growing conditions. The box plots show the heights of all the plants after 3 weeks. How do the two populations compare? What inferences can be drawn?

The median heights are the same.

50% of the plants in 7D are between 8 and 14 inches tall IQR = 6.

50% of the plants in 7G are between 10 and 16 inches tall IQR = 6.

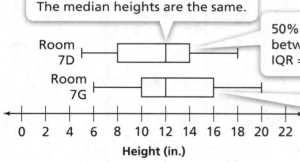

While the median heights of the plants are the same, the plants in Room 7G are generally taller. You can infer that the growing conditions in Room 7G are more favorable for plant growth than in Room 7D.

☑ Try It!

A local recreation center offers a drop-in exercise class in the morning and in the evening. The attendance data for each class over the first month is shown in the box plots at the right. What can you infer about the class attendance?

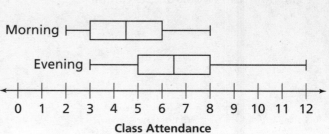

You can use data displays, such as box plots, to make informal comparative inferences about two populations. You can compare the shapes of the data displays or the measures of center and variability.

The medians of the two data sets appear to be the same.

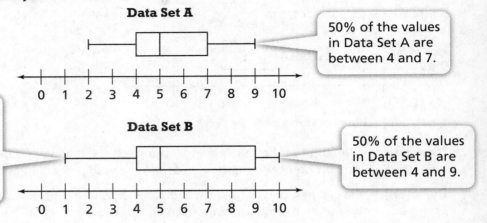

Data Set A

50% of the values in Data Set A are between 4 and 7.

0 1 2 3 4 5 6 7 8 9 10

The length of the box, the IQR, for Data Set B is greater than the length of the box, the IQR, for Data Set A. So Data Set B has greater variability.

Data Set B

50% of the values in Data Set B are between 4 and 9.

0 1 2 3 4 5 6 7 8 9 10

Do You Understand?

1. **Essential Question** How can data displays be used to compare populations?

2. **Generalize** What measures of variability are used when comparing box plots? What do these measures tell you?

3. **Make Sense and Persevere** Two data sets both have a median value of 12.5. Data Set A has an interquartile range of 4 and Data Set B has an interquartile range of 2. How do the box plots for the two data sets compare?

Do You Know How?

The box plots describe the heights of flowers selected randomly from two gardens. Use the box plots to answer 4 and 5.

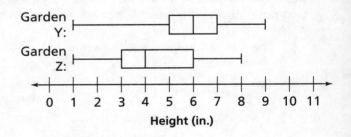

Garden Y:

Garden Z:

0 1 2 3 4 5 6 7 8 9 10 11
Height (in.)

4. Find the median of each sample.

Garden Y median = ☐ inches

Garden Z median = ☐ inches

5. Make a comparative inference about the flowers in the two gardens.

Name: _____

Practice & Problem Solving

Leveled Practice For 6–8, complete each statement.

6. Water boils at lower temperatures as elevation increases. Rob and Ann live in different cities. They both boil the same amount of water in the same size pan and repeat the experiment the same number of times. Each records the water temperature just as the water starts to boil. They use box plots to display their data. Compare the medians of the box plots.

The median of Rob's data is [_____] the median of Ann's data.

This means Rob is at [_____] elevation than Ann.

Rob's Temperature Data

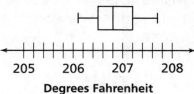

205   206   207   208
Degrees Fahrenheit

Ann's Temperature Data

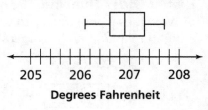

205   206   207   208
Degrees Fahrenheit

7. Liz is analyzing two data sets that compare the amount of food two animals eat each day for one month.

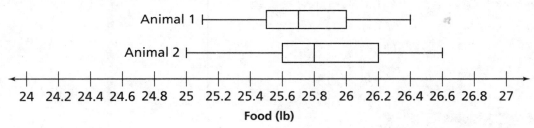

Animal 1

Animal 2

24 24.2 24.4 24.6 24.8 25 25.2 25.4 25.6 25.8 26 26.2 26.4 26.6 26.8 27
Food (lb)

a. The median of Animal 2's data is [_____] than the median of Animal 1's data.

b. Liz can infer that there is [_____] variability in the data for Animal 1 than for Animal 2.

c. Liz can infer that Animal [_____] generally eats more food.

8. The box plots show the heights of a sample of two types of trees.

The median height of Tree [____] is greater.

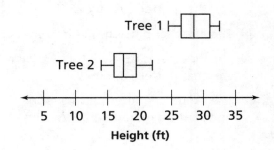

Tree 1

Tree 2

5   10   15   20   25   30   35
Height (ft)

9. Reasoning A family is comparing home prices in towns where they would like to live. The family learns that the median home price in Hometown is equal to the median home price in Plainfield and concludes that the homes in Hometown and Plainfield are similarly priced.

What is another statistical measure that the family might consider when deciding where to purchase a home?

10. Higher Order Thinking The box plots show the daily average high temperatures of two cities from January to December. Which city should you live in if you want a greater variability in temperature? Explain.

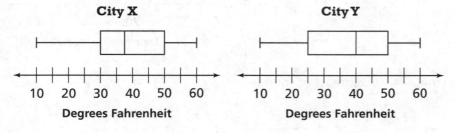

Assessment Practice

11. Paul compares the high temperatures in City 1 and City 2 for one week. In City 1, the range in temperature is 10°F and the IQR is 5°F. In City 2, the range in temperature is 20°F and the IQR is 5°F.

What might you conclude about the weather pattern in each city based on the ranges and interquartile ranges?

Ⓐ The weather pattern in City 1 is more consistent than the weather pattern in City 2.

Ⓑ The weather patterns in City 1 and City 2 are equally consistent.

Ⓒ The weather pattern in City 2 is more consistent than the weather pattern in City 1.

Ⓓ The range and interquartile range do not provide enough information to make a conclusion.

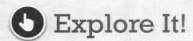 Explore It!

 ACTIVITY

Jackson and his brother Levi watch Jewel Geyser erupt one afternoon. They record the time intervals between eruptions. The dot plot shows their data.

Jackson estimates that the average time between eruptions is 8 minutes. Levi estimates that the average time between eruptions is $8\frac{1}{2}$ minutes.

Jewel Geyser Eruptions

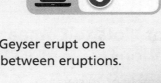

6½ 7 7½ 8 8½ 9 9½ 10

Minutes

Lesson 6-4
Make More Comparative Inferences About Populations

 Go Online

I can...
compare populations using the mean, median, mode, range, interquartile range, and mean absolute deviation.

© **Common Core Content Standards**
7.SP.B.3, 7.SP.B.4

Mathematical Practices
MP.2, MP.3, MP.4, MP.8

A. Construct Arguments Construct an argument to support Jackson's position.

B. Construct Arguments Construct an argument to support Levi's position.

Focus on math practices

Reasoning How can you determine the best measure of center to describe a set of data?

347

VISUAL LEARNING ASSE

EXAMPLE 1 Use Dot Plots to Compare Populations

Quinn collects data from a random sample of 20 seventh-grade students who participate in a youth fitness program. She compares the number of curl-ups each student completed in thirty seconds last year and this year. What can Quinn infer from her comparison of the data sets?

Scan for Multimedia

Number of Curl-Ups That 20 Students Completed

Last Year	20	27	21	26	22	25	23	23	26	23	24	24	25	24	22	24	23	24	21	25
This Year	21	30	22	24	29	26	28	26	30	27	27	29	27	28	25	28	25	28	29	23

STEP 1 Display the two data sets in dot plots.

Model with Math Why are dot plots an appropriate representation for the data sets?

Curl-Ups Completed Last Year

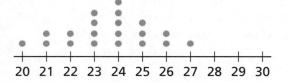

Curl-Ups Completed This Year

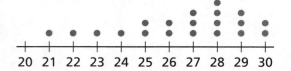

STEP 2 Use the dot plots to compare the two data sets.

Curl-Ups Completed Last Year

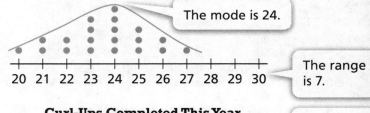

The mode is 24.

The range is 7.

Curl-Ups Completed This Year

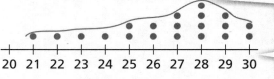

The mode is 28.

The range is 9.

The number of curl-ups completed this year is generally greater than last year. But, based on the shape of the data, not all students made the same progress.

Quinn can infer that most of her classmates were able to do more curl-ups this year.

✓ Try It!

Quinn also collects data about push-ups. Does it appear that students generally did more push-ups last year or this year? Explain your reasoning.

Push-Ups Completed Last Year

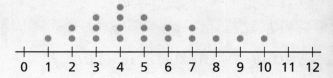

Convince Me! How does the range of these data sets affect the shape of the dot plots?

Push-Ups Completed This Year

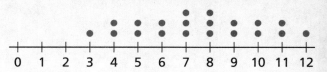

EXAMPLE **2**

Use Measures of Center and Variability to Compare Populations

ACTIVITY ASSESS

Quinn computes the mean and mean absolute deviation (MAD) for each data set. How do these measures support Quinn's inference from the data displays?

Curl-Ups Completed Last Year

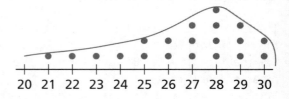

	Mean	MAD
Curl-Ups Completed Last Year	23.6	1.4
Curl-Ups Completed This Year	26.6	2.1

20 21 22 23 24 25 26 27 28 29 30

> The mean can be used to describe the data because the data sets do not have outliers.

Curl-Ups Completed This Year

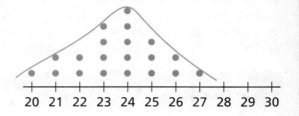

20 21 22 23 24 25 26 27 28 29 30

The mean number of curl-ups completed this year is greater than the mean number of curl-ups completed last year. This supports Quinn's inference.

The mean absolute deviation is greater for the number of curl-ups completed this year. This suggests that not all students made the same progress.

EXAMPLE **3**

Use Statistical Measures to Make Predictions

Rafi, one of Quinn's classmates, reported the numbers of curl-ups he completed this year and last year. He did not tell Quinn which number is for which year. Based on the data that Quinn gathered, which number *most likely* represents the curl-ups he completed last year?

Based on the data that Quinn gathered, she inferred that most students could complete more curl-ups this year than last year.

So, Rafi *most likely* completed 19 curl-ups last year and 23 curl-ups this year.

Total curl-ups **19**

Total curl-ups **23**

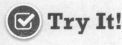 **Try It!**

Peter surveyed a random sample of adults and a random sample of teenagers about the number of hours that they exercise in a typical week. He recorded the data in the table below. What comparative inference can Peter make from the data sets?

Hours of Exercise

	Mean	MAD
Adults	4.4	3.0
Teenagers	7.9	2.8

You can use dot plots to make informal comparative inferences about two populations. You can compare the shapes of the data displays or the measures of center and variability.

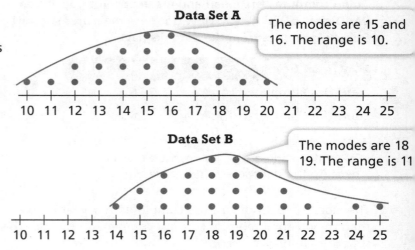

Data Set A — The modes are 15 and 16. The range is 10.

Data Set B — The modes are 18 19. The range is 11

	Mean	Mean Absolute Deviation (MAD)
Data Set A	15.04	1.9648
Data Set B	18.56	2.1024

The modes of Data Set B are greater than the modes of Data Set A.

The mean of Data Set B is greater than the mean of Data Set A.

You can infer that data points are generally greater in Data Set B.

The ranges and the MADs of the data sets are similar. You can infer that the variabilities of the two data sets are about the same.

Do You Understand?

1. **? Essential Question** How can dot plots and statistical measures be used to compare populations?

2. **Reasoning** How can you make predictions using data from samples from two populations?

3. **Construct Arguments** Two data sets have the same mean but one set has a much larger MAD than the other. Explain why you may want to use the median to compare the data sets rather than the mean.

Do You Know How?

For 4 and 5, use the information below.

Coach Fiske recorded the number of shots on goal his first-line hockey players made during two weeks of hockey scrimmage.

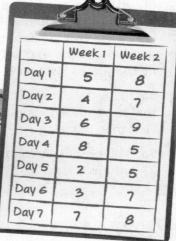

	Week 1	Week 2
Day 1	5	8
Day 2	4	7
Day 3	6	9
Day 4	8	5
Day 5	2	5
Day 6	3	7
Day 7	7	8

4. Find the mean number of shots on goal for each week.

5. a. Based on the mean for each week, in which week did his first line take more shots on goal?

   b. Based on the comparison of the mean and the range for Week 1 and Week 2, what could the coach infer?

PRACTICE   TUTORIAL

Practice & Problem Solving

Scan for
Multimedia

Leveled Practice In 6 and 7, complete each statement.

6. A study is done to compare the fuel efficiency of cars. Cars in Group 1 generally get about 23 miles per gallon. Cars in Group 2 generally get about 44 miles per gallon. Compare the groups by their means. Then make an inference and give a reason the inference might be true.

The mean for Group ☐ is less than the mean for

Group ☐.

The cars in Group ☐ generally are more fuel-efficient.

The cars in Group ☐ may be smaller.

Group 1

23 miles
per gallon

Group 2

44 miles
per gallon

7. The dot plot shows a random sample of vertical leap heights of basketball players in two different basketball camps. Compare the mean values of the dot plots. Round to the nearest tenth.

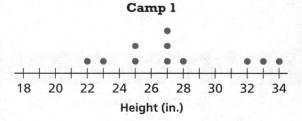

Camp 1

Height (in.)

Vertical Leap Samples

Camp	Mean
1	$303 \div 11 =$ ☐
2	☐ $\div 11 =$ ☐

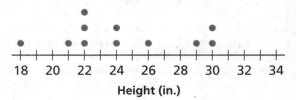

Camp 2

Height (in.)

The mean values tell you that participants in Camp ☐ jump higher in general.

8. A researcher divides some marbles into two data sets. In Data Set 1, the mean mass of the marbles is 13.6 grams. In Data Set 2, the mean mass of the marbles is 14 grams. The MAD of both data sets is 2. What can you infer about the two sets of marbles?

9. **Generalize** Brianna asks 8 classmates how many pencils and erasers they carry in their bags. The mean number of pencils is 11. The mean number of erasers is 4. The MAD of both data sets is 2. What inference could Brianna make using this data?

10. **Higher Order Thinking** Two machines in a factory are supposed to work at the same speed to pass inspection. The number of items built by each machine on five different days is recorded in the table. The inspector believes that the machines should not pass inspection because the mean speed of Machine X is much faster than the mean speed of Machine Y.

Number of Items Built

Machine X	20	16	21	18	19
Machine Y	23	2	18	21	19

a. Which measures of center and variability should be used to compare the performances of each machine? Explain.

b. Is the inspector correct? Explain.

✓ Assessment Practice

11. The dot plots show the weights of a random sample of fish from two lakes.

Which comparative inference about the fish in the two lakes is most likely correct?

Ⓐ There is about the same variation in weight between small and large fish in both lakes.

Ⓑ There is less variation in weight between small and large fish in South Lake than between small and large fish in Round Lake.

Ⓒ There is less variation in weight between small and large fish in Round Lake than between small and large fish in South Lake.

Ⓓ There is greater variability in the weights of fish in Round Lake.

Sample from Round Lake

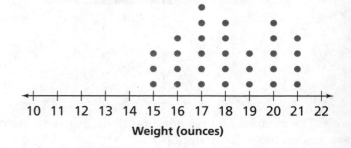

Weight (ounces)

Sample from South Lake

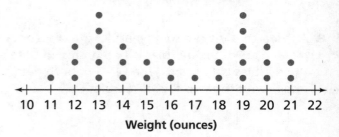

Weight (ounces)

© **Common Core Content Standards**
7.SP.A.1, 7.SP.A.2, 7.RP.A.3

Mathematical Practices
MP.4, MP.1, MP.2, MP.3, MP.5, MP.7, MP.8

ACT 1

1. After watching the video, what is the first question that comes to mind?

2. Write the Main Question you will answer.

3. Make a prediction to answer this Main Question.

4. Construct Arguments Explain how you arrived at your prediction.

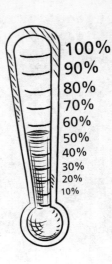

5. What information in this situation would be helpful to know? How would you use that information?

6. Use Appropriate Tools What tools can you use to solve the problem? Explain how you would use them strategically.

7. Model with Math Represent the situation using mathematics. Use your representation to answer the Main Question.

8. What is your answer to the Main Question? Does it differ from your prediction? Explain.

9. Write the answer you saw in the video.

10. Reasoning Does your answer match the answer in the video? If not, what are some reasons that would explain the difference?

11. Make Sense and Persevere Would you change your model now that you know the answer? Explain.

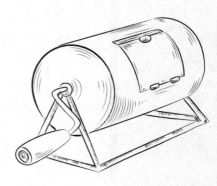

Reflect

12. Model with Math Explain how you used a mathematical model to represent the situation. How did the model help you answer the Main Question?

13. Critique Reasoning Explain why you agree or disagree with each of the arguments in Act 2.

SEQUEL

14. Use Appropriate Tools You and your friends are starting a new school club. Design a sampling method that is easy to use to help you estimate how many people will join your club. What tools will you use?

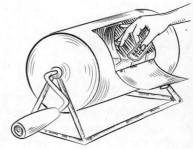

? Topic Essential Question

How can sampling be used to draw inferences about one or more populations?

Vocabulary Review

Complete each definition, and then provide an example of each vocabulary word used.

| **Vocabulary** | inference | population | random sample |
| | representative sample | sample | valid inference |

Definition	Example
1. A(n) [_____] is an entire group of objects from which data can be collected.	
2. Making a conclusion by interpreting data is called making a(n) [_____].	
3. A(n) [_____] is one that is true about a population based on a representative sample.	
4. A(n) [_____] accurately reflects the characteristics of an entire population.	

Use Vocabulary in Writing

Do adults or teenagers brush their teeth more? Nelson surveys two groups: 50 seventh-grade students from his school and 50 students at a nearby college of dentistry. Use vocabulary words to explain whether Nelson can draw valid conclusions.

Concepts and Skills Review

Quick Review

A **population** is an entire group of people, items, or events. Most populations must be reduced to a smaller group, or **sample**, before surveying. A **representative sample** accurately reflects the characteristics of the population. In a **random sample**, each member of the population has an equal chance of being included.

Example

Describe the sample and the population.

Honey Bee Florist Customer Survey: Favorite Flowers

Rose	Daisy	Tulip
15	9	16

Sample: 40 customers of Honey Bee Florist

Population: All Honey Bee Florist customers

Practice

1. Anthony opened a new store and wants to conduct a survey to determine the best store hours. Which is the best representative sample?

   Ⓐ A group of randomly selected people who come to the store in one week

   Ⓑ A group of randomly selected people who visit his website on one night

   Ⓒ Every person he meets at his health club one night

   Ⓓ The first 20 people who walk into his store one day

2. Becky wants to know if she should sell cranberry muffins at her bakery. She asks every customer who buys blueberry muffins if they would buy cranberry muffins. Is this a representative sample? Explain.

3. Simon wants to find out which shop has the best frozen fruit drink in town. How could Simon conduct a survey with a sample that is representative of the population?

Quick Review

An **inference** is a conclusion about a population based on data from a sample or samples. Patterns or trends in data from representative samples can be used to make **valid inferences**. Estimates can be made about the population based on the sample data.

Example

There are 400 students at Polly's school. She surveyed a random sample of 80 students to find their favorite hobby.

19 said they like to read.

30 said they like to be with friends.

8 said they like to do crafts.

23 said they like to play sports.

Make an inference from the data.

Doing crafts is the least popular hobby at Polly's school.

Practice

1. Refer to the example. Polly surveys two more samples. Do the results from these samples support the inference made from the example?

Random Samples of Students' Favorite Hobbies

Sample 2		Sample 3	
Hobby	Number of Students	Hobby	Number of Students
Read	24	Read	32
Friends	35	Friends	41
Crafts	11	Crafts	16
Sports	30	Sports	31

2. Refer to the example. Yovani estimates that about 200 students in the school favor playing sports as a hobby. Do you agree? Explain.

Quick Review

Box plots and dot plots are common ways to display data gathered from samples of populations. Using these data displays makes it easier to visually compare sets of data and make inferences. Statistical measures such as mean, median, mode, MAD, interquartile range (IQR), and range can also be used to draw inferences when comparing data from samples of two populations.

Example

The box plots show how long it took students in Ms. Huang's two math classes to complete their math homework last night. Use the median time to make an inference.

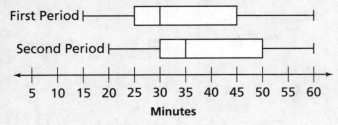

Median for First Period: 30

Median for Second Period: 35

Students in the second-period class tended to take longer to complete their math homework.

Janelle collected data for runs scored for two baseball teams in the first 8 games of the season.

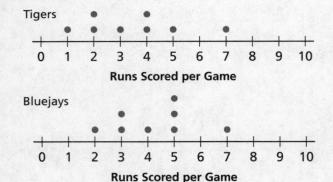

What can Janelle infer from the data sets?

The Bluejays are a higher scoring team. The mode is greater for them than it is for the Tigers.

Practice

1. The two data sets show the number of days that team members trained before a 5K race.

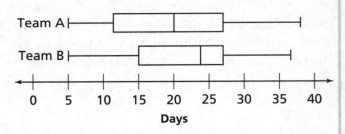

a. What inference can you draw by comparing the medians?

b. What inference can you draw by comparing the interquartile ranges?

2. The dot plots show how long it took students in Mr. Chauncey's two science classes to finish their science homework last night. Find the means to make an inference about the data.

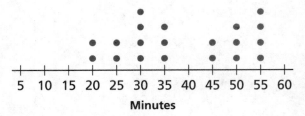

First Period

Second Period

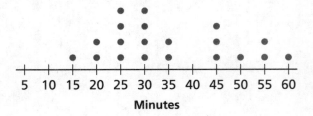

Riddle Rearranging

Find each percent change or percent error. Round to the nearest whole percent as needed. Then arrange the answers in order from least to greatest. The letters will spell out the answer to the riddle below.

I can...
use the percent equation to solve problems. © 7.RP.A.3

V A young tree is 16 inches tall. One year later, it is 20 inches tall. What is the percent increase in height?

A A ship weighs 7 tons with no cargo. With cargo, it weighs 10.5 tons. What is the percent increase in the weight?

R The balance of an account is $500 in April. In May it is $440. What is the percent decrease in the balance?

B Ben thought an assignment would take 20 minutes to complete. It took 35 minutes. What is the percent error in his estimate of the time?

N Natalie has $250 in savings. At the end of 6 months, she has $450 in savings. What is the percent increase in the amount of her savings?

I The water level of a lake is 22 feet. It falls to 18 feet during one month. What is the percent decrease in the water level?

R Shamar has 215 photos on his cell phone. He deletes some so that only 129 photos remain. What is the percent decrease in the number of photos?

K Lita estimates she will read 24 books during the summer. She actually reads 9 books. What is the percent error of her estimate?

E Camden estimates his backpack weighs 9 pounds with his books. It actually weighs 12 pounds. What is the percent error of his estimate?

Where do fish keep their money?

◯ ◯ ◯ ◯ ◯   ◯ ◯ ◯ ◯

PROBABILITY

How can you investigate chance processes and develop, use, and evaluate probability models?

Topic Overview

7-1 Understand Likelihood and Probability

7-2 Understand Theoretical Probability

7-3 Understand Experimental Probability

7-4 Use Probability Models

3-Act Mathematical Modeling: Photo Finish

7-5 Determine Outcomes of Compound Events

7-6 Find Probabilities of Compound Events

7-7 Simulate Compound Events

Topic Vocabulary

- compound event
- event
- experimental probability
- outcome
- probability
- probability model
- relative frequency
- sample space
- simulation
- theoretical probability

Lesson Digital Resources

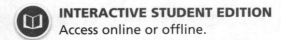

INTERACTIVE STUDENT EDITION
Access online or offline.

INTERACTIVE ANIMATION
Interact with visual learning animations.

ACTIVITY Use with *Solve & Discuss It, Explor* and *Explain It* activities, and to explore Exam

VIDEOS Watch clips to support *3-Act Mathematical Modeling Lessons* and *STEM P*

 Go online

Photo Finish

Photo Finish

Have you ever watched a race that was so close you couldn't tell who won? That's what a photo finish is for. In shorter races, such as the 100-meter sprint, all the runners could finish within half a second of each other. That's why it's important for athletes to consider every possible way to improve their race times. Think about this during the 3-Act Mathematical Modeling lesson.

PRACTICE Practice what you've learned.

TUTORIALS Get help from *Virtual Nerd*, right when you need it.

MATH TOOLS Explore math with digital tools.

GAMES Play Math Games to help you learn.

KEY CONCEPT Review important lesson content.

GLOSSARY Read and listen to English/Spanish definitions.

ASSESSMENT Show what you've learned.

enVision STEM Project

 VIDEO

Did You Know?

China and India are the two **most populated** nations in the world. More than $\frac{1}{3}$ of all people live in one of these countries.

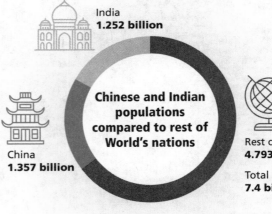

India
1.252 billion

Chinese and Indian populations compared to rest of World's nations

China
1.357 billion

Rest of the World
4.793 billion

Total Population
7.4 billion

California has a greater **population** than Canada.

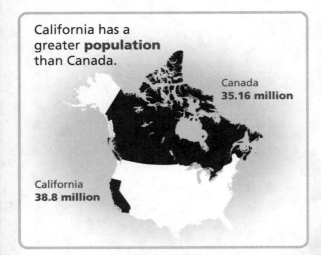

Canada
35.16 million

California
38.8 million

Nearly **ten million more** people live in the metropolitan area of Tokyo, Japan, than in the entire State of Texas.

JAPAN

Tokyo

TEXAS

The population of the world has nearly **doubled** in the last 40 years, but is expected to take at least 100 years to double again.

World population

1975: 4.1 billion

2016: 7.4 billion

2125: 15 billion (estimated)

There are more than **100,000 residents per square mile** in Manila, the capital city of the Philippines. There is approximately **1 human** inhabitant per square mile in Alaska.

Your Task: International Trending

Demography is the science of populations. Demographers — scientists who study populations — follow trends in populations, including birth rates and immigration statistics, to learn more about how countries are changing around the world. You and your classmates will use population data like birth rate, age range, and life expectancy to compare and contrast the characteristics of populations.

Review What You Know!

Vocabulary

Choose the best term from the box to complete each definition.

> equivalent
>
> frequency
>
> diagram
>
> ratio

1. A(n) [   ] is a drawing that can be used to visually represent information.

2. The number of times a specific value occurs is referred to as [   ].

3. A(n) [   ] is a relationship between one quantity and another quantity.

4. Quantities that have the same value are [   ].

Operations with Fractions

Solve for x.

5. $\frac{2}{5} + x = 1$

6. $225 \cdot \frac{1}{3} = x$

7. $1 = \frac{1}{8} + x + \frac{2}{8}$

Ratios

Write each ratio in fraction form. Then write the percent equivalent.

8. 72 out of 96

9. 88 out of 132

10. 39 out of 104

11. 23 out of 69

12. 52 out of 208

13. 25 out of 200

Order Fractions and Decimals

Plot the following fractions and decimals on the number line.

$$0.7, \frac{1}{3}, \frac{7}{8}, 0.4, 0.125, \frac{5}{6}$$

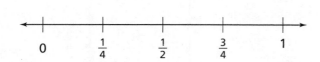

Language Development

Sort the vocabulary words into categories. Explain your categories.

compound event	event	experimental probability	outcome
probability	probability model	relative frequency	sample space
simulation	theoretical probability		

Category:

Category:

Category:

PROJECT 7A

What makes a carnival game fun and successful?

PROJECT: DEVELOP A GAME OF CHANCE

PROJECT 7B

If you could invent a character for an adventure, what would that character be like?

PROJECT: DESIGN AN ADVENTURE

PROJECT 7C

What is the silliest sentence you can think of? Why is it silly?

PROJECT: GENERATE A FUNNY SENTENCE

PROJECT 7D

How could you teach a math concept through a performance?

PROJECT: PERFORM YOUR KNOWLEDGE

Solve & Discuss It!  **ACTIVITY**

For a game show, Jared has to choose 1 of 8 boxes to win a prize. One of the boxes has a big prize, 3 boxes have a medium prize, 3 boxes have smaller prizes, and 1 box is empty. How confident should Jared be that whatever box he chooses, he will win a prize? Support your response with a mathematical argument.

I can...
describe the likelihood that an event will occur.

© **Common Core Content Standards**
7.SP.C.5, 7.EE.B.3

Mathematical Practices
MP.1, MP.2, MP.3, MP.4

Make Sense and Persevere
What are the chances that Jared will choose a box with a prize?

Focus on math practices

Construct Arguments Suppose the empty box is taken out of the game. How confident should Jared be that he will win a prize? Explain.

VISUAL LEARNING ASSES

EXAMPLE 1   Use Probability to Describe Chance

Scan for Multimedia

Alisa and Cheri spin the pointer to the right and record the color that it lands on. The table shows their results after 100 spins. How can Alisa and Cheri explain their results?

Color	Frequency
Red	23
Yellow	24
Green	27
Blue	26

There are 4 possible results, or **outcomes**, when Alisa and Cheri spin the pointer:

- The pointer lands on the red section.
- The pointer lands on the yellow section.
- The pointer lands on the green section.
- The pointer lands on the blue section.

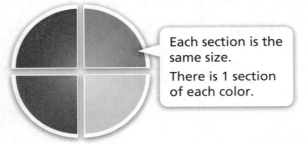

Each section is the same size.

There is 1 section of each color.

Each of the 4 outcomes is equally likely because the pointer has an equal chance of landing on any of the 4 sections.

Each time they spin the pointer, the likelihood, or **probability**, of the pointer landing on red, yellow, green, or blue is the same.

Each of the equal-sized sections is shaded 1 of 4 colors, so the probability of the pointer landing on any given color is 1 out of 4, or $\frac{1}{4}$. Since $\frac{1}{4} = 25\%$, the probability can also be written as 25%.

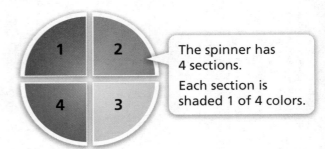

The spinner has 4 sections.

Each section is shaded 1 of 4 colors.

The pointer should land on each color about 1 out of 4 times, or about 25 times out of 100 spins.

☑ Try It!

How might the probability of the pointer landing on a given color change for the spinner shown at the right?

Convince Me! How would the probability of the pointer landing on a given color change if the spinner had six equal-sized sections with each section a different color?

EXAMPLE 2 — Use Probability and Likelihood to Describe Situations

Carrie will roll a number cube with sides labeled 1 to 6.

a. What is the probability that she will roll a 2?
Only 1 out of 6 total sides is a 2.
So, the probability is 1 out of 6, or $\frac{1}{6}$.

b. What is the probability that she will roll a number less than 7?
All 6 numbers on the cube are less than 7.
So, it is certain that she will roll a number less than 7.
The probability is 6 out of 6, or 1.

c. What is the probability that she will roll a number greater than 6?
None of the 6 numbers on the cube is greater than 6.
So, it is impossible to roll a number greater than 6.
The probability is 0 out of 6, or 0.

Try It!

The game piece shown has 12 sides, labeled 1 to 12.

a. What is the probability of rolling an 11?

b. What is the probability of rolling a number greater than 5?

c. What is the probability of rolling a number greater than 12?

EXAMPLE 3 —  Use Probability to Examine Fairness

Marisol designed a spinner for a game. The spinner is fair if there is an equal chance for the pointer to land on each letter. Is the spinner a fair spinner?

> The spinner has 6 equal-sized sections. Two sections are labeled "A."

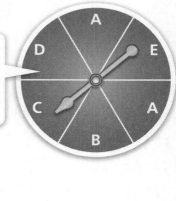

The probability of the pointer landing on "A" is 2 out of 6, which is equivalent to 1 out of 3, or $\frac{1}{3}$.

The probability of the pointer landing on "B" is 1 out of 6, or $\frac{1}{6}$.

Each of the probabilities of the pointer landing on "C", "D", or "E" is also 1 out of 6, or $\frac{1}{6}$.

It is more likely that the pointer will land on "A" than on any other number. So, it is not a fair spinner.

 Try It!

Is the spinner shown a fair spinner? If yes, explain why. If not, describe a change that could make the spinner fair.

The probability that something will occur is a value from 0 to 1, which describes its likelihood. You can write probability as a ratio, such as 1 out of 2, or $\frac{1}{2}$, or as a percent, such as 50%.

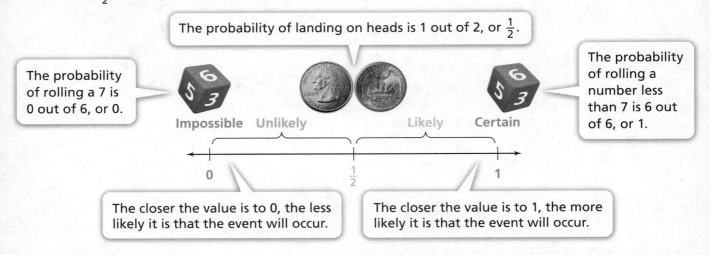

The probability of landing on heads is 1 out of 2, or $\frac{1}{2}$.

The probability of rolling a 7 is 0 out of 6, or 0.

The probability of rolling a number less than 7 is 6 out of 6, or 1.

Impossible   Unlikely   Likely   Certain

0          $\frac{1}{2}$ 1

The closer the value is to 0, the less likely it is that the event will occur.

The closer the value is to 1, the more likely it is that the event will occur.

Do You Understand?

1. **? Essential Question** What is probability?

2. **Construct Arguments** How can you use probability to draw conclusions about the likelihood that something will occur?

3. **Reasoning** Why is probability limited to numbers between 0 and 1?

Do You Know How?

Allie is going to select a card from the group of cards shown. Complete each statement.

4. The probability that Allie will select a card labeled 3 is _____ out of 10, or _____ %.

5. Because the probability that each number will be selected is not _____, the group of cards is not fair.

6. It is _____ that Allie will select a card labeled with a number less than 6.

7. It is _____ that Allie will select a card labeled 4.

Name: _____

Practice & Problem Solving

Leveled Practice In 8–10, fill in the boxes to complete each statement.

8. A spinner has 8 equal-sized sections. Six of the sections are green.

  a. What is the probability that the spinner will land on green?

  [ ] out of 8, or $\dfrac{\boxed{}}{4}$, or [ ] %

  b. Use words to describe the probability.

  It is [ ] that the spinner will land on green.

9. Marcus is rolling a number cube with sides labeled 1 to 6.

  a. The probability that the number cube will show 10 is [ ] .

  b. It is [ ] that the number cube will show 10.

10. Of the marbles in a bag, 3 are yellow, 2 are red, and 2 are blue. Sandra will randomly choose one marble from the bag.

  a. The probability that Sandra will choose a blue marble from the bag is [ ] out of [ ] , or $\dfrac{\boxed{}}{\boxed{}}$.

  b. It is [ ] that Sandra will choose a blue marble from the bag.

11. Suppose you have a bag with 20 letter tiles in it, and 3 of the tiles are labeled Y. Suppose a second bag has 500 letter tiles in it, and 170 of the tiles are labeled Y. From which bag are you more likely to pick a tile that is labeled Y? Explain.

12. Make Sense and Persevere Suppose you have a bag of 40 marbles, and 20 of them are white. If you choose a marble without looking, the probability that you choose a white marble is $\frac{20}{40}$. Describe the probability.

13. Suppose Nigel has a bag of colored wristbands, and he chooses one without looking. The bag contains a total of 25 wristbands and 6 of the wristbands are blue.

   a. What is the probability that Nigel will choose a blue wristband?

   b. Is it likely, unlikely, or neither likely nor unlikely that Nigel will choose a blue wristband?

14. A box contains four equal-sized cards labeled 1, 3, 5, and 7. Tim will select one card from the box.

   a. What is the probability that Tim will select a card labeled 4?

   b. What is the probability that Tim will select a card labeled with a number less than 6?

   c. What is the probability that Tim will select a card labeled with an odd number?

15. **Model with Math** Henry is going to color a spinner with 10 equal-sized sections. Three of the sections will be orange and 7 of the sections will be purple. Is this spinner fair? If so, explain why. If not, explain how to make it a fair spinner.

16. **Higher Order Thinking** Without being able to calculate probability, describe the likelihood that the following event will occur.

   All 21 students in a class share the same birthday.

✓ Assessment Practice

17. After many studies, a researcher finds that the probability that a word recognition app correctly interprets a handwritten word is $\frac{9}{10}$. Which statement is true?

   Ⓐ It is impossible that the handwritten word will be correctly interpreted.

   Ⓑ It is unlikely that the handwritten word will be correctly interpreted.

   Ⓒ It is likely that the handwritten word will be correctly interpreted.

   Ⓓ It is certain that the handwritten word will be correctly interpreted.

18. A bag contains 8 letter tiles of the same size. The tiles are labeled either A, B, C, D, E, or F. Three of the tiles are labeled C. If Corey selects 1 tile from the bag without looking, is the selection of letters fair? Explain.

Solve & Discuss It!

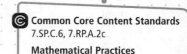 ACTIVITY

Betty and Carl will conduct an experiment. They will flip
a coin 100 times and record the result of each flip. What
should they expect the results of their experiment to be?
Justify your answer.

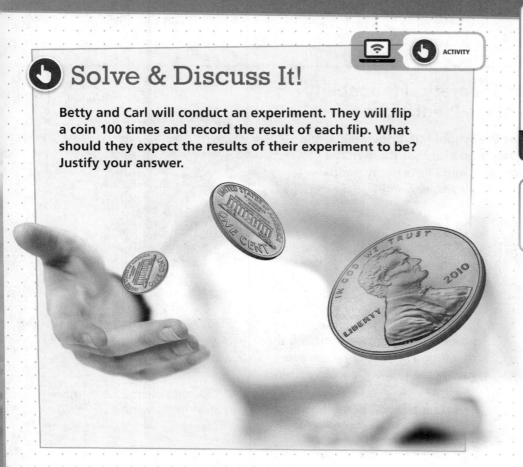

Lesson 7-2
Understand
Theoretical
Probability

Go Online

I can...
determine the theoretical
probability of an event.

© **Common Core Content Standards**
7.SP.C.6, 7.RP.A.2c

Mathematical Practices
MP.1, MP.2, MP.3, MP.4, MP.7

Focus on math practices

Look for Relationships How would their expected results change if Betty
and Carl flipped a coin 500 times?

? Essential Question How can the probability of an event help make predictions?

 VISUAL LEARNING ASSES

EXAMPLE 1 **Use Theoretical Probability to Make Predictions**

Scan for Multimedia

Talia and Yoshi design a game for the school fair. Contestants spin the pointer and win a prize if it lands on either of the two red sections. How can Talia and Yoshi determine how many people are likely to be winners if 500 people play their game?

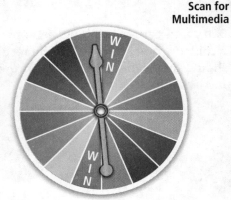

Model with Math How can you use probability to predict the number of winners?

STEP 1 Determine the total number of possible outcomes from one spin of the pointer.

There are 16 sections that are all the same size. There are 2 sections of each color.

The pointer could land on any of the 16 sections, so there are 16 possible equally likely outcomes.

STEP 2 Because you know all the possible outcomes, you can find the **theoretical probability** of an event, such as the pointer landing on red.

P represents theoretical probability. An **event** is a single outcome or group of outcomes.

$$P(\text{event}) = \frac{\text{number of favorable outcomes}}{\text{total number of possible outcomes}}$$

The event is *landing on red*.

$$P(\text{red}) = \frac{\text{number of red sections}}{\text{total number of sections}}$$
$$= \frac{2}{16} = \frac{1}{8}$$

The theoretical probability that a contestant will win this game is $\frac{1}{8}$ or 12.5%.

STEP 3 Use proportional reasoning to predict the number of likely winners.

w represents the number of likely winners.

$$\frac{1}{8} = \frac{w}{500}$$
$$\frac{1}{8} \cdot 500 = \frac{w}{500} \cdot 500$$
$$62.5 = w$$

Of the 500 contestants, about 62 are likely to be winners.

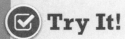 **Try It!**

If Talia and Yoshi redesign their spinner to have 14 sections instead of 16 sections, would they likely have more or fewer winners? Explain why.

Convince Me! If there are always 2 red sections, how does the number of total sections in the spinner relate to the theoretical probability of winning this game?

EXAMPLE 2 ▶ 👆 Determine Theoretical Probability

ACTIVITY   ASSESS

Archie plays a word board game. He places 98 lettered tiles and 2 blank tiles in a bag. Players will draw tiles from the bag one at a time without looking.

What is the probability that the first tile drawn will be a blank tile? Labeled with a letter? A vowel? A consonant?

$P(\text{blank}) = \frac{2}{100} = \frac{1}{50}$

$P(\text{vowel}) = \frac{42}{100} = \frac{21}{50}$

$P(\text{letter}) = \frac{98}{100} = \frac{49}{50}$

$P(\text{consonant}) = \frac{56}{100} = \frac{28}{50}$

Look for Relationships How are the probabilities related to each other?

A A A A A A A A A A A E
E E E E E E E E E E
E I I I I I I I I I
O O O O O O O O U U
U U B B C C D D D D
F F G G H H J K L
L L L M M N N N N N
N P P Q R R R R R R
S S S S T T T T T T
V V W W X Y Y Z

EXAMPLE 3 ▶ 👆 Use Theoretical Probability to Make More Predictions

Joaquin also designs a game for the school fair. Contestants roll two number cubes at the same time. If the sum of the numbers on the two cubes is 7, the player wins. About how many winners should Joaquin expect if 500 contestants play his game?

STEP 1 Find all possible outcomes and all winning outcomes.

favoirble out comes over Possible

2nd number cube

	1	2	3	4	5	6
1	2	3	4	5	6	7
2	3	4	5	6	7	8
3	4	5	6	7	8	9
4	5	6	7	8	9	10
5	6	7	8	9	10	11
6	7	8	9	10	11	12

1st number cube

There are 6 ways to win out of a total of 36 possible combinations of rolls.

STEP 2 Find the theoretical probability of rolling a sum of 7.

$P(\text{sum of 7}) = \frac{6}{36} = \frac{1}{6}$

STEP 3 Use proportional reasoning to predict the number of winners, w.

$$\frac{1}{6} = \frac{w}{500}$$

$$\frac{1}{6} \cdot 500 = \frac{w}{500} \cdot 500$$

$$83.\overline{3} = w$$

Of 500 contestants, Joaquin should expect about 83 winners.

☑ Try It!

Joaquin wants to reduce the number of winners so he does not have to prepare as many prizes. Choose another sum he could use as a winning sum, and predict the number of winners if 500 people play his game.

You can determine the theoretical probability of an event, *P*(event), if you know all the possible outcomes and they are equally likely.

$$P(event) = \frac{number\ of\ favorable\ outcomes}{total\ number\ of\ possible\ outcomes}$$

You can use theoretical probability and proportional reasoning to make predictions, such as in a game situation.

$$\frac{number\ of\ favorable\ outcomes}{total\ number\ of\ possible\ outcomes} = \frac{number\ of\ winning\ outcomes}{total\ number\ of\ possible\ outcomes}$$

Do You Understand?

1. **? Essential Question** How can the probability of an event help make predictions?

2. **Construct Arguments** A game board has a spinner with 10 equal-sized sections, of which 4 are green, 3 are blue, 2 are yellow, and 1 is red. What is the sum of the probabilities of the pointer landing in the green, blue, yellow, and red sections? Explain.

3. **Reasoning** What does it mean that there is an equal theoretical probability of each outcome? Explain.

Do You Know How?

In 4–6, Monique rolls a six-sided number cube labeled 1 to 6.

4. Find *P*(rolling a 4).

5. Find *P*(rolling an odd number).

6. If Monique rolls the number cube 12 times, how many times would she expect a number greater than 4 to be rolled?

Name: _____

Practice & Problem Solving

Scan for
Multimedia

Leveled Practice In 7–9, complete each statement.

7. A spinner has 8 equal-sized sections. To win the game, the pointer
must land on a yellow section.

$P(\text{yellow}) = \dfrac{\text{favorable outcomes}}{\text{total number of possible outcomes}} = \dfrac{2}{8} = \boxed{\dfrac{1}{4}}$

8. Natalie is playing a game using a fair coin.
Contestants win the game if the fair coin lands
tails up.

The theoretical probability that the coin will

land tails up is $\boxed{\dfrac{1}{2}}$.

If 250 contestants play the game, about $\boxed{1.05}$
of them are expected to win.

9. In a different game, the probability of correctly
guessing which of 5 boxes contains a tennis
ball is $\frac{1}{5}$. About how many winners would be
expected if 60 contestants play the game?

$\dfrac{1}{5} = \dfrac{x}{\boxed{60}}$

$x = \boxed{12}$ winners

10. **Make Sense and Persevere** A 12-sided solid has equal-sized
faces numbered 1 to 12.

a. Find P(number greater than 10).   a number greater than
10 is 11

b. Find P(number less than 5).   Less than 5 is
4 3 2 1

c. If the 12-sided solid is rolled 200 times, how many times would you
expect either a 4, 6, or 9 to be rolled?

4 6 9 becase it would $\dfrac{42}{200}$
be very Like Le to
get is 92 times

11. Tamara finds the sum of two number cubes rolled at the same time. The chart below shows all possible sums from the 36 possible combinations when rolling two number cubes. How many times should Tamara expect the sum of the two cubes to be equal to 5 if she rolls the two number cubes 180 times?

Sum	2	3	4	5	6	7	8	9	10	11	12
Possible Combinations	1	2	3	4	5	6	5	4	3	2	1

12. Higher Order Thinking A store is giving every customer who enters the store a scratch-off card labeled with numbers from 1 to 10. It is equally likely that any of the numbers from 1 to 10 will be labeled on a given card. If the card is an even number, the customer gets a 15% discount on a purchase. If the card is an odd number greater than 6, the customer gets a 30% discount. Otherwise, the discount is 20%.

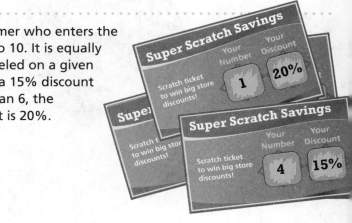

a. What is the probability for each discount?

15% discount: ☐   20% discount: ☐

30% discount: ☐

b. The store manager gives out 300 scratch-off cards. Which discount will the greatest number of customers likely receive? Explain.

✅ Assessment Practice

13. A spinner is divided into 4 equal parts. 1 part is colored red, 2 parts are colored blue, and 1 part is colored yellow. The spinner is spun 1,000 times. Select all of the reasonable possible outcomes.

☐ The spinner lands on blue 445 times.

☐ The spinner lands on red 430 times.

☐ The spinner lands on blue 290 times.

☐ The spinner lands on yellow 200 times.

☐ The spinner lands on red 290 times.

14. One thousand five hundred runners have signed up for a marathon. The probability of a runner finishing the race is $\frac{11}{12}$. Approximately how many runners are expected to finish the race?

Solve & Discuss It!

Kevin is awarded a penalty shot. He will either score a goal or not score a goal. Are both outcomes equally likely? Explain.

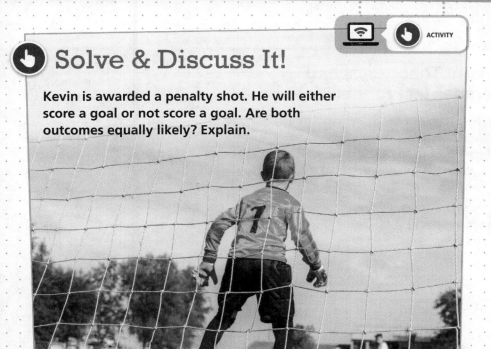

Look for Relationships
What might affect the outcome?

Lesson 7-3
Understand Experimental Probability

 Go Online

I can...
determine the experimental probability of an event.

© **Common Core Content Standards**
7.SP.C.6, 7.SP.C.7

Mathematical Practices
MP.2, MP.3, MP.7

Focus on math practices

Construct Arguments Lowe Senior High School's soccer team won 12, lost 5, and tied in 3 of their first 20 games this season. Which outcome is most likely for the team's next game? Explain your reasoning.

Essential Question ▶ How is experimental probability similar to and different from theoretical probability?

  VISUAL LEARNING ASSES

EXAMPLE 1 Compare Theoretical and Experimental Probability

Scan for Multimedia

Talia and Yoshi plan for 1 out of 8, or 12.5%, of the players winning a prize. During the school fair, they kept track of the numbers of total players and winners and recorded the data in the table below. How does the actual number of winners compare to the expected number of winners?

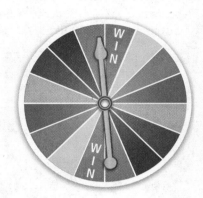

Time Period	Total Players	Winners
10 A.M.–noon	213	22
Noon–2 P.M.	262	36
TOTAL	**475**	**58**

STEP 1 Determine the *relative frequency* of winners during each time period. The **relative frequency** is the ratio of the number of times an event occurs to the total number of trials.

Ratio of Winners to Total Players

Time Period	Total Players	Winners	Relative Frequency
10 A.M.–noon	213	22	$\frac{22}{213} \approx 10.3\%$
Noon–2 P.M.	262	36	$\frac{36}{262} \approx 13.7\%$
TOTAL	475	58	$\frac{58}{475} \approx 12.2\%$

STEP 2 The relative frequency of an event can also be called **experimental probability**. Compare the experimental probability based on the data to the theoretical probability of winning the game.

Theoretical Probability   Experimental Probability

$P(\text{red}) = \frac{1}{8} = 12.5\%$ $\frac{58}{475} \approx 12.2\%$

In the previous lesson, Talia and Yoshi expected about 63 winners for 500 players, based on theoretical probability. Based on the data, there were actually 58 winners out of 475 players.

The experimental probability is slightly lower than the theoretical probability of winning this game. There were slightly fewer winners than expected.

☑ Try It!

During the second day of the school fair, Talia and Yoshi recorded 43 winners out of a total of 324 players. How does the actual number of winners compare to the expected number of winners?

Theoretical Probability

$P(\text{red}) = \frac{1}{8} = 12.5\%$

Experimental Probability

$\dfrac{\boxed{}}{324} \approx \boxed{}\%$

This experimental probability is [ ] than the theoretical probability.

There were [ ] winners than expected.

Convince Me! Will experimental probability always be close to theoretical probability? Explain.

EXAMPLE **2**

Use Experimental Probability to Make Predictions

Joaquin also kept track of players and winners for his game during the fair. Based on the results shown in the table, how many winners should he expect if 300 people play his game?

Use proportional reasoning to predict the number of likely winners, w, based on the experimental probability.

$$\frac{71}{416} = \frac{w}{300}$$

$$\frac{71}{416} \cdot 300 = \frac{w}{300} \cdot 300$$

$$51.2 \approx w$$

Time Period	Total Players	Winners	Relative Frequency
10 A.M.–noon	174	28	$\frac{28}{174} \approx 16.1\%$
Noon–2 P.M.	242	43	$\frac{43}{242} \approx 17.8\%$
TOTAL	**416**	**71**	$\frac{71}{416} \approx 17.1\%$

Joaquin should expect about 51 winners out of 300 players.

EXAMPLE **3**

Explain Differences Between Theoretical and Experimental Probability

Amir and Marvin each flip a coin 50 times and record the result of each flip. The tables show their results.

Amir's Results

Heads	Tails
26	24

Marvin's Results

Heads	Tails
30	20

A. Based on theoretical probability, what are the expected results of 50 coin flips?

There are two possible outcomes—heads or tails—and both outcomes are equally likely. For each coin flip, the probability of landing heads up (or tails up) is 1 out of 2, or $\frac{1}{2}$.

After 50 flips, the results should be *about* 25 heads and 25 tails.

B. Why might their results be different from the expected results based on theoretical probability?

Theoretical probability can be used to estimate results, but does not guarantee results. The more times they flip their coins, the more likely it is that their results will be closer to the theoretical probability.

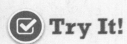 **Try It!**

Amir and Marvin continue until they each flip a coin 200 times. How do you expect Amir's results and Marvin's results to compare? How will their results compare with expected results based on theoretical probability?

Relative frequency, or experimental probability, is based on the actual results of an experiment, while theoretical probability is based on calculated results from the knowledge of the possible outcomes. Experimental probability and theoretical probability may be close but are rarely exactly the same.

Experimental probability = $\dfrac{\text{number of times an event occurs}}{\text{total number of times the experiment is carried out}}$

> This value changes each time an experiment is carried out.

The experimental probability tends to get closer to the theoretical probability of an experiment as more trials are conducted.

Do You Understand?

1. **? Essential Question** How is experimental probability similar to and different from theoretical probability?

2. **Construct Arguments** How can experimental probability be used to make predictions?

3. **Reasoning** Is experimental probability always close to theoretical probability? Explain.

Do You Know How?

In 4–6, complete each statement.

Kelly flips a coin 20 times. The results are shown in the table, where "H" represents the coin landing heads up and "T" represents the coin landing tails up.

Flip	1	2	3	4	5
Result	H	T	T	H	H
Flip	6	7	8	9	10
Result	H	H	T	H	T
Flip	11	12	13	14	15
Result	H	T	T	T	H
Flip	16	17	18	19	20
Result	T	H	H	T	H

4. The theoretical probability that the coin will land heads up is $\boxed{50}$.

5. Based on the data, the experimental probability that the coin will land heads up is $\boxed{50}$.

6. The experimental probability is $\boxed{}$ than the theoretical probability.

Name: _____

Practice & Problem Solving

Scan for
Multimedia

Leveled Practice In **7** and **8**, complete each statement.

7. The table shows the results of spinning a wheel 80 times.
What is the relative frequency of the event "spin a 3"?

Wheel Spins				
Outcomes	1	2	3	4
Frequency	8	22	18	32

The relative frequency of the wheel landing on 3 is

$$\frac{\text{number of times an event occurs}}{\text{total number of trials}} = \frac{\boxed{}}{\boxed{}} = \boxed{} \%$$

8. Liz flips a coin 50 times. The coin lands heads up
20 times and tails up 30 times. Complete each
statement.

The theoretical probability of the coin landing

heads up is $\boxed{}$. $\frac{25}{50}$

Based on Liz's results, the experimental probability

of the coin landing heads up is $\boxed{\frac{20}{50}}$.

The theoretical probability is $\boxed{}$ than

the experimental probability in this experiment.

9. Jess spins a pointer 25 times and finds an
experimental probability of the pointer landing
on 3 to be $\frac{4}{25}$, or 16%. The theoretical probability
of the spinner landing on 3 is $\frac{1}{4}$, or 25%. Why
might there be a significant difference between
the theoretical and experimental probabilities?

10. The table shows the results of a survey of 100 people
randomly selected at an airport. Find the experimental
probability that a person is going to City E.

Airport Destinations

Destination	Number of Responses
City A	28
City B	34
City C	16
City D	14
City E	8

7-3 Understand Experimental Probability **385**

11. The theoretical probability of selecting a consonant at random from a list of letters in the alphabet is $\frac{21}{26}$. Wayne opens a book, randomly selects a letter on the page, and records the letter. He repeats the experiment 200 times. He finds $P(\text{consonant}) = 60\%$. How does the theoretical probability differ from the experimental probability? What are some possible sources for this discrepancy?

$$\frac{21}{26} = 50\% , 0.50$$

12. **Higher Order Thinking** Seven different names are written onto sticks and placed into a cup. A stick is chosen 100 times, out of which the name Grace is chosen 23 times. How do the theoretical probability and experimental probability compare? Explain why there is a discrepancy between them, if there is any.

13. Each of three friends flips a coin 36 times. Angel records "tails" 20 times. Michael records "tails" 17 times. Fernanda records "tails" 23 times.

   a. Find the relative frequency with which each friend records "tails".

   b. Which friend has a relative frequency that is closest to the theoretical probability of flipping "tails" 36 times? Explain.

✓ Assessment Practice

14. In a survey, 125 people were asked to choose one card out of five cards labeled 1 to 5. The results are shown in the table. Compare the theoretical probability and experimental probability of choosing a card with the number 1.

Cards Chosen					
Number	1	2	3	4	5
Frequency	15	30	35	20	25

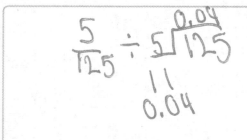

15. A basketball player makes 65% of all free throws in her first 5 seasons. In her 6th season she makes 105 out of 150 free throws. How does the observed frequency of her 6th season compare to the expected frequency? Provide a possible explanation for any similarities or differences in the frequencies.

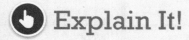 **Explain It!**

The Chess Club has 8 members. A new captain will be chosen by randomly selecting the name of one of the members. Leah and Luke both want to be captain. Leah says the chance that she will be chosen as captain is $\frac{1}{2}$ because she is either chosen for captain or she is not. Luke says the chance that he is chosen is $\frac{1}{8}$.

I can...
use probability models to find probabilities of events.

© **Common Core Content Standards**
7.SP.C.7a, 7.SP.C.7b, 7.EE.B.3
Mathematical Practices
MP.2, MP.3, MP.4, MP.6, MP.7

A. Construct Arguments Do you agree with Leah's statement? Use a mathematical argument to justify your answer.

B. Construct Arguments Do you agree with Luke's statement? Use a mathematical argument to justify your answer.

Focus on math practices
Look for Relationships How does the probability of Leah being chosen captain compare to the probability of Luke being chosen captain?

Essential Question How can a model be used to find the probability of an event?

VISUAL LEARNING   ASSESS

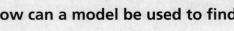 **EXAMPLE 1** Develop a Probability Model

Scan for Multimedia

Mr. Campbell has a jar on his desk that contains 10 marbles. At the end of class, each student draws a marble from the jar without looking, notes its color, and then puts it back in the jar. If a student draws the red marble, the student gets a pass on that day's homework. How can the students determine the probability of drawing the red marble?

> **Model with Math** How can you use a model to help you predict what color marble will be drawn?

Develop a *probability model* based on theoretical probability.

A **probability model** consists of:

• the *sample space*, and

• events within the sample space and their probabilities.

A **sample space** is the set of all possible outcomes.

When a marble is drawn, there are 10 possible outcomes.

Sample space, $S = \{R, G, G, G, P, P, P, P, P, P\}$

This is one way to represent the sample space.

R represents a red marble.
G represents a green marble.
P represents a purple marble.

List the three possible events and their probabilities.

– Drawing a ● $P(R) = \frac{1}{10}$

– Drawing a ● $P(G) = \frac{3}{10}$

– Drawing a ● $P(P) = \frac{6}{10}$

The students in Mr. Campbell's class can use a probability model to determine that the probability of drawing the red marble is $\frac{1}{10}$.

✓ Try It!

Mr. Campbell decides that too many students are getting a pass on homework. He adds 10 yellow marbles to the jar. Tell whether each part of the probability model **does** or **does not** change.

The sample space ☐ change. Each event within the sample space

☐ change. The probability of each event ☐ change.

The new probability of drawing a red marble is $P(R) = \dfrac{1}{\boxed{}}$.

Convince Me! How does a probability model help you predict how likely an event is to occur?

EXAMPLE 2 — Use a Probability Model to Evaluate a Situation

Ms. Stillman has a marble jar for the same purpose, but students do not know the number of marbles, or their colors. Each of 30 students draws a marble, notes its color, and then puts it back in the jar. Based on the results shown in the table, what can the students conclude about the probability of drawing a red marble?

Color	Red	Blue	Green
Number of Marbles Drawn	4	11	15

Develop a probability model based on experimental probability.

List the three possible events and their experimental probabilities.

- Drawing a red marble: $\dfrac{4}{30}$

- Drawing a blue marble: $\dfrac{11}{30}$

- Drawing a green marble: $\dfrac{15}{30}$

> The sum of the probabilities of all the possible outcomes in the sample space of a probability model is equal to 1.

Based on this experimental probability, Ms. Stillman's students can conclude that the probability of drawing a red marble is about $13\frac{1}{3}$%.

EXAMPLE 3 — Use a Probability Model to Make an Estimate

Ms. Stillman tells her students that the jar contains 100 marbles. Based on the table of marble colors after 60 draws, about how many marbles of each color are in the jar?

Color	Red	Blue	Orange	Green
Number of Marbles Drawn	7	20	1	32

Develop a probability model based on experimental probability.

List the four possible events and their experimental probabilities.

- Drawing a red marble: $\dfrac{7}{60}$

- Drawing a blue marble: $\dfrac{20}{60}$

- Drawing an orange marble: $\dfrac{1}{60}$

- Drawing a green marble: $\dfrac{32}{60}$

> Use proportional reasoning and the probability model to estimate the number of marbles of each color.

The estimated number of marbles in the jar is:

$\dfrac{7}{60} = \dfrac{11.\overline{6}}{100}$ or about 12 red marbles

$\dfrac{20}{60} = \dfrac{33.\overline{3}}{100}$ or about 33 blue marbles

$\dfrac{1}{60} = \dfrac{1.\overline{6}}{100}$ or about 2 orange marbles

$\dfrac{32}{60} = \dfrac{53.\overline{3}}{100}$ or about 53 green marbles

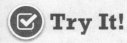 **Try It!**

To reduce the number of homework passes, which color of marble should Ms. Stillman use as the pass on homework? Explain.

A probability model can help you evaluate a chance process and its outcomes. You can develop a model using theoretical or experimental probability.

A probability model consists of the sample space of an action, events within the sample space, and probabilities associated with each event.

For rolling a number cube labeled from 1 through 6:

Sample space, $S = \{1, 2, 3, 4, 5, 6\}$

$P(1) = \frac{1}{6}$ $P(4) = \frac{1}{6}$

$P(2) = \frac{1}{6}$ $P(5) = \frac{1}{6}$

$P(3) = \frac{1}{6}$ $P(6) = \frac{1}{6}$

Do You Understand?

1. **Essential Question** How can a model be used to find the probability of an event?

2. **Construct Arguments** How can you check the sample space of a probability model?

3. **Reasoning** How does developing a probability model based on experimental probability help you evaluate a situation or make an estimate? Explain.

Do You Know How?

4. Develop a probability model for the spinner shown.

5. Mr. Henry has a basket full of fruit. He does not know how many pieces of fruit are in the basket or the types of fruit. Each of the 20 students in his class selects one piece of fruit from the basket without looking, notes its fruit type, and then puts it back in the basket. Based on the results shown in the table, what can the students conclude about the probability of selecting an apple?

Fruit	Apple	Orange	Pear
Number of Pieces of Fruit	5	2	13

6. The probability model based on experimental probability for randomly selecting a marble from a bag is $P(\text{green}) = \frac{18}{40}$, $P(\text{blue}) = \frac{14}{40}$, and $P(\text{white}) = \frac{8}{40}$. About how many marbles of each color are in the bag if there are 60 total marbles?

Practice & Problem Solving

7. Murray spins the pointer of the spinner shown at the right.

    a. What is the sample space for the probability model?

    b. What is the probability of each event in the sample space?

8. Rafael spins the pointers of the two spinners shown at the right. Find the probability of each possible sum.

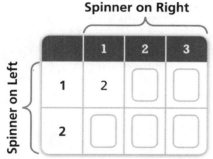

Spinner on Right

		1	2	3
Spinner on Left	**1**	2		
	2			

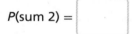

$P(\text{sum 2}) =$ [ ] $P(\text{sum 3}) =$ [ ] $P(\text{sum 4}) =$ [ ] $P(\text{sum 5}) =$ [ ]

9. Be Precise An arts and crafts store has a crate that contains glass, wood, and brass beads. Friends take turns choosing a bead without looking, recording the bead type, and returning the bead to the crate. The table shows the results of 300 selections.

Choosing Beads	
Glass	60
Wood	96
Brass	144

    a. Write a probability model for choosing a bead.

    b. Based on the frequencies in the table, estimate the number of each type of bead that will be chosen if the friends select a total of 450 beads from the crate.

10. A bag contains 14 green, 12 orange, and 19 purple tennis balls.

    a. Create a probability model for choosing a tennis ball from the bag.

    b. Suppose a tennis ball is randomly selected and then replaced 75 times. How many orange tennis balls do you expect? Explain.

11. Given that $P(\text{red pepper}) = \frac{3}{5}$, write another probability statement to complete the probability model of a random pepper selection from the box below.

12. **Higher Order Thinking** A survey asked 600 people for their favorite genre of book. The table shows the number of people who preferred four possible genres.

    a. How many people surveyed responded with a genre that is not listed in the table?

    b. Find the probabilities and complete a probability model to describe each response, including "other genre".

Genre	Number of People
Adventure	90
Comedy	102
Mystery	150
Romance	132

13. One hundred people buy gum balls from a gum ball machine. 45 of them get a red gum ball, 40 get a blue gum ball and 15 get a yellow gum ball.

    PART A

    Develop a probability model to predict the color of the next gum ball purchased. Compare the probability of getting a red gum ball to the probability of getting a yellow gum ball.

    PART B

    Of the next 10 people to buy gum balls, 7 get yellow, 1 gets red and 2 get blue. Explain a possible reason for this outcome.

Name: _____

1. **Vocabulary** How does the theoretical probability of the event "flip heads" change when a coin is flipped more times in an experiment? *Lesson 7-2*

   Ⓐ increases; there are more chances for heads to be flipped

   Ⓑ decreases; there are more chances for tails to be flipped

   Ⓒ does not change

   Ⓓ increases; all values increase

In 2–4, use the information given.

Brianna has a bag of marbles that are all the same size. Of all the marbles in the bag, there are 6 red, 7 white, 3 black, and 4 green marbles.

2. Select all the likelihood statements that are true. *Lesson 7-1*

   ☐ It is impossible that Brianna will draw a blue marble.

   ☐ It is more likely that Brianna will draw a black marble than a green marble.

   ☐ It is certain that Brianna will draw either a red, white, black, or green marble.

   ☐ It is unlikely that Brianna will draw a black marble.

   ☐ It is neither likely nor unlikely that Brianna will draw a green marble.

3. Ryan asks 80 people to choose a marble, note the color, and replace the marble in Brianna's bag. The results of the random marble selections in this experiment are: 34 red, 18 white, 9 black, and 19 green marbles. How does the theoretical probability compare with the experimental probability of drawing a white marble? *Lessons 7-2 and 7-3*

Theoretical Probability	Experimental Probability
%	%

4. Write a probability model for this experiment, and use the probability model to predict how many times Brianna would pick a green marble if she chose a marble 50 times. Give the probabilities as simplified fractions. *Lesson 7-4*

   Drawing a red marble: _____   Drawing a white marble: _____

   Drawing a black marble: _____   Drawing a green marble: _____

   Brianna would draw _____ green marbles in 50 tries.

5. Jewel spins the pointer of a spinner. The spinner has 7 equal-sized sections labeled 1 to 7. What is the probability that Jewel will spin a 7? *Lessons 7-2 and 7-4*

How well did you do on the Mid-Topic Checkpoint? Fill in the stars.

MID-TOPIC PERFORMANCE TASK

Viet, Quinn, and Lucy are going to play Bingo, using a standard game set. They make some predictions before the game begins. The table shows how the numbers match with the letters B, I, N, G, and O.

Letter	Numbers
B	1–15
I	16–30
N	31–45
G	46–60
O	61–75

PART A

Viet makes a probability model to describe the probability of each number being called first. Quinn makes a probability model to describe the probability of any particular letter being called first. Compare the probability models.

PART B

Lucy makes a probability model to determine whether the first number drawn will be even or odd. Compare the different probabilities.

PART C

Suppose the game changed to have 90 numbers, instead of 75 numbers, matched with the letters B, I, N, G, and O. How would Viet's, Quinn's, and Lucy's probability models change? Explain.

3-ACT MATH ▶ ▶ ▶

3-Act Mathematical Modeling:
Photo Finish

 Go Online

© Common Core Content Standards
7.SP.C.5, 7.SP.C.6, 7.SP.C.7
Mathematical Practices
MP.4, MP.1, MP.2, MP.3, MP.5, MP.6, MP.7, MP.8

ACT **1**

1. After watching the video, what is the first question that comes to mind?

2. Write the Main Question you will answer.

3. Construct Arguments Predict an answer to this Main Question. Explain your prediction.

4. On the number line below, write a number that is too small to be the answer. Write a number that is too large. Plot your prediction on the same number line.

Too small   Too large

5. What information in this situation would be helpful to know? How would you use that information?

6. **Use Appropriate Tools** What tools can you use to solve the problem? Explain how you would use them strategically.

7. **Model with Math** Represent the situation using mathematics. Use your representation to answer the Main Question.

8. What is your answer to the Main Question? Is it higher or lower than your prediction? Explain why.

9. Write the answer you saw in the video.

10. Reasoning Does your answer match the answer in the video? If not, what are some reasons that would explain the difference?

11. Make Sense and Persevere Would you change your model now that you know the answer? Explain.

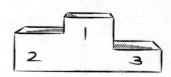

Reflect

12. Model with Math Explain how you used a mathematical model to represent the situation. How did the model help you answer the Main Question?

13. Be Precise What vocabulary have you learned in this topic that helps you communicate the answer to the Main Question?

SEQUEL

14. Generalize How would your answer change if a fifth person joined the race? A sixth person? If *n* people are running in the race?

Solve & Discuss It! ACTIVITY

Cameron packed two pairs of shorts and three T-shirts for a weekend trip. What are some combinations of shirts and shorts that Cameron can wear while on his trip? How many days will he have a different outfit to wear?

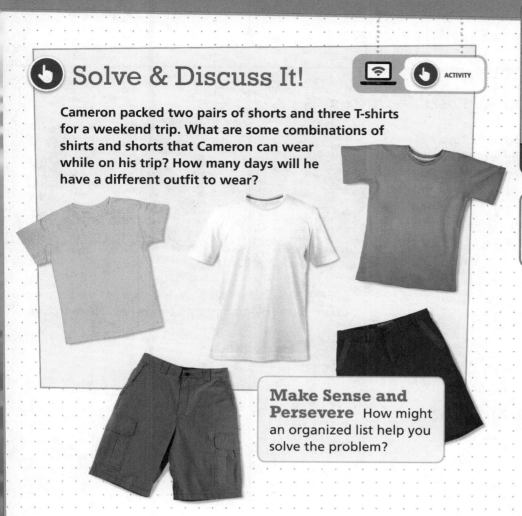

Make Sense and Persevere How might an organized list help you solve the problem?

 I can...
find all possible outcomes of a compound event.

Common Core Content Standards
7.SP.C.8b

Mathematical Practices
MP.1, MP.2, MP.7, MP.8

Focus on math practices

Reasoning How would the number of different outfits change if Cameron packed a pair of khaki shorts? Explain.

? Essential Question How can all the possible outcomes, or sample space, of a compound event be represented?

EXAMPLE 1 **Find All Possible Outcomes**

Scan for Multimedia

Hailey has two sisters and no brothers. Josh has two brothers and no sisters. They wonder what the chances are, in a family with three children, that the children will be all boys or all girls. How can they determine all possible combinations of boys and girls in a family with three children?

STEP 1 List the different events.

Child 1 is either a boy or a girl.

B   G

Child 2 is either a boy or a girl.

B   G

Child 3 is either a boy or a girl.

B   G

This is a *compound event*. A **compound event** consists of two or more events. This compound event consists of three events.

STEP 2 Make a tree diagram to represent the sample space. A tree diagram shows all the possible outcomes.

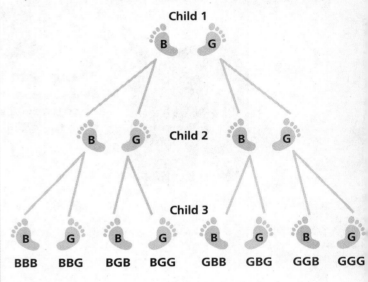

Child 1
B   G

Child 2
B   G   B   G

Child 3
B   G   B   G   B   G   B   G
BBB BBG BGB BGG GBB GBG GGB GGG

Hailey and Josh can make a tree diagram to show the sample space of boys and girls in a family with three children.

✓ Try It!

Jorge will flip two quarters at the same time. Complete the tree diagram, and then list the sample space of this compound event. Use H for heads and T for tails.

The sample space is: ☐

Convince Me! How does the sample space change when the number of quarters that Jorge flips is increased by 1?

Quarter 1   Quarter 2

H ⟨ H
    ☐

☐ ⟨ ☐
    T

EXAMPLE **2** **Use a Table to Represent Sample Spaces**

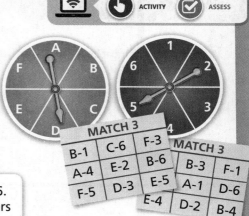

A game is played by spinning the two spinners shown. Players match the results of the spinners to combinations on their game cards. How many different combinations are possible?

Use a table to represent the sample space.

> Remember: The sample space shows all the possible outcomes.

	1	2	3	4	5	6
A	A-1	A-2	A-3	A-4	A-5	A-6
B	B-1	B-2	B-3	B-4	B-5	B-6
C	C-1	C-2	C-3	C-4	C-5	C-6
D	D-1	D-2	D-3	D-4	D-5	D-6
E	E-1	E-2	E-3	E-4	E-5	E-6
F	F-1	F-2	F-3	F-4	F-5	F-6

> The table is 6 × 6. There are 6 letters and 6 numbers.

MATCH 3

B-1	C-6	F-3
A-4	E-2	B-6
F-5	D-3	E-5

MATCH 3

B-3	F-1
A-1	D-6
E-4	D-2	B-4

There are 36 different letter-number combinations.

The sample space consists of 36 possible outcomes.

EXAMPLE **3** **Use an Organized List to Represent Sample Spaces**

Stan will roll a number cube labeled 1 to 6 and flip a coin.

What are all the possible outcomes?

Use an organized list to represent the sample space.

{(1, H), (1, T),
(2, H), (2, T),
(3, H), (3, T),
(4, H), (4, T),
(5, H), (5, T),
(6, H), (6, T)}

> For each of the 6 possible outcomes of the number cube, there are 2 possible outcomes for the coin.

There are 12 different combinations.

The sample space consists of 12 possible outcomes.

☑ Try It!

The bag contains tiles labeled with the letters A, B, and C. The box contains tiles labeled with the numbers 1, 2, and 3. June draws one letter tile and one number tile. Represent the sample space using either a table or an organized list.

A compound event is a combination of two or more events.

An organized list, table, or tree diagram can be used to represent the sample space of a compound event. The sample space for flipping two coins consists of 4 outcomes.

Organized List

{(H, H), (H, T), (T, H), (T, T)}

Table

	H	T
H	H, H	H, T
T	T, H	T, T

Tree Diagram

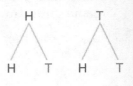

Do You Understand?

1. **Essential Question** How can all the possible outcomes, or sample space, of a compound event be represented?

2. **Generalize** Will a list, a table, and a tree diagram always give you the same number of outcomes for the same compound event? Explain.

3. **Use Structure** Shari is drawing a tree diagram to represent the sample space of rolling a 12-sided game piece and spinning the pointer of a 4-section spinner. Does it matter if Shari starts the tree diagram with the game piece outcomes or the spinner outcomes? Explain.

Do You Know How?

4. Both Spinner A and Spinner B have equal-sized sections, as shown at the right. Make a table to represent the sample space when both spinners are spun.

Spinner A

Spinner B

5. Tiles labeled with the letters X, Y, and Z are in a bag. Tiles labeled with the numbers 1 and 2 are in a box.

Make a tree diagram to represent the sample space of the compound event of selecting one tile from each container.

Practice & Problem Solving

Scan for
Multimedia

Leveled Practice In 6 and 7, find the number of outcomes for each event.

6. Oliver is playing a game in which he has to choose one of two numbers (2 or 7) and then one of five vowels (a, e, i, o, or u). How many possible outcomes are there?

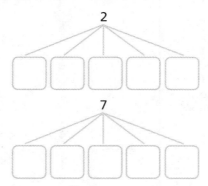

2

7

There are ☐ possible outcomes.

7. There are four stores that sell school supplies (S1, S2, S3, and S4) and three stores that sell sporting goods (G1, G2, and G3) nearby. How many possible combinations of stores could you visit to buy a tennis racquet and then a backpack?

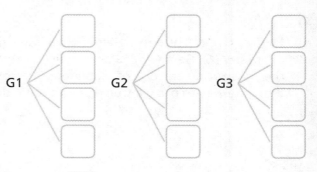

G1   G2   G3

There are ☐ possible combinations.

8. A bakery sells wheat, multigrain, rye, and oat bread. Each type of bread is available as a loaf or as dinner rolls.

a. Complete the table to show all the possible outcomes for the types and styles of bread sold by the bakery.

b. Find the number of possible outcomes.

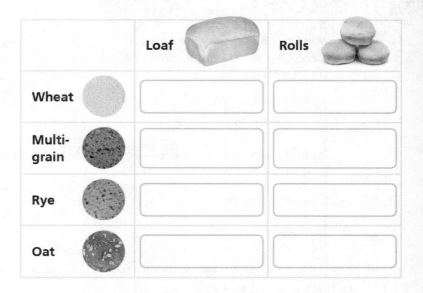

	Loaf	Rolls
Wheat		
Multi-grain		
Rye		
Oat		

9. Generalize How does the number of possible outcomes of a single event help you determine the total number of possible outcomes of a compound event?

10. A new car can be purchased with a choice of four exterior colors (A, B, C, and D) and three interior colors (1, 2, and 3). Make an organized list of all the possible color combinations for the car.

11. Two friends each plan to order a fruit drink at the diner. The available flavors are kiwi (K), lemon (L), and watermelon (W). Make a list to represent all the possible outcomes of the friends' fruit drink order. Write each outcome in the format (Friend 1, Friend 2).

12. Plastic souvenir cups come in three different sizes: small (S), medium (M), and large (L). The available colors are red (R), white (W), and blue (B). Make a list to represent all the possible combinations of the different cups based on size and color. Write each outcome in the format (Size, Color).

13. **Higher Order Thinking** Heidi's older sister needs to take either Chemistry (C), Geometry (G), or Physics (P) this year. She can take the class during any one of six periods (1 through 6). Is there more than one way to draw a tree diagram to model this situation? Explain.

Assessment Practice

14. A fruit basket has 6 oranges, 4 apples and 2 pears in it. 5 people each select a piece of fruit and eat it. Which of the following outcomes could represent this selection?

☐ All 5 people eat an orange.

☐ 1 person eats an orange, 4 people eat an apple.

☐ 2 people eat an orange, 3 people eat a pear.

☐ 3 people eat an orange, 1 person eats an apple, 1 person eats a pear.

☐ All 5 people eat an apple.

15. Royce has a collection of trading cards. 16 of his cards are baseball cards, 21 are football cards and 13 are basketball cards. He selects half of this collection and gives them to his friend. Which of the following represent possible outcomes of this selection?

☐ He gives his friend 6 baseball cards, 10 football cards and all of his basketball cards.

☐ He gives his friend 4 baseball cards and all of his football cards.

☐ He gives his friend only football cards.

☐ He gives his friend 8 baseball cards, 10 football cards and 7 basketball cards.

☐ He gives his friend all of his baseball and basketball cards.

Lesson 7-6
Find Probabilities of Compound Events

  Go Online

I can...
find the probability of a compound event.

© **Common Core Content Standards**
7.SP.C.8a

Mathematical Practices
MP.1, MP.4, MP.7, MP.8

 ## Solve & Discuss It!  ACTIVITY

Talia is playing a game in which she must choose Option 1 or Option 2 and then spin the game wheel, flip the coin, and roll the number cube labeled 1 through 6. For her to win a prize, all the conditions listed under the chosen option must occur. Which option should Talia choose? Explain.

Option 1	Option 2
• The game wheel lands on S.	• The game wheel lands on Z.
• The coin lands on tails.	• The coin lands on either side.
• An even number is rolled.	• The number 3 is rolled.

Look for Relationships
How can you use what you know about sample spaces to choose the best option?

Focus on math practices

Make Sense and Persevere Suppose an Option 3 was added to the game, with the conditions that the game wheel lands on Q, the coin lands on either side, and an odd number is rolled. Should Talia change her choice to Option 3? Explain.

? **Essential Question** How can a model help find the probability of a compound event?

 EXAMPLE 1 **Find the Probability of Compound Events Using a Table**

Scan for Multimedia

Sadie has one ticket left at the school fair and she hasn't yet won a prize. She decides between two games. Which game should she play?

> **Use Structure** Does having more possible outcomes make it more likely or less likely that Sadie will win?

Flip to Win
Flip two heads to win a prize!

Flip 'n' Spin
Flip a head and spin blue to win a prize!

STEP 1 Use a table to determine the probability of winning a prize playing *Flip to Win*.

	Heads (H)	Tails (T)
Heads (H)	H, H	H, T
Tails (T)	T, H	T, T

There are 4 possible outcomes.

There is 1 favorable outcome: {H, H}.

$P(H, H) = \frac{1}{4}$, or 25%

STEP 2 Use a table to determine the probability of winning a prize playing *Flip 'n' Spin*.

	Heads (H)	Tails (T)
Red (R)	R, H	R, T
Yellow (Y)	Y, H	Y, T
Blue (B)	B, H	B, T
Green (G)	G, H	G, T

There are 8 possible outcomes.

There is 1 favorable outcome: {B, H}.

$P(B, H) = \frac{1}{8}$, or 12.5%

STEP 3 Compare the probabilities of winning each game.

The probability of winning a prize at *Flip to Win* is 25%.

The probability of winning a prize at *Flip 'n' Spin* is 12.5%.

Sadie is more likely to win a prize playing *Flip to Win*.

So, she should use her last ticket to play *Flip to Win*.

☑ **Try It!**

The designer of *Flip 'n' Spin* creates a new game using a 5-section spinner, as shown. How does the new spinner change the probability of winning a prize?

Using the 5-section spinner, the probability of winning a prize

is ☐.

It is ☐ likely that a player will win a prize when using the 5-section spinner than when using the 4-section spinner.

Convince Me! What generalization can you make about the number of sections on the spinner and the probability of winning a prize while playing the *Flip 'n' Spin* game?

EXAMPLE 2 **Find the Probability Using a Tree Diagram**

What is the probability that a coin flipped 3 times will land heads up exactly 2 times?

Flip 1

Flip 2

Flip 3

Outcomes   HHH   HHT   HTH   HTT   THH   THT   TTH   TTT

> Each of the 8 outcomes is equally likely.
>
> **Three** of the 8 outcomes are favorable.

P(exactly 2 heads) $= \frac{3}{8}$, or 37.5%

 Try It!

Is it more likely that a coin flipped 3 times will land heads up exactly once, or will land heads up exactly 2 twice? Explain using probability.

EXAMPLE 3  **Find the Probability Using an Organized List**

The names of all middle school students with perfect attendance are entered into a drawing for one of two tickets to a baseball game. This year, Angie, Phil, Marc, Carly, and Josie attended school every day. What is the probability that Marc's name will be drawn to win one of the two tickets?

Make an organized list of possible outcomes for the winners of the two tickets.

If Angie wins the first ticket:	**If Phil wins the first ticket:**	**If Marc wins the first ticket:**
Angie and Phil	Phil and Angie	Marc and Angie
Angie and Marc	Phil and Marc	Marc and Phil
Angie and Carly	Phil and Carly	Marc and Carly
Angie and Josie	Phil and Josie	Marc and Josie

If Carly wins the first ticket:	**If Josie wins the first ticket:**
Carly and Angie	Josie and Angie
Carly and Phil	Josie and Phil
Carly and Marc	Josie and Marc
Carly and Josie	Josie and Carly

There are 20 possible outcomes. Of the 20 outcomes, 8 are favorable.

P(Marc wins one of the tickets) $= \frac{8}{20}$, or 40%

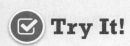 **Try It!**

Does Marc have a greater chance than Carly of winning the tickets to Carly? Explain using probability.

The probability of a compound event can be represented by a ratio of the number of favorable outcomes to the total number of possible equally likely outcomes. You can use an organized list, a table, or a tree diagram to determine the number of favorable outcomes and the total number of possible outcomes.

Do You Understand?

1. **? Essential Question** How can a model help find the probability of a compound event?

2. **Generalize** What do you know about the outcomes of a compound event displayed in an organized list, a table, or a tree diagram?

3. How does finding the probability of a compound event compare with finding the probability of a simple event?

Do You Know How?

4. One of three contestants will be randomly selected to win a prize. One of three different prizes will be randomly awarded to the contestant whose name is selected to win. The tree diagram shows all possible outcomes of this contest.

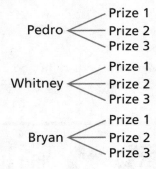

Pedro — Prize 1, Prize 2, Prize 3
Whitney — Prize 1, Prize 2, Prize 3
Bryan — Prize 1, Prize 2, Prize 3

What is the probability that Whitney will win Prize 2?

5. The table shows all the possible outcomes for flipping a coin and spinning the pointer of a spinner with four equal-sized sections labeled 1 through 4.

	1	2	3	4
heads	heads, 1	heads, 2	heads, 3	heads, 4
tails	tails, 1	tails, 2	tails, 3	tails, 4

a. What is the probability that the pointer will stop on 3 and the coin will land on heads?

b. What is the probability that the pointer will stop on an odd number and the coin will land on heads?

Practice & Problem Solving

Leveled Practice In **6** and **7**, find the probability of each event.

6. A fair coin is tossed twice in succession. The sample space is shown, where H represents heads up and T represents tails up. Find the probability of getting exactly one tail.

(Toss 1, Toss 2)	
(H, H)	(T, H)
(H, T)	(T, T)

There are [ ] outcomes that have exactly

one tail. There are [ ] possible outcomes,

which are equally likely.

P(exactly one tail) = [ ] , or [ ] %

7. The tree diagram shows the sample space of two-digit numbers that can be created using the digits 2, 6, 7, and 9. What is the probability of choosing a number from the sample space that contains both 9 and 6?

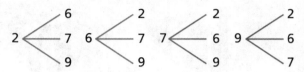

There are [ ] outcomes that include both

9 and 6. There are [ ] possible outcomes,

which are equally likely

P(9 and 6) = [ ] , or [ ] %

8. The table shows the possible outcomes of spinning the given spinner and flipping a fair coin. Find the probability of the coin landing heads up and the pointer landing on either 1, 2, or 4.

	1	2	3	4	5
H	H, 1	H, 2	H, 3	H, 4	H, 5
T	T, 1	T, 2	T, 3	T, 4	T, 5

9. The organized list shows all the possible outcomes when three fair coins are flipped. The possible outcomes of each flip are heads (H) and tails (T).

What is the probability that at least 2 fair coins land heads up when 3 are flipped?

Sample Space

HHH

HHT

HTH

HTT

THH

THT

TTH

TTT

10. **Look for Relationships** Gary spins two game wheels at the carnival. He will win a prize if both of the wheels land on any red section. How does the chance of winning change if different game wheels are used with more sections that aren't red?

11. **Model with Math** Each week, a clothing store gives away a shirt to a lucky customer. The shirts vary by sleeve type (Long, Short, No Sleeve) and color (Gray, Blue, Pink). Draw a tree diagram to represent the sample space. What is the probability that the free shirt will have either long or short sleeves and be either pink or blue?

12. **Higher Order Thinking** The table shows the sample space of picking a 2-character password using the letters Y, B, R, O, G, and P. If double letters are not allowed, what is the probability of choosing a password with no Y's? With no O's? Is one probability greater than the other? Explain.

Possible Combinations					
Y, B	B, R	R, O	O, G	G, P	P, Y
Y, R	B, O	R, G	O, P	G, Y	P, B
Y, O	B, G	R, P	O, Y	G, B	P, R
Y, G	B, P	R, Y	O, B	G, R	P, O
Y, P	B, Y	R, B	O, R	G, O	P, G

☑ **Assessment Practice**

13. A single number cube is rolled twice.

PART A

Determine the number of possible outcomes. Explain how you know you have found all the possible outcomes.

PART B

Find the probability of rolling two numbers that have a sum equal to 10.

Solve & Discuss It!

ACTIVITY

Jillian lands the beanbag on the board in about half of her attempts in a beanbag toss game. How can she predict the number of times she will get the beanbag in the hole in her next 5 attempts using a coin toss?

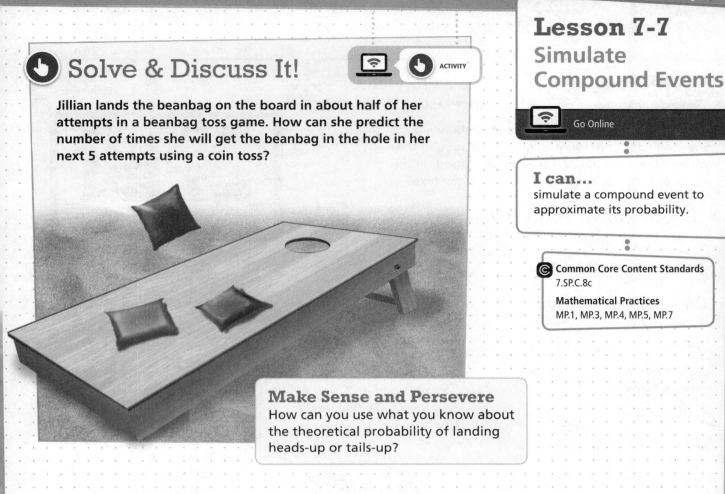

I can...
simulate a compound event to approximate its probability.

© **Common Core Content Standards**
7.SP.C.8c

Mathematical Practices
MP.1, MP.3, MP.4, MP.5, MP.7

Make Sense and Persevere
How can you use what you know about the theoretical probability of landing heads-up or tails-up?

Focus on math practices

Use Appropriate Tools When might it be useful to model a scenario with a coin or other tool?

? **Essential Question** How can you use simulations to determine the probability of events?

VISUAL LEARNING   ASSE

EXAMPLE 1 Simulate a Probability Situation Using a Spinner

Scan for Multimedia

Nikki is planning a hike for the end of the week. She really does not want to hike if it is raining the whole time, but is okay if it is cloudy. Based on the weather forecast, should she postpone the hike?

> **Model with Math** How can you use a model to represent the situation?

STEP 1 Develop a probability model for rain on a given day.

Sample space, S = {rain, no rain}

List the two possible events and their probabilities.

P (rain) = 40%, or $\frac{4}{10}$

P (no rain) = $1 - \frac{4}{10}$

$\qquad\qquad = \frac{6}{10}$

> The sum of the probabilities of the outcomes in a probability model is 1.
> P(rain) + P(no rain) = 1

STEP 2 Design a *simulation* using a spinner. A **simulation** is a model of a real-world situation that can be used to find probabilities. The spinner has outcomes and probabilities that match the real-world situation.

> P(rain) = $\frac{4}{10}$, or $\frac{2}{5}$

STEP 3 Run the simulation.

Spin the spinner 3 times—once for each day—and record the results.

Trial 1: R, N, N

Conduct additional trials.

Trial 2: N, R, N
Trial 3: R, R, N
Trial 4: N, N, N
Trial 5: R, N, N

Based on this simulation, Nikki should expect rain on one day of the three days.

She should not postpone her hike.

✓ **Try It!**

There is a 50% chance that a volleyball team will win any one of its four remaining games this year. A spinner with 2 equal sections numbered 1 (win) and 2 (loss) is used to simulate the probability that the team will win exactly two of its last four games. The results of the simulation are shown below.

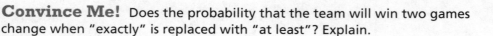

1221   1121   2211   2121   2221   2212   1122   1111   1222   1112

Out of 10 trials, there are ☐ favorable outcomes. Based on the simulation,

the probability that the team will win exactly 2 of its last 4 games is ☐.

Convince Me! Does the probability that the team will win two games change when "exactly" is replaced with "at least"? Explain.

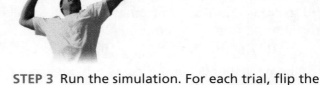
EXAMPLE 2 — Simulate a Probability Situation Using a Coin

The Hornets and the Tigers will play a 5-game series, with the winner of 3 games named the state volleyball champion. The two teams are evenly matched. Use a simulation to find the probability that the Hornets will win the 5-game series.

STEP 1 Develop a probability model.

Sample space, S = {Hornets win, Tigers win}

List the events and their probabilities.
P (Hornets win) = 50%
P (Tigers win) = 50%

STEP 2 Design a simulation using a coin. The outcomes and probabilities of flipping a coin can be matched with those of the game.

Heads (H) = Hornets win
Tails (T) = Tigers win

STEP 3 Run the simulation. For each trial, flip the coin 5 times to represent the 5 games.

Trial 1: H, H, T, H, T – The Hornets win.
Trial 2: T, T, H, H, T – The Tigers win.
Trial 3: H, T, H, H, T – The Hornets win.
Trial 4: T, H, T, H, T – The Tigers win.
Trial 5: H, H, T, H, T – The Hornets win.
Trial 6: T, H, T, H, H – The Hornets win.
Trial 7: H, T, T, T, T – The Tigers win.

STEP 4 Find the probability.

Based on 7 trials of the simulation, the probability that the Hornets will win the series is $\frac{4}{7}$.

EXAMPLE 3 — Simulate a Probability Situation with a Random Number Generator

An energy bar company is printing equal quantities of 6 different collectible cards. The company will randomly package one card inside the wrapper of each energy bar. What is the probability that all 6 collectible cards will be packaged in a box of 10 energy bars?

Use a random number generator to simulate the situation. The numbers 1 through 6 represent each of the trading cards.

Each trial has 10 numbers to represent the 10 bars.

Trial 1: 4, 4, 6, 3, 5, 6, 1, 6, 6, 1 – Not a full set of cards
Trial 2: 1, 1, 1, 2, 1, 3, 5, 5, 2, 6 – Not a full set of cards
Trial 3: 6, 1, 2, 1, 6, 2, 3, 1, 4, 5 – Full set of cards
Trial 4: 3, 4, 3, 1, 6, 3, 2, 4, 1, 6 – Not a full set of cards
Trial 5: 5, 6, 1, 5, 4, 5, 6, 1, 4, 2 – Not a full set of cards
Trial 6: 2, 1, 3, 2, 5, 5, 2, 4, 3, 4 – Not a full set of cards
Trial 7: 3, 6, 1, 5, 6, 3, 5, 1, 2, 5 – Not a full set of cards
Trial 8: 5, 6, 4, 5, 6, 3, 6, 2, 4, 5 – Not a full set of cards

1 out of 8 trials result in a full set of cards.

Based on 8 trials of the simulation, the probability that all 6 cards will be packaged in a box of 10 energy bars is $\frac{1}{8}$, or 12.5%.

Try It!

In a tennis tournament, 25% of Sarah's serves were aces. Design a simulation to predict how many aces you expect Sarah to serve out of 50 serves.

A simulation is a model of a real-world situation that can be used to predict results or outcomes when the actual event is difficult to perform or record.

A simulation uses a tool, such as a spinner, number cube, coin, or random number generator, for which outcomes have the same probabilities as the actual event.

> A greater number of trials will usually give results that are closer to the theoretical probability of the actual event.

Do You Understand?

1. **? Essential Question** How can you use simulations to determine the probability of events?

2. **Look for Relationships** What is the connection between the tool used to simulate an event and the probability of the actual event?

3. Why are the results of simulations usually close to the probabilities of their related events?

Do You Know How?

4. Carl hits the target 50% of the time he throws a ball at it. Carl uses a coin to simulate his next three pitches. He assigns H for a hit and T for a miss. The results of 12 trials are shown below.

   HHT HTH TTH HTT THT THH

   HHT HTT HTH HTT TTH THT

   Based on the results, what is the probability that Carl will hit the target with exactly two of his next three throws?

5. On average, Margo scores a goal for her field hockey team every 2 out of 3 shots. Margo uses a number cube to simulate her next three shots. She assigns 1 to 4 as "goals" and 5 and 6 as "missed shots." Why does this assignment of numbers on the number cube make it a valid simulation?

Practice & Problem Solving

Scan for
Multimedia

Leveled Practice In **6** and **7**, estimate the probability for each event.

6. Molly makes 70% of her free throws. The random numbers below represent 20 trials of a simulation of two free throws, using the numbers 0 through 9.

38 38 21 50 64
71 66 42 47 90
80 92 29 98 27
87 89 89 93 03

Let the numbers from ☐ to ☐ represent a successful free throw.

Let the numbers from ☐ to ☐ represent a missed free throw.

Based on the simulated results, the probability that Molly makes both free throws is

☐ , or ☐ %.

7. Survey results state that 80% of people enjoy going to the beach. The random numbers below represent 10 trials of a simulation of asking two people if they enjoy going to the beach, using the numbers 0 through 9 for their responses.

86 54 22 09 40
53 07 65 56 15

Let the numbers from ☐ to ☐ represent people who enjoy going to the beach.

Let the numbers ☐ to ☐ represent people who do not enjoy going to the beach.

Based on the simulated results, the probability that exactly one of two people enjoys going to the beach is ☐ , or ☐ %.

8. In Stacia's town, 60% of registered people vote regularly. A spinner with equal-sized sections numbered 0 to 9 can be used to represent those who do and do not vote.

a. What numbers can be assigned to represent those who do vote and those who do not vote?

b. Based on the simulated results below, what is the probability that at least one person out of three does not vote?

380 799 331 205 851
182 117 768 715 410

9. Inspection of items at a company shows that an item has a 50% chance of being defective. A spinner with equal-sized sections numbered 0 to 9 can be used to simulate the event that the next 2 items inspected are defective.

a. How would you assign numbers to represent the defective and non-defective items?

b. Based on the simulated results below, what is the probability that the next 2 items are defective?

88 92 87 70 49
44 43 55 32 12

10. Julie used a number cube to simulate a flower seed sprouting, for which the success rate is 50%. She used even numbers to represent success and odd numbers to represent failure. The results of 8 trials that simulate the sprouting of five seeds are shown below.

31534   35635   43631   35633

25143   25643   64133   53113

Based on the simulated results, what is the probability that none of the next five flower seeds will sprout successfully?

11. **Construct Arguments** How is the difference between the simulated probability and the theoretical probability of an actual event related to the number of simulated trials conducted?

12. **Higher Order Thinking** Suppose Arun has an 80% chance of winning a game. For a simulation, the numbers 0 to 7 represent winning, and the numbers 8 and 9 represent losing. Write three different trial results that show 5 wins in a row out of 6 games played.

☑ Assessment Practice

13. About 50% of the people surveyed in a certain county work for a small business. A random number generator was used to simulate the results of the next four people surveyed.

The numbers 0 to 4 represent people who work for a small business, and the numbers 5 to 9 represent people who do not work for a small business.

6411   0501   7582   0403   3074

7383   5250   2235   0803   3750

7694   9225   7121   4493   7596

8223   1288   8121   7652   3154

PART A

Based on the simulated results shown above, what is the probability that at least one of the next four people surveyed works for a small business?

PART B

How would the design of the simulation change if the percent of people who work for a small business was 70%?

? Topic Essential Question

How can you investigate chance processes and develop, use, and evaluate probability models?

Vocabulary Review

Complete each definition, and then provide an example of each vocabulary word.

| Vocabulary | event | outcome | probability |
| | relative frequency | sample space | simulation |

Definition	Example
1. The ratio of the number of times an event occurs to the total number of trials is the _____.	
2. The set of all possible outcomes is the _____.	
3. A model of a real-world situation that is used to find probabilities is a(n) _____.	
4. A single outcome or a group of outcomes is a(n) _____.	

Use Vocabulary in Writing

A restaurant serves either skim milk or whole milk in glasses that are either small, medium, or large. Use vocabulary words to explain how you could determine all the possible outcomes of milk choices at the restaurant. Use vocabulary words in your explanation.

Concepts and Skills Review

LESSON 7-1 **Understand Likelihood and Probability**

Quick Review

The **probability** of an event describes the likelihood an **event** will occur. The likelihood of an event ranges from impossible to certain, but more common descriptions are likely or unlikely. An event is a single **outcome** or group of outcomes. An outcome is a possible result of an action. Probability can be represented as a fraction, as a decimal, or as a percent. Something is fair if there is an equal chance for each outcome to occur.

Example

Luke rolls a 10-sided solid with equal-sized faces labeled 1 to 10. What is the probability of rolling a 4?

1 out of 10, or $\frac{1}{10}$. It is unlikely to occur.

Practice

1. Use Luke's 10-sided solid from the example. Describe an event that is certain and one that is impossible using this solid.

2. A spinner with 8 equal-sized sections is used for a game. Based on the descriptions below, is the spinner fair? Explain.
   The probability the pointer will land on yellow is 1 out of 4.
   The probability the pointer will land on blue is 2 out of 8.
   The probabilities that the pointer will land on green or red are both 25%.

LESSON 7-2 **Understand Theoretical Probability**

Quick Review

The **theoretical probability** of an **event** can be found if the possible outcomes are known and are all equally likely. Theoretical probability can be used to make predictions.

Example

The numbers from 1 to 5 are written on slips of paper and placed in a bucket. What is the theoretical probability of drawing a 2?

$P(2) = \dfrac{\text{number of slips labeled "2"}}{\text{number of possible outcomes}} = \dfrac{1}{5}$

Practice

1. Using the example, fifteen people take out a slip of paper from the bucket without looking and record the results before replacing the slip back into the bucket. How many times is a slip labeled "5" expected to be drawn?

Quick Review

The **experimental probability** or **relative frequency** **is based on actual results from an experiment and may differ from the theoretical probability of an event occurring. This discrepancy decreases as the number of trials of an experiment increases. You can use experimental probability and proportional reasoning to make predictions.**

experimental probability =

$$\frac{\text{number of times an event occurs}}{\text{total number of trials}}$$

Example

Four people conduct an experiment to find how often a flipped coin lands heads up. The results are shown in the table below.

Name	Total Flips	Heads
Ashley	55	26
Brent	70	38
Carey	50	22
David	80	41
TOTAL	**255**	

Based on the results from each person's coin flips, find the experimental probability of a flipped coin landing heads up.

The flipped coin landed heads-up in 127 of 255 trials. The experimental probability is about 49.8%.

How does the experimental probability compare to the theoretical probability of a flipped coin landing heads up?

The experimental probability, 49.8%, is very close to the theoretical probability of 50%.

Practice

1. Jaylon and Paula spin the pointer 30 times and get the results shown in the table.

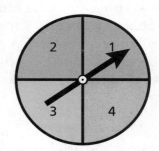

	1	2	3	4
Jaylon	6	8	9	7
Paula	8	5	7	10

What is the theoretical probability of the pointer landing on the number 2?

Based on the results in the table, how does the experimental probability of the pointer landing on 2 compare to the theoretical probability?

2. Based on the results in the table, about how many times should Jaylon and Paula expect the pointer to land on 4 out of a total of 130 spins? Explain your answer.

Quick Review

A **probability model** consists of a **sample space**, or all possible outcomes of an action, and a list of events within the sample space with the probability of each. The sum of the probabilities in the model is 1. A probability model can be used to make conclusions about probabilities of events or to make estimates or predictions.

Example

Jenna spins the pointer on her spinner 20 times. Develop a probability model for the situation. What is the sum of the probabilities in the probability model?

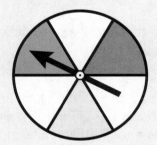

Sample space, S = {white section, blue section, white section, red section, white section, yellow section}

List the events and their probabilities.

P(white) = $\frac{1}{2}$; P(blue) = $\frac{1}{6}$;

P(red) = $\frac{1}{6}$; P(yellow) = $\frac{1}{6}$

Find the sum of the probabilities.

$$\frac{1}{2} + \frac{1}{6} + \frac{1}{6} + \frac{1}{6} = 1$$

The sum of the probabilities is 1.

Practice

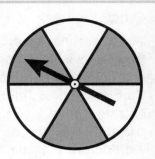

1. Abe has a different spinner. He also wants to develop a probability model.

How will his probability model be the same as, and how will it differ from, Jenna's model?

2. Walter has a different spinner.

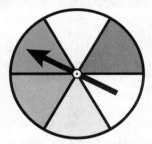

What is the probability that the pointer will land on a color that is not red?

3. What is the sample space of Walter's spinner?

4. Walter will spin the pointer 50 times. About how many times will the pointer land on each color?

Quick Review

A **compound event** is a combination of two or more events. An organized list, table, or tree diagram can be used to represent the sample space of a compound event.

Example

The student shop sells red and black bags printed with the school logo. Students can choose a backpack, duffel bag, or cinch sack of either color. Make a tree diagram to show all the styles of bags sold at the shop.

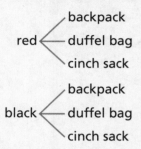

The shop sells 6 different styles of bags.

Practice

1. A basket contains a red, a yellow, and a green apple. A second basket contains an orange, a lemon, and a peach. Use an organized list to show all the outcomes in the sample space.

2. Simon is playing a game with letter tiles. He has 5 tiles remaining and will spell a new word by placing two tiles–first a consonant and then a vowel–in front of a Y already on the board. Complete the table below to describe all combinations of tiles that Simon can use to spell a new word.

	A	O
B		
S		
J		

Quick Review

The probability of a compound event can be represented by a ratio of the favorable outcomes to all possible outcomes. The probability can be calculated using an organized list, a table, or a tree diagram.

Example

If it is equally likely that a soccer team wins or loses any game, what is the probability that the team will win its next two games? Make a tree diagram to list the outcomes.

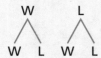

Only 1 of the 4 outcomes shows the team winning each of its next two games.

P(winning the next two games) $= \frac{1}{4} = 25\%$

Practice

1. One set of cards has a beach, a road, a desert, a mountain, and an island. A second set of cards has a car, a truck, and a van. Complete the table below to find the probability of randomly drawing a mountain card and a truck card.

	Car	Truck	Van
Beach			
Road			
Desert			
Mountain			
Island			

Simulate Compound Events

Quick Review

An actual event is sometimes difficult to perform or record. A simulation can be used to model the outcomes of a real-world event. Based on simulated results, you can approximate the probability and predict the future outcomes of an event.

Example

Mr. Jones assigns homework 60% of the days that school is in session. His students use a random number generator to simulate five trials representing Mr. Jones's homework assignments next week. The numbers 0 to 5 represent days on which homework is assigned, and the numbers 6 to 9 represent days without homework. What is the probability that Mr. Jones will assign homework on 3 or more days next week?

14528   62807   53290   24375   40681

Number of weeks simulated: 5

Number of weeks in which homework is assigned on 3 or more days: 4

Based on the simulation, the probability that Mr. Jones will assign homework on 3 or more days next week is $\frac{4}{5}$, or 80%.

Practice

1. Felix's favorite cereal includes 1 of 3 different prizes inside each box. The chance of getting each prize is equally likely. Felix conducts a simulation to see what his chances are of collecting all 3 prizes if he buys 5 boxes over time. Each section of the spinner represents the possible prizes in a single box.

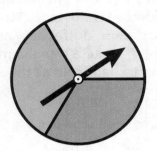

YGGBB   GBGBG   YGGYB   BGGYG

BGBYB   GYBYY   YYGYG   GYYGB

Based on the simulation, what is the probability that Felix will collect all three prizes?

2. Reece is playing a carnival game in which he must guess under which of 2 cups a ball is hidden. To simulate the results of this game, he flips a coin with heads up (H) representing wins and tails up (T) representing losses. Based on the simulation below, what is the probability that Reece will win at least 2 of his next 4 games?

HHTT   HTTT   HTTT   THTH   TTHT
HHHT   TTHH   TTHH   HTTH   HHTH

Hidden Clue

For each ordered pair, one coordinate is given. Find the second coordinate by determining the sale price after the percent markup or markdown. Then locate and label the corresponding point on the graph. Draw line segments to connect the points in alphabetical order. Use the completed picture to help you answer the riddle below.

I can...
use the percent equation to solve problems.

© 7.RP.A.3

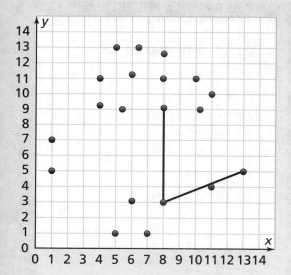

What do you throw out when you want to use it, but take in when you don't want to use it?

A (13, 25% markup on $4) 13, _____

B (30% markdown on $10, 1) _____, 1

C (20% markdown on $1.25, 5) _____, 5

D (6, 40% markdown on $5.10) 6, _____

E (35% markup on $4, 9) _____, 9

F (4, 50% markdown on $18.50) 4, _____

G (60% markup on $2.50, 11) _____, 11

H (6, 25% markdown on $15) 6, _____

I (60% markup on $4, 13) _____, 13

J (8, 30% markdown on $18) 8, _____

K (50% markup on $5.30, 11) _____, 11

L (10, 45% markdown on $20) 10, _____

M (35% markup on $7.60, 9) _____, 9

N (8, 30% markdown on $13) 8, _____

TOPIC 8

SOLVE PROBLEMS INVOLVING GEOMETRY

? Topic Essential Question

How can geometry be used to solve problems?

Topic Overview

8-1 Solve Problems Involving Scale Drawings

8-2 Draw Geometric Figures

8-3 Draw Triangles with Given Conditions

8-4 Solve Problems Using Angle Relationships

8-5 Solve Problems Involving Circumference of a Circle

8-6 Solve Problems Involving Area of a Circle

3-Act Mathematical Modeling: Whole Lotta Dough

8-7 Describe Cross Sections

8-8 Solve Problems Involving Surface Area

8-9 Solve Problems Involving Volume

Topic Vocabulary

- adjacent angles
- circumference
- complementary angles
- composite figure
- cross section
- scale drawing
- supplementary angles
- vertical angles

Go online

Lesson Digital Resources

INTERACTIVE STUDENT EDITION
Access online or offline.

VISUAL LEARNING ANIMATION
Interact with visual learning animations.

ACTIVITY Use with *Solve & Discuss It, Explo*
and *Explain It* activities, and to explore Exam

VIDEOS Watch clips to support *3-Act Mathematical Modeling Lessons* and *STEM P*

Whole Lotta Dough

▶ Whole Lotta Dough

In 2012, a team of Italian chefs baked a pizza that was 131 feet across and weighed more than 50,000 pounds! Imagine how many people it would take to eat one slice of that pizza, assuming you can find a tool big enough to cut it. Think about this during the 3-Act Mathematical Modeling lesson.

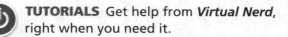 **PRACTICE** Practice what you've learned.

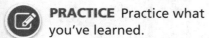 **TUTORIALS** Get help from *Virtual Nerd*, right when you need it.

MATH TOOLS Explore math with digital tools.

GAMES Play Math Games to help you learn.

 **KEY CONCEPT** Review important lesson content.

GLOSSARY Read and listen to English/Spanish definitions.

ASSESSMENT Show what you've learned.

⊙enVision® STEM Project

Did You Know?

The Rail-Trail Hall of Fame includes these exemplary rail-trails.

The High Line in NYC allows New Yorkers to float over busy streets in an innovative park. A decaying urban eyesore for decades, this 30-foot high freight line carried goods in and out of Manhattan's industrial district from 1934 to 1980.

The Fred Marquis Pinellas Trail in FL was built along a railroad right of way which was abandoned in the mid 1980's. Designed with safety in mind, the trail allows users to travel easily between numerous parks and provides a variety of beautiful scenic vistas.

The Paul Bunyan State Trail in MN is built on a former Burlington Northern corridor dating back to 1893. Towns along this 115-mile trail come in 10 to 15-mile intervals—a byproduct of the railroading era.

France has experimented with paying people to bike to work. They hope to reduce air pollution and cut fossil fuel consumption while at the same time boosting people's health.

Copenhagen is the most bike-friendly city in the world.

41%
of residents bike to school or work

55%
bike every day

Your Task:
Upscale Design

Review your survey results on the needs of walkers and bicyclists in your area. Choose an existing path or bikeway and make a scale drawing of the route. Add improvements or extensions to your drawing that enhance the trails and better meet the needs of users. If your area lacks a trail, choose a possible route and make a scale drawing that proposes a new path. How will your proposal enhance the quality of life and provide solutions for potential users?

Review What You Know!

Vocabulary

Choose the best term from the box to complete each definition.

area
base
diameter
height
radius
volume

1. The number of square units that a figure covers is its _____ .

2. The _____ of a triangle is the length of the perpendicular line segment from a vertex to the opposite side.

3. The _____ of a solid figure is the number of cubic units needed to fill it.

4. Any line segment that connects the center of a circle to a point on the circle is called a _____ .

Area and Volume

Find each measure.

5. Area of a triangle with a base 6 feet and height 9 feet

6. Volume of a rectangular prism with length 4 inches, width 2 inches, and height 2 inches

Measure Angles

Use a protractor to find the measure of each angle.

7.

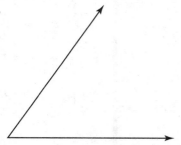

8.

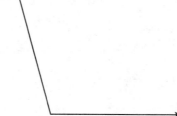

Describe Characteristics of Shapes

Describe this figure using as many geometry terms as you can.

9.

A _____ B
| 90°   90° |
| 90°   90° |
D _____ C

Language Development

Fill in the word web to connect key words you learn in this topic. A sample key word and its connections are given.

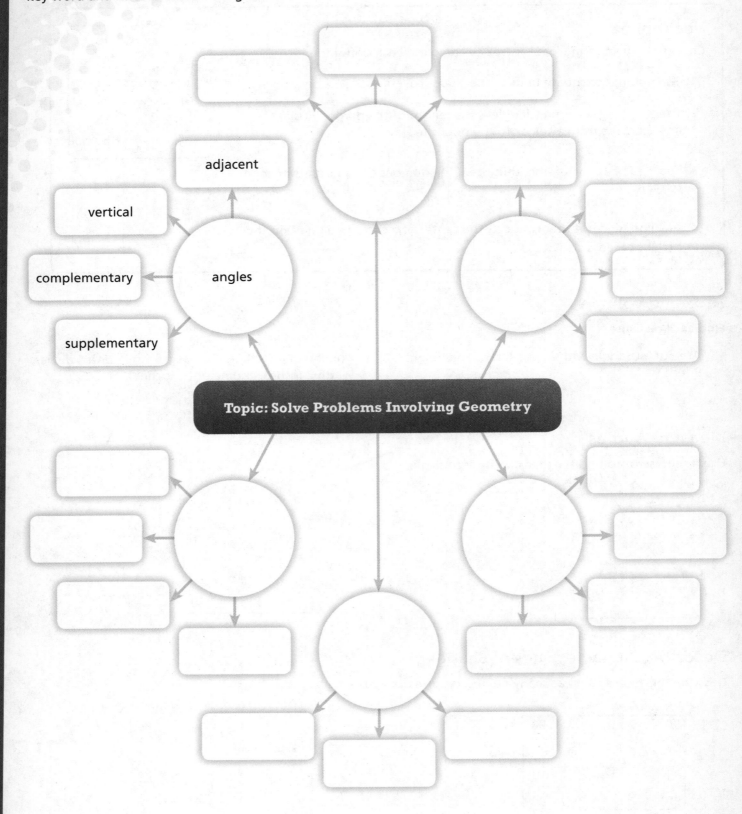

PROJECT 8A

If you built a sculpture, what materials would you use?

PROJECT: CONSTRUCT A THREE-DIMENSIONAL SCULPTURE

PROJECT 8B

If you made a pizza, what kind of pizza would it be?

PROJECT: ANALYZE A PEPPERONI PIZZA

PROJECT 8C

What places have you visited where being a tour guide would be fun?

PROJECT: PLAN A GUIDED TOUR

PROJECT 8D

How could you determine which is larger—a tall building or a wide building?

PROJECT: BUILD A SCALE MODEL

Explore It!

Calvin made a scale model of the plane shown.

240 ft

15 in.

I can...
use the key in a scale drawing to find missing measures.

© **Common Core Content Standards**
7.G.A.1

Mathematical Practices
MP.2, MP.7, MP.8

A. How can you represent the relationship between the model of the plane and the actual plane?

B. What do you notice about the relationship between the model of the plane and the actual plane?

Focus on math practices

Look for Relationships If the model and the actual plane are to scale, what do you know about the relationship between all the other parts of the model and the actual plane, aside from the total length?

EXAMPLE 1 **Find Actual Lengths Using a Scale Drawing**

Scan for Multimedia

The island in the blueprint is 6 inches long. What is the actual length of the island in the kitchen?

A **scale drawing** is an enlarged or reduced drawing of an object that is proportional to the actual object.

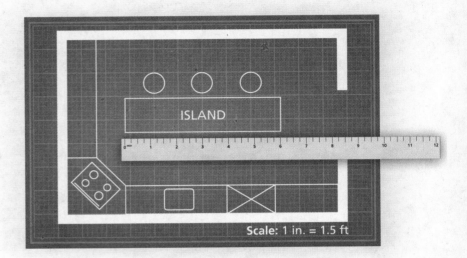

ISLAND

Scale: 1 in. = 1.5 ft

Use a double number line to represent the scale drawing length and the actual length.

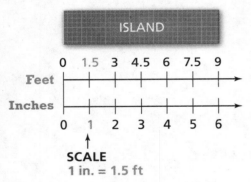

ISLAND

Feet: 0 1.5 3 4.5 6 7.5 9

Inches: 0 1 2 3 4 5 6

↑ SCALE
1 in. = 1.5 ft

Use a proportion to find the actual length, x, of the island.

$$\frac{1.5}{1} = \frac{x}{6}$$

Use the scale $\frac{1.5 \text{ ft}}{1 \text{ in.}}$ to write the proportion.

$$\frac{1.5}{1} \cdot 6 = \frac{x}{6} \cdot 6$$

$$9 = x$$

Look for Relationships The ratio $\frac{1.5 \text{ ft}}{1 \text{ in.}}$ will be the constant scale factor for all lengths in the drawing relative to the actual lengths.

The actual length of the island is 9 feet.

☑ Try It!

What is the actual width, w, of the island if the width in the drawing is 2.5 inches?

Convince Me! How would the proportion for Example 1 change if the scale changed?

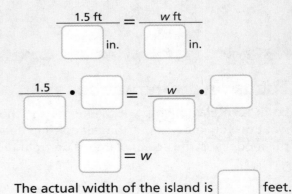

$$\frac{1.5 \text{ ft}}{\boxed{} \text{ in.}} = \frac{w \text{ ft}}{\boxed{} \text{ in.}}$$

$$\frac{1.5}{\boxed{}} \cdot \boxed{} = \frac{w}{\boxed{}} \cdot \boxed{}$$

$$\boxed{} = w$$

The actual width of the island is $\boxed{}$ feet.

EXAMPLE 2 ▶ 👆 Use Scale Factors to Solve Area Problems

ACTIVITY   ASSESS

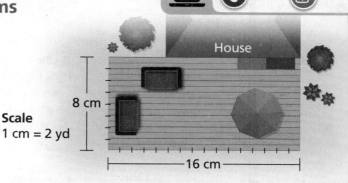

House

What is the area, in square yards, of the deck represented by the scale drawing?

8 cm

Scale
1 cm = 2 yd

16 cm

> **Use Structure** You can use an equation in the form $y = kx$ to represent the proportional relationship between lengths in the scale drawing, x, and actual lengths, y. The constant of proportionality, k, is the scale factor.

STEP 1 Find the actual length, L, of the deck using the length, ℓ, in the scale drawing.

$L = k\ell$

 Use the scale factor of $\frac{2 \text{ yd}}{1 \text{ cm}}$ for k.

$= 2 \cdot 16$

$= 32$

The actual length is 32 yards.

STEP 2 Find the actual width, W, of the deck using the width, w, in the scale drawing.

$W = kw$

$= 2 \cdot 8$

$= 16$

The actual width is 16 yards.

STEP 3 Calculate the actual area of the deck.

Area = Length × Width

$= 32 \times 16$

$= 512$

The actual area of the deck is 512 square yards.

EXAMPLE 3 ▶ 👆 **Reproduce a Scale Drawing at a Different Scale**

Students are recreating the landscape drawing shown at the right for a mural. They want the length of the drawing on the mural to be 80 inches. What will be the new scale and the height of the drawing on the mural?

Scale
1 in. = 4 ft

8 in.

10 in.

> **Look for Relationships** What is the scale factor, k, that relates the actual lengths to the lengths in the scale drawing?

STEP 1 Find the actual length, L, and actual height, H, of the landscape.

$L = k \cdot 10 \qquad H = k \cdot 8$

$= 4 \cdot 10 \qquad = 4 \cdot 8$

$= 40 \qquad = 32$

The actual dimensions of the landscape are 40 feet by 32 feet.

STEP 2 Find the new scale for the mural to the actual landscape.

÷ 80

$\dfrac{40 \text{ ft}}{80 \text{ in.}} = \dfrac{? \text{ ft}}{1 \text{ in.}} \qquad ? =$
0.5

÷ 80

The new scale of 1 in. = 0.5 ft means 1 inch on the mural represents 0.5 feet in the actual landscape.

STEP 3 Find the height, h, of the drawing on the mural using the new scale.

$H = kh$

$32 = 0.5 \cdot h$

$64 = h$

The dimensions of the drawing on the mural are 80 inches by 64 inches.

👆 **Try It!**

The scale drawing shown represents an existing barn. The shortest side of the barn measures 150 meters. If a new barn that is $\frac{2}{3}$ its size replaces the existing barn, what will be the scale of this drawing to the new barn?

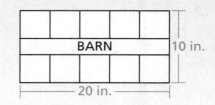

BARN   10 in.

20 in.

KEY CONCEPT

The scale factor of a scale drawing is the ratio of an actual length, y, to the corresponding length, x, in the drawing. The ratio is the constant of proportionality, k, that relates the actual figure to the scale drawing. You can use a proportion or use an equation of the form $y = kx$ to solve problems involving scale drawings.

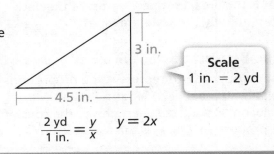

Scale
1 in. = 2 yd

$$\frac{2 \text{ yd}}{1 \text{ in.}} = \frac{y}{x} \qquad y = 2x$$

Do You Understand?

1. **Essential Question** How do scale drawings and actual measurements represent proportional relationships?

2. **Generalize** Describe the ratio of corresponding measures in scale drawings and the actual measures they represent.

3. **Reasoning** Mikayla is determining the actual distance between Harrisville and Lake Town using a map. The scale on her map reads.
1 inch = 50 miles. She measures the distance to be 4.5 inches and writes the following proportion:

$$\frac{1 \text{ in.}}{4.5 \text{ in.}} = \frac{50 \text{ mi}}{x \text{ mi}}$$

Explain why her proportion is equivalent to
$$\frac{50 \text{ mi}}{1 \text{ in.}} = \frac{x \text{ mi}}{4.5 \text{ in.}}.$$

Do You Know How?

4. What is the actual base length of the triangle depicted in the scale drawing?

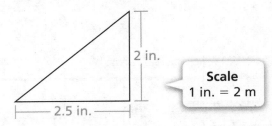

Scale
1 in. = 2 m

5. What is the area of the actual square window shown in the scale drawing?

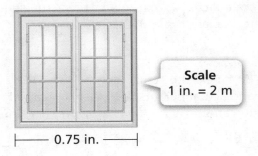

Scale
1 in. = 2 m

6. A distance of 30 miles on a map is represented by a 2-inch line. If the map is enlarged to 3 times its size, what will be the scale of the enlarged map?

Practice & Problem Solving

Scan for
Multimedia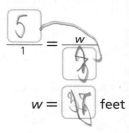

Leveled Practice For **7** and **8**, fill in the boxes to find the actual measures.

7. On a map, 1 inch equals 5 miles. Two cities are 8 inches apart on the map.

What is the actual distance between the cities?

$$\frac{\boxed{40}}{\boxed{8}} = \frac{x}{8}$$

$$x = \boxed{40} \text{ miles}$$

8. Ryan makes a scale drawing of a banner for a school dance. He uses a scale of 1 inch = 3 feet, and the width of the drawing is 5 inches.

What is the actual width, *w*, of the banner?

$$\frac{\boxed{5}}{1} = \frac{w}{\boxed{3}}$$

$$w = \boxed{15} \text{ feet}$$

9. On a map, 1 inch equals 7.2 miles. Two houses are 1.5 inches apart on the map. What is the actual distance between the houses?

10. The original blueprint for the Morenos' living room has a scale of 2 inches = 5 feet. The family wants to use a new blueprint that shows the length of the living room to be 15 inches. If the width of the living room on the original blueprint is 6 inches and the length is 9.6 inches, what are the scale and the width of the new blueprint?

$$\frac{5}{2} \times \frac{1}{15} = \frac{5}{30}$$

11. The scale for a drawing of the tennis court is 1 centimeter = 2 meters. What is the area of the actual tennis court?

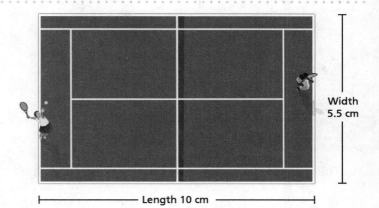

Width
5.5 cm

Length 10 cm

12. The scale for the drawing of a rectangular playing field is 2 inches = 5 feet.

a. Write an equation you can use to find the dimensions of the actual field, where *x* is a dimension of the scale drawing (in inches) and *y* is the corresponding dimension of the actual field (in feet).

b. What is the area of the field?

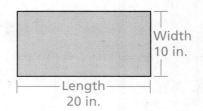

Width
10 in.

Length
20 in.

13. How many square feet of flooring are needed to cover the entire floor of Bedroom 1?

Bedroom 1

Scale: 1 in. = 4 ft
The gridlines are spaced 1 inch apart.

14. The actual distance between Point A and Point B is 200 meters. A length of 1.9 feet represents this distance on a certain wall map. Point C and Point D are 3.8 feet apart on this map. What is the actual distance between Point C and Point D?

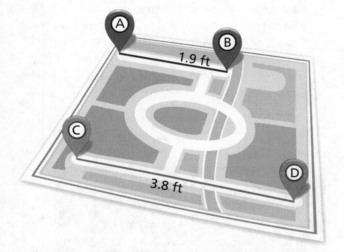

A
B
1.9 ft

C

D
3.8 ft

15. Higher Order Thinking A map of a highway has a scale of 2 inches equals 33 miles. The length of the highway on the map is 6 inches. There are 11 rest stops equally spaced on the highway, including one at each end. You are making a new map with a scale of 1 inch equals 30 miles. How far apart are the rest stops on the new map?

 Assessment Practice

16. The original blueprint of a concrete patio has a scale of 2 inches = 3 feet.

Victoria wants to make a new blueprint of the patio with a length of 16.8 inches.

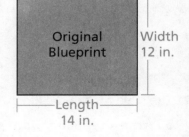

Original Blueprint

Width
12 in.

Length
14 in.

PART A
What is the scale for the new blueprint?

1 inch = [ ] feet

PART B
What is the width, in inches, of the blueprint with the new scale?

[ ]

Solve & Discuss It! ACTIVITY

Students in the Art Club are designing a flag with the school's mascot and emblem. The flag has four sides, with two sides that are twice as long as the other two sides. What shape could the flag be, and what dimensions could it have? Make and label a scale drawing as part of your answer.

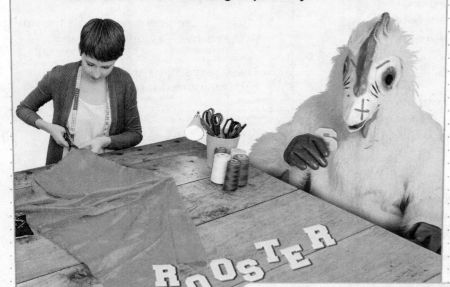

Make Sense and Persevere Is there more than one shape that could represent the flag?

Go Online

I can...
draw figures with given conditions.

© **Common Core Content Standards**
7.G.A.2

Mathematical Practices
MP.1, MP.2, MP.3, MP.5

Focus on math practices

Reasoning How did you decide what lengths to use for the four sides of the flag you drew? What lengths could the actual flag be, based on your drawing?

Essential Question How can a shape that meets given conditions be drawn?

  VISUAL LEARNING ASSE

 EXAMPLE 1 Draw a Quadrilateral with Given Conditions

Scan for Multimedia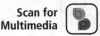

The school's landscaping club is designing a 4-sided patio and garden. The patio has 2 perpendicular sides that each measure 4 yards, and a third side that is perpendicular to one of the equal sides but twice as long. One angle of the patio measures 135°. Make a scale drawing of the patio using a scale of 1 cm = 1 yd.

Use Appropriate Tools You can use rulers and protractors to construct precise drawings.

STEP 1 Use a ruler to draw three sides that meet the given conditions.

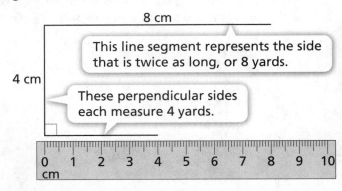

8 cm

This line segment represents the side that is twice as long, or 8 yards.

4 cm

These perpendicular sides each measure 4 yards.

STEP 2 Use a protractor to draw a 135° angle that connects and completes the shape.

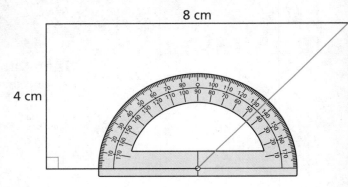

8 cm

4 cm

The scale drawing shows that the patio is the shape of a trapezoid.

Try It!

Use a ruler and protractor to draw a quadrilateral with two equal sides that meet at a right angle, and two nonadjacent angles of the same measure. What is the name of the quadrilateral you drew?

The quadrilateral I drew is a [   ].

Convince Me!
Could you have drawn more than one shape that fits the given conditions? Explain.

EXAMPLE **2** Draw a Figure to Solve a Problem

ACTIVITY   ASSESS

Mr. Miller's classroom has desks shaped like equilateral triangles. He is planning to arrange the desks for a lunch for 10 people. If one person can sit at each edge of each desk, make a sketch to show how many desks he needs.

Use Appropriate Tools Why is a freehand drawing precise enough for the table arrangement?

ONE WAY Mr. Miller can arrange the desks in one row to make a long lunch table.

He will need 8 desks to make this arrangement.

ANOTHER WAY Mr. Miller can arrange the desks in two rows to make a wider lunch table.

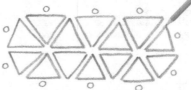

He will need 14 desks to make this arrangement.

EXAMPLE **3** **Draw a Figure Using Technology**

An engineer makes a scale drawing of the floor of a building. The floor has two pairs of parallel sides that are 50 feet and 80 feet. Two of the four angles measure 60°. Use geometry software to make a scale drawing. What is the name of the floor's shape?

Use Appropriate Tools Why would the engineer use technology, rather than a freehand sketch?

STEP 1 Draw two line segments at a 60° angle. Using a scale of 1 unit = 10 feet, the segments should be 5 units and 8 units long.

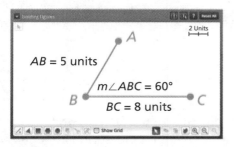

STEP 2 Duplicate each line segment to create pairs of parallel sides, and move them to construct a closed figure.

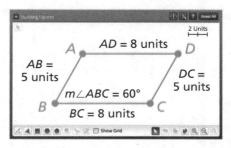

The floor shape of the building is a parallelogram.

 Try It!

a. Make a sketch to show another way Mr. Miller can arrange the desks to seat 10 people for lunch.

b. Use geometry software to make a rhombus with a side length of 6 units and two angles that measure 45°.

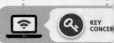

You can draw shapes that meet given conditions freehand, with a ruler and protractor, or with technology. The given conditions may include properties of geometric figures and relationships between parts of the figures.

> **Use Appropriate Tools** Deciding how precise the drawing of the shape should be will help you choose the method you use to draw the shape.

Do You Understand?

1. **Essential Question** How can a shape that meets given conditions be drawn?

2. **Use Appropriate Tools** How can you decide whether to draw a shape freehand, with a ruler and protractor, or using technology?

3. **Construct Arguments** Why can you draw more than one quadrilateral using four right angles?

Do You Know How?

4. Draw, freehand, a quadrilateral with exactly one pair of parallel sides and at least one angle measuring 45°.

5. Use a ruler and protractor to draw a quadrilateral with four right angles, two side lengths each measuring 3 inches, and two side lengths each measuring 4 inches. What is the most descriptive name of the figure you drew?

6. Use geometry software to draw a quadrilateral with two angles measuring 80° and two angles measuring 100°. What is the name of the figure you drew?

Practice & Problem Solving

7. What quadrilaterals can you draw that have exactly four right angles?

8. A four-sided sandbox has more than two right angles, two side lengths of 2 feet, and two side lengths of 5 feet. What geometric shape best describes the shape of the sandbox?

9. What quadrilateral can you draw that has exactly one pair of parallel sides?

10. A friend is building a 4-sided garden with two side lengths of 19 feet and exactly one right angle. What quadrilaterals could describe the garden?

11. What quadrilaterals can you draw that have two side lengths of 9 centimeters and two side lengths of 4 centimeters?

12. A park has a pond shaped like a quadrilateral with side lengths of 17 feet and no right angles. What other geometric shapes could describe the shape of the pond?

13. Draw a quadrilateral that has one angle measure of 20° and exactly one side length of 4 units.

14. Which of the following shapes are trapezoids that have side lengths of 7 inches and 5 inches and a right angle? Select all that apply.

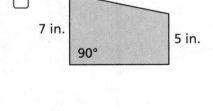

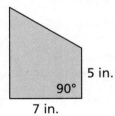

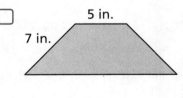

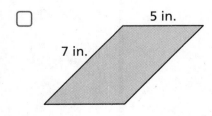

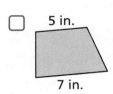

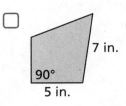

15. Using computer software, draw a quadrilateral with two sets of parallel sides and two angles measuring 135 degrees.

16. Higher Order Thinking Draw a rhombus with side lengths of 6 units and angle measures of 100°, 80°, 100°, and 80°.

 Assessment Practice

17. Thomas is painting a geometry mural. He is painting quadrilaterals that have at least 1 line of symmetry.

PART A

Which could be a quadrilateral that Thomas painted? Select all that apply.

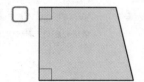

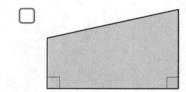

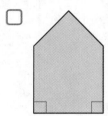

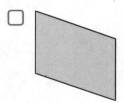

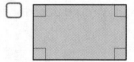

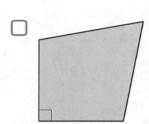

PART B

Which of the following figures can he also include in his painting?

Ⓐ A quadrilateral with no equal sides

Ⓑ A quadrilateral with only 2 equal sides that are perpendicular to each other

Ⓒ A quadrilateral with 2 pairs of equal sides and 1 right angle

Ⓓ A quadrilateral with 2 pairs of parallel equal sides, with no right angles

Solve & Discuss It!

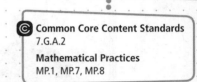 ACTIVITY

Kane has 4 pieces of wood available to build a triangle-shaped garden. Which pieces of wood can he use?

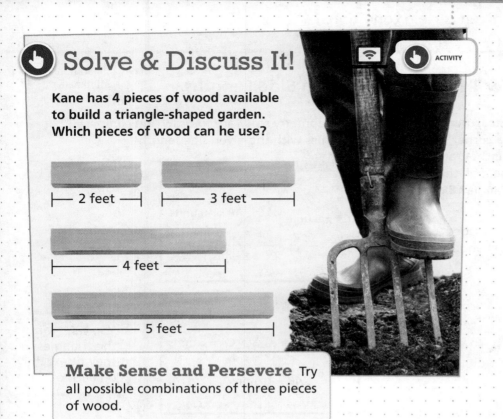

├── 2 feet ──┤   ├────── 3 feet ──────┤

├──────── 4 feet ────────┤

├──────────── 5 feet ────────────┤

Make Sense and Persevere Try all possible combinations of three pieces of wood.

I can...
draw triangles when given information about their side lengths and angle measures.

Ⓒ Common Core Content Standards
7.G.A.2

Mathematical Practices
MP.1, MP.7, MP.8

Focus on math practices

Use Structure Are there any combinations of three pieces of wood that will not create a triangle? Explain.

? Essential Question How can you determine when it is possible to draw a triangle given certain conditions?

 VISUAL LEARNING ASSES

EXAMPLE 1 Draw Triangles with Given Side Lengths

Scan for Multimedia

Students in woodshop class are measuring and cutting out a triangular base for a corner shelf, with sides measuring 6 inches, 8 inches, and 10 inches. How can you determine if all the students will cut out the same triangle? Explain.

Look for Relationships Does the orientation of a triangle change its shape?

Use geometry software to draw and compare triangles with the given side lengths.

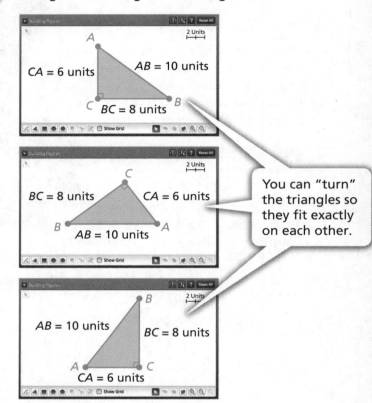

You can "turn" the triangles so they fit exactly on each other.

Triangles with the same side lengths are the same shape and size, no matter how they are positioned.

So, all the students will cut out the same triangle.

☑ Try It!

How many unique triangles can be drawn with given side lengths of 8 inches, 10.3 inches, and 13 inches?

[ ] unique triangle(s) can be drawn with the given side lengths.

Convince Me! When two sides of a triangle are switched, why is it still considered the same triangle?

EXAMPLE 2 — Determine Possible Side Lengths of Triangles

Steve gathers three pieces of wood from the scrap pile in woodshop class.

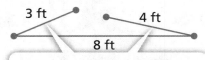

| 3 feet | 4 feet | 8 feet |

a. Can Steve make a triangle with these three wood pieces? Explain.

No. The 3-ft and 4-ft wood pieces are not long enough to form a triangle. $3 + 4 < 8$

b. Generalize What can you conclude about the lengths that make a triangle possible?

3 ft 5 ft
8 ft

The sum of the lengths of the two shortest sides must be greater than the length of the third side in order to form a triangle.

EXAMPLE 3 — Draw a Triangle with a Combination of Given Side Lengths and Angle Measures

Can more than one triangle be drawn with the following conditions?

a. side lengths of 5 inches and 6 inches which make an angle of 45°

Draw a 45° angle with line segments of 5 inches and 6 inches.

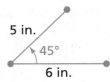

5 in.
45°
6 in.

Connect the sides by drawing the third side.

5 in.
45°
6 in.

Generalize Is there more than one way to connect the two ends of the given sides?

Only one triangle can be drawn with the given measures.

b. a side length of 6 inches with angles at each end measuring 40° and 60°

Draw a 6-inch line segment and rays that form the 40° and 60° angles.

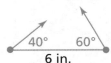

40° 60°
6 in.

Extend the rays until they intersect.

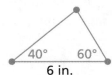

40° 60°
6 in.

Generalize Is there more than one way to draw the two other sides?

Only one triangle can be drawn with the given measures.

✓ Try It!

a. Write three side lengths that will form a triangle. Write three side lengths that will NOT form a triangle. **Sample answer: Triangle: 3 ft, 9 ft, 10 ft; No triangle: 2 ft, 4 ft, 8 ft**

b. Can a triangle be drawn with a side length of 3 inches and angles at each end measuring 90° and 89°? Explain. **Yes; Sample answer: The third angle will be 1°.**

EXAMPLE 4 **Draw a Triangle with Two Given Side Lengths and a Nonincluded Angle Measure**

Can more than one triangle be drawn using two side lengths of 6 units and 9 units, and a 40° angle that is not formed by their intersection?

Draw △ABC with side lengths 6 units and 9 units, and a nonincluded angle of 40°.

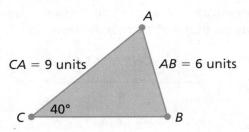

Swing side AB left to create an obtuse triangle, keeping m∠C at 40°.

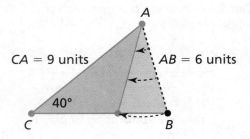

The new triangle still has the given side lengths and angle measure, but it is a different triangle.

So, more than one triangle can be made with the given measures.

EXAMPLE 5 **Draw a Triangle with Three Given Angle Measures**

Is there a unique triangle with angle measures of 30°, 60°, and 90°?

Draw a triangle with the given angle measures. Notice that side lengths are not required.

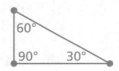

Enlarge and reduce your drawing, keeping the angle measures the same but changing the side lengths to proportional measurements.

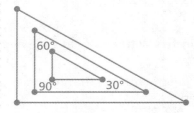

Generalize Is there more than one way to draw a triangle with three given angles?

Many different triangles can be drawn with the given angle measures.

So, there is not one unique triangle with angle measures of 30°, 60°, and 90°.

 **Try It!**

Can more than one triangle be drawn with two side lengths of 6 inches and a nonincluded angle of 60°? Explain.

You can analyze given conditions of side lengths and angle measures to determine whether one unique triangle, more than one unique triangle, or no triangle can be drawn.

There is more than one possible triangle given these cases: all three angles, or two sides and a nonincluded angle.

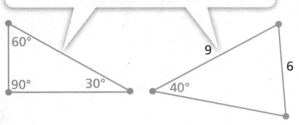

There is one unique triangle given these cases: all three sides, two sides and an included angle, or two angles and an included side.

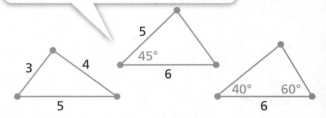

Do You Understand?

1. **? Essential Question** How can you determine when it is possible to draw a triangle given certain conditions?

2. **Look for Relationships** What is the relationship between all triangles that can be drawn given the same three angle measures?

3. Why can there be only one way to draw a triangle if two sides and an included angle are given?

Do You Know How?

4. How many triangles can be drawn with side lengths 4 centimeters, 4.5 centimeters, and 9 centimeters? Explain.

5. Can more than one triangle be drawn with side lengths of 5 inches and 7 inches and an included angle with a measure of 50°? Explain.

6. Sketch two different triangles that have angle measures of 45°, 45°, and 90°.

Practice & Problem Solving

7. Draw two different triangles with angle measurements 90°, 35°, and 55°.

8. If you form a triangle from three given side lengths, will you always get one triangle or more than one triangle?

9. How can you make different-looking triangles given two of the angle measures and the included side lengths?

10. If you form a triangle from two given angle measures and the length of the included side, will you always get one triangle or will you get more than one triangle?

11. How can you make different triangles with the same angle measures?

12. Given two side lengths of 15 units and 9.5 units, with a nonincluded angle of 75°, can you draw no triangles, only one triangle, or more than one triangle?

13. A student was asked to form different triangles with angle measures of 90°, 30°, and 60°. She incorrectly said this triangle is the only triangle with angle measures of 90°, 30°, and 60°. What mistake might she have made?

14. In triangle *QRS*, *m∠QSR* = 100°, *m∠SQR* = 45°, and *QR* = 4 units. In triangle *XYZ*, *m∠XYZ* = 100°, *m∠ZXY* = 45°, and *XY* = 4 units. Are triangles *QRS* and *XYZ* the same? Explain.

15. You are asked to make a triangular sign using the given information about triangle *WXY*. In triangle *WXY*, *m∠WXY* = 45°, *m∠YWX* = 90°, and *WX* = 5 feet.

   a. Which triangle is correct? Each square on the grid is equal to 1 square foot.

   Ⓐ 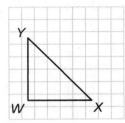   Ⓑ 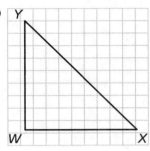   Ⓒ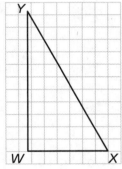

   b. Explain why only one triangle can be formed with these three pieces of information.

16. **Look for Relationships** Two different triangles have side lengths of 13 and 16 units and a nonincluded angle of 50°. Explain how the triangles are different.

17. **Higher Order Thinking** Two triangles have side lengths of 12 units and 15 units and the non-included angle of 45°. Draw two different triangles with these conditions.

18. For triangle *RST*, *RS* is 12 centimeters, *ST* is 16 centimeters, and *RT* is 19 centimeters. How many triangles can be drawn with the given side lengths?

19. A triangle has two side lengths of 8.5 centimeters and 9.5 centimeters. What is a possible length for the third side? Explain why this is a possible length.

20. Can a triangle be formed with side lengths of 4, 5, and 7 units?

21. Which of the following combinations of side lengths would form a triangle? Select all that apply.

☐ 7 in., 10 in., 2.5 in.

☐ 4.5 ft, 8 ft, 5 ft

☐ 5 yd, 11 yd, 5 yd

☐ 12 in., 5 in., 9.5 in.

☐ 7 m, 7 m, 9 m

☐ 6 ft, 16 ft, 9 ft

22. Which of the following combinations of side lengths would NOT form a triangle?

Ⓐ 7 cm, 10 cm, 13 cm

Ⓑ 10 ft, 13 ft, 15 ft

Ⓒ 10 yd, 11 yd, 13 yd

Ⓓ 10 in., 13 in., 23 in.

23. Draw a triangle that has exactly one line of symmetry.

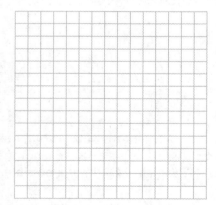

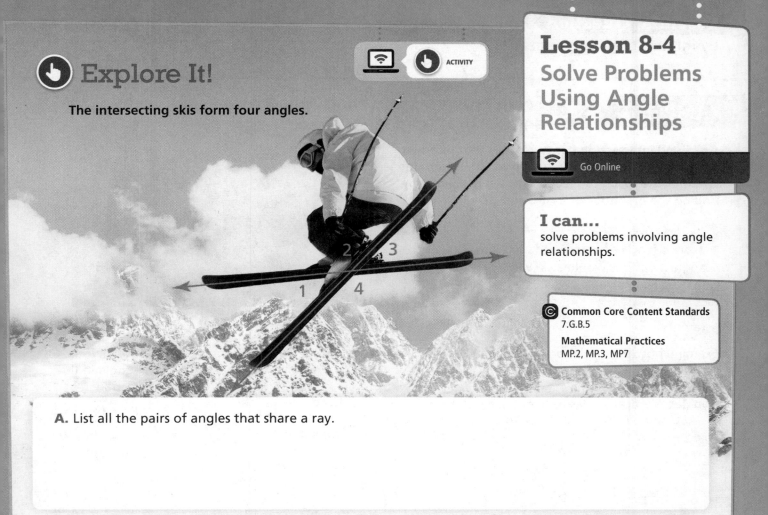

Lesson 8-4
Solve Problems Using Angle Relationships

Go Online

I can...
solve problems involving angle relationships.

© **Common Core Content Standards**
7.G.B.5

Mathematical Practices
MP.2, MP.3, MP7

⊙ Explore It!

ACTIVITY

The intersecting skis form four angles.

A. List all the pairs of angles that share a ray.

B. Suppose the measure of ∠1 increases. What happens to the size of ∠2? ∠3?

C. How does the sum of the measures of ∠1 and ∠2 change when one ski moves? Explain.

Focus on math practices

Construct Arguments Why does the sum of all four angle measures stay the same when one of the skis moves?

EXAMPLE 1 Solve Problems Involving Adjacent and Vertical Angles

Scan for Multimedia

A skewed intersection has two roads that intersect at more than 20 degrees away from 90°. Determine whether the road intersection shown is skewed by finding the measures of ∠ABC and ∠DBE.

Look for Relationships What angle measures would a skewed intersection have?

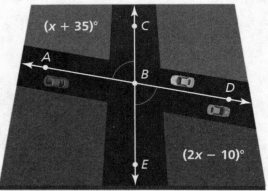

Examine how the angles are related.

Angles opposite each other are called **vertical angles**. Vertical angles have equal measures. ∠ABC and ∠DBE are vertical angles.

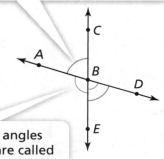

Non-overlapping angles that share a ray are called **adjacent angles**. ∠ABE and ∠EBD are adjacent angles, sharing ray BE.

Write and solve an equation to find the value of x.

Read "m" as "the measure of" the named angle.

$m\angle ABC = m\angle DBE$

$x + 35 = 2x - 10$

$x + 35 + 10 = 2x - 10 + 10$

$x + 45 = 2x$

$x - x + 45 = 2x - x$

$45 = x$

Find the measure of an angle in the intersection.

$m\angle ABC = (x + 35)°$

$= (45 + 35)°$

$= 80°$

∠ABC and ∠DBE both measure 80°.

Since 80° is within 20° of 90°, the road intersection is not skewed.

☑ **Try It!**

∠MNQ and ∠PNR are vertical angles. What is the value of x?

Vertical angles are [   ], so the equation [   ] can be used to find x. The value of x is [   ].

Convince Me! Why can you use an equation when solving for x in the diagram?

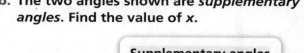

EXAMPLE 2 — Solve Problems Involving Complementary and Supplementary Angles

a. Ray *EG* splits right angle *DEF* into two angles, ∠*DEG* and ∠*GEF*. Find the value of *x*.

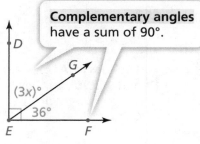

> **Complementary angles** have a sum of 90°.

$$m\angle DEG + m\angle GEF = 90$$
$$3x + 36 = 90$$
$$3x + 36 - 36 = 90 - 36$$
$$3x = 54$$
$$\frac{3x}{3} = \frac{54}{3}$$
$$x = 18$$

b. The two angles shown are *supplementary angles*. Find the value of *x*.

> **Supplementary angles** have a sum of 180°.

$$\left(\frac{x}{2} - 4\right) + 50 = 180$$
$$\frac{x}{2} + 46 = 180$$
$$\frac{x}{2} + 46 - 46 = 180 - 46$$
$$\frac{x}{2} = 134$$
$$2 \cdot \frac{x}{2} = 2 \cdot 134$$
$$x = 268$$

EXAMPLE 3 — Find the Measure of an Unknown Angle

Find the measure of ∠*PAR*.

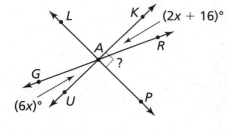

STEP 1 Use vertical angles to find the value of *x*.

$$m\angle UAG = m\angle KAR$$
$$6x = 2x + 16$$
$$6x - 2x = 2x - 2x + 16$$
$$4x = 16$$
$$\frac{4x}{4} = \frac{16}{4}$$
$$x = 4$$

> $m\angle UAG = (6x)°$
> $= (6 \cdot 4)° = 24°$
> So $m\angle KAR = 24°$.

STEP 2 Use complementary angles to find the measure of ∠*PAR*.

$$m\angle KAR + m\angle PAR = 90°$$
$$24° + m\angle PAR = 90°$$
$$m\angle PAR = 66°$$

 **Try It!**

m∠1 is 4 times *m*∠2. ∠1 and ∠2 are complementary. ∠1 and ∠3 are vertical angles. ∠3 and ∠4 are supplementary. What are the measures of the four angles?

This ray is shared by Angles 1 and 2, so they are *adjacent*.

Angles 4 and 5 form a straight line and add up to 180°, so they are *supplementary*.

The sum of Angles 2 and 3 is 90°, so they are *complementary*.

Angles 1 and 4 are opposite each other, so they are *vertical*.

Angle 1

Angle 5

Angle 2

Angle 3

Angle 4

Do You Understand?

1. **Essential Question** How are angles formed by intersecting lines related?

2. **Use Structure** Can vertical angles also be adjacent angles? Explain.

3. **Reasoning** Do complementary and supplementary angles also have to be adjacent angles? Explain.

Do You Know How?

Use the diagram below for 4–6.

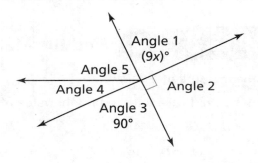

Angle 1 (9x)°

Angle 5

Angle 4

Angle 2

Angle 3 90°

4. List two pairs of adjacent angles.

5. List all pairs of vertical angles.

6. If ∠1 and ∠3 are the same measure, what is the value of x?

Practice & Problem Solving

Scan for Multimedia

7. List each angle adjacent to ∠w.

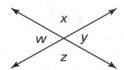

8. List two pairs of adjacent angles.

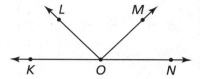

9. Find the value of x.

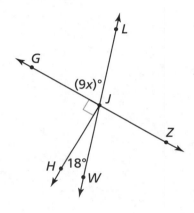

10. Find the value of x.

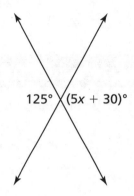

$125°$ $(5x + 30)°$

11. ∠1 and ∠2 are complementary angles. The measure of ∠1 is 42°. The measure of ∠2 is $(3x)°$. Find the value of x.

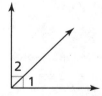

12. Two streets form an intersection. ∠C and ∠D are supplementary angles. If the measure of ∠C is 128° and the measure of ∠D is two times the value of x, what is the value of x?

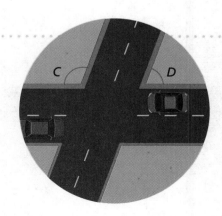

13. If ∠A and ∠B are supplementary angles and ∠A is three times as large as ∠B, find the measures of ∠A and ∠B.

14. Higher Order Thinking The measure of ∠DBE is $(0.1x - 22)°$ and the measure of ∠CBE is $(0.3x - 54)°$. Find the value of x.

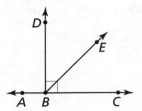

15. Reasoning ∠1 and an angle that measures 50° are supplementary. Another angle that measures 50° and ∠3 are supplementary. Show that $m∠1$ and $m∠3$ are equal.

☑ Assessment Practice

16. Using the diagram at the right, Martin incorrectly writes $m∠b = 125°$.

What mistake did Martin likely make? Find the correct measure of ∠b.

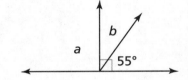

17. What is the measure, in degrees, of angle x?

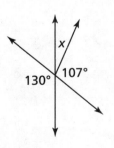

18. What is the measure, in degrees, of the highlighted angle?

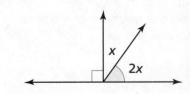

🖱 Explore It!

ACTIVITY

The distance around a circle and the distance across a circle are related.

I can...
solve problems involving radius, diameter, and circumference of circles.

© **Common Core Content Standards**
7.G.B.4, 7.EE.B.4a

Mathematical Practices
MP.1, MP.3, MP.6, MP7, MP.8

A. Use string to measure the distance across each circle. How many of these lengths does it take to go completely around the circle?

B. Use the string and a ruler to measure the distance across the circle and the distance around the circle. Complete the table. Round each measurement to the nearest quarter inch.

	Button	Disk	Dartboard
Distance Around the Circle			
Distance Across the Circle			

C. What do you notice about the ratio of the distance around the circle to the distance across the circle for each circle?

Focus on math practices

Look for Relationships How can you estimate the distance around any circle when given the distance across the circle?

VISUAL LEARNING ASSESS

Scan for Multimedia

Mark recently replaced his front bicycle wheel. How far does the bike travel with each revolution of his new front wheel?

Look for Relationships
How is one revolution of the wheel related to linear distance?

Diameter = 26 inches

Relate the given information to the parts of a circle.

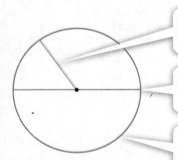

The *radius* is the distance from the outside of the circle to the center.

The *diameter* is the distance across the circle through the center.

The **circumference** is the distance around the circle.

$\frac{C}{d} = \pi$

$C = \pi d$

π is the ratio of the circumference, *C*, of a circle to its diameter, *d*.

π is a decimal that never repeats or terminates. $\pi = 3.14159...$

Use the circumference formula to calculate the distance around the wheel.

$C = \pi d$

$C = \pi(26)$

The diameter of the wheel is 26 inches.

$C = 26\pi$

The circumference is exactly 26π.

$C \approx 26(3.14)$

$= 81.64$

To approximate the distance, use 3.14 for π.

The distance around the wheel is about 81.64 inches. So the bike travels about 81.64 inches with each revolution of the wheel.

Try It!

What is the circumference of the rim of a basketball hoop with a radius of 9 inches?

First, multiply the radius by [ ] to get the diameter, [ ] inches.

Then, multiply the diameter by 3.14 (an approximation for π) to get

a circumference of about [ ] inches.

Convince Me! If the diameter is doubled, what happens to the circumference? Explain.

9 in.

EXAMPLE 2 Find the Diameter Using the Circumference

Kayla and Theo got on the Ferris wheel shown. About how high will they be at the top of the Ferris wheel?

Use the circumference formula to find the diameter of the Ferris wheel.

Circumference: 220 ft

ONE WAY Use 3.14 as an approximation for π.

$C = \pi d$

$220 \approx (3.14)d$ ← Substitute 3.14 for π.

$\dfrac{220}{3.14} = \dfrac{3.14d}{3.14}$

$70 \approx d$

ANOTHER WAY Use $\dfrac{22}{7}$ as an approximation for π.

$C = \pi d$

$220 \approx \left(\dfrac{22}{7}\right)d$ ← Substitute $\dfrac{22}{7}$ for π.

$\dfrac{7}{22} \cdot 220 = \dfrac{7}{22} \cdot \dfrac{22}{7}d$

$70 = d$

Kayla and Theo will be about 70 feet above the ground when at the top of the Ferris wheel.

EXAMPLE 3 Use Circumference to Solve a Problem

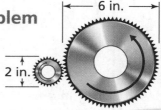

6 in.

2 in.

The larger gear turns twice per second. It causes the smaller gear to turn. How fast does the smaller gear turn per second?

STEP 1 Use the circumference formula to find the circumferences of the larger gear and the smaller gear.

Larger gear	Smaller gear
$C = \pi d$	$C = \pi d$
$C \approx (3.14)(6)$	$C \approx (3.14)(2)$
$C = 18.84$	$C = 6.28$

STEP 2 Divide to find the number of full turns the smaller gear makes when the larger gear makes one full turn.

$\dfrac{18.84}{6.28} = 3$

The smaller gear makes three full turns for every full turn of the larger gear.

STEP 3 Multiply to find the number of full turns the smaller gear makes in one second.

$3 \times 2 = 6$

The larger gear turns two times per second.

The smaller gear makes 6 full turns per second.

Try It!

The circle has a circumference of 9.42 units. What is the area of the square? Use 3.14 for π. Explain how you found the answer.

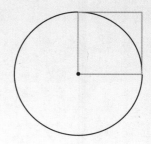

The parts of a circle and their relationships are summarized in the diagram below.

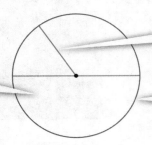

The radius of a circle is half the length of its diameter.

The ratio of the circumference of a circle to its diameter is π. The value of π is approximately 3.14 or $\frac{22}{7}$.

Circumference is the distance around a circle. It can be calculated using the formula $C = \pi d$ or equivalently $C = 2\pi r$.

Do You Understand?

1. **Essential Question** How is the circumference of a circle related to the length of its diameter?

2. **Construct Arguments** Are there any circles for which the relationship between the diameter and circumference cannot be represented by π? Explain.

3. **Be Precise** Can you find the exact circumference of a circle when you multiply the diameter by $\frac{22}{7}$? Explain.

Do You Know How?

4. What is the circumference of a circle with a radius of 5 inches?

5. What is the diameter of a circle with a circumference of 10.99 feet?

6. How many full revolutions does a car tire with a diameter of 25 inches make when the car travels one mile?

← 25 in.

Practice & Problem Solving

Scan for
Multimedia

7. Find the circumference of the circle. Use π as part of the answer.

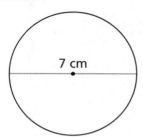

7 cm

8. Find the circumference of the circle. Use 3.14 for π. Round to the nearest hundredth.

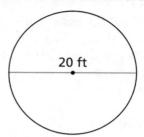

20 ft

9. Find the circumference of the circle. Use π as part of the answer.

12 mi

10. Find the circumference of the circle. Use 3.14 for π. Round to the nearest hundredth.

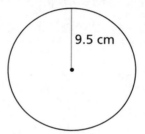

9.5 cm

11. Find the diameter of a circle with a circumference of 27 centimeters. Use 3.14 for π. Round to the nearest tenth.

12. The distance around a meteor crater is 9,687 feet. Find the diameter of the crater. Use $\frac{22}{7}$ for π. Round to the nearest tenth.

13. Make Sense and Persevere The circumference of the inner circle is 44 feet. The distance between the inner circle and the outer circle is 3 feet. By how many feet is the circumference of the outer circle greater than the circumference of the inner circle? Use $\frac{22}{7}$ for π. Round to the nearest hundredth of a foot.

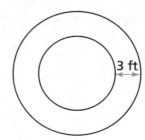

3 ft

14. Generalize What is the ratio of the radius to the circumference of any circle, using 3.14 for π?

15. What is the radius of a circle with a circumference of 26.69 centimeters?

16. Higher Order Thinking A unicycle wheel makes five rotations. The unicycle travels 37.94 feet. Find the diameter of the wheel in inches. Use 3.14 for π. Round to the nearest tenth of an inch.

5 rotations

✓ Assessment Practice

17. Camille drew the figure shown at the right.

Which of the following is the best estimate of the perimeter of the figure?

Ⓐ 36 feet

Ⓑ 81 feet

Ⓒ 45 feet

Ⓓ 50 feet

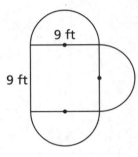

9 ft

9 ft

18. A cabin on a ferris wheel has traveled one fourth of the circumference of the wheel, a distance of 117.75 feet. What is the radius, in feet, of the ferris wheel? Use 3.14 for π.

19. The diagram shows a track composed of a rectangle with a semicircle on each end. The area of the rectangle is 7,200 square meters. What is the perimeter, in meters, of the track? Use 3.14 for π.

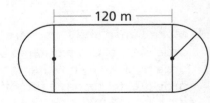

120 m

1. Vocabulary How are *adjacent angles* and *vertical angles* alike? How are they different? *Lesson 8-4*

2. On a map, 1 inch equals 150 miles. The border between two states is 5.5 inches long on the map. What is the actual length of the border? *Lesson 8-1*

In 3 and 4, use the figure to the right.

3. What is the measure of ∠BZD? *Lesson 8-4*

Ⓐ 58°

Ⓑ 148°

Ⓒ 32°

Ⓓ 90°

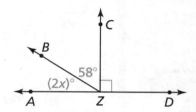

4. Find the value of *x*. *Lesson 8-4*

5. Pierce draws a circle with a radius of 3 centimeters. Gianna draws a circle with a radius that is twice as long as the radius of Pierce's circle. How will the circumference of Gianna's circle compare with the circumference of Pierce's circle? *Lesson 8-5*

The circumference of Gianna's circle is _____ times the circumference of Pierce's circle.

6. Draw a triangle with one side length of 5 units and another side length of 7 units. What additional piece of information will guarantee that only one triangle can be drawn? *Lessons 8-2 and 8-3*

How well did you do on the mid-topic checkpoint? Fill in the stars.

☆☆☆

MID-TOPIC PERFORMANCE TASK

Mrs. Thomas has two rolls of garden edging that are each 96 inches long. She wants to make two new flower beds in her back yard. Each flower bed will be bordered by one roll of the edging. One flower bed will be in the shape of a quadrilateral. The other will be in the shape of a triangle.

PART A

Mrs. Thomas decides to make a scale drawing of each flower bed using a scale of 1 centimeter = 5 inches. What will be the total length of each roll of edging in her scale drawings?

PART B

Mrs. Thomas wants the quadrilateral flower bed to have at least two 90° angles. Draw a possible plan for this flower bed using the scale from Part A. Make sure to use a complete roll of edging in the border. Label your drawing with all the angle measures and with the scaled length of each side. Name the shape of the flower bed you drew. What will be its actual dimensions?

PART C

Mrs. Thomas began to make a drawing for the triangular flower bed. In her drawing, the length of one side of the triangle is 4.8 centimeters, the length of a second side is 6.4 centimeters, and the included angle is a right angle. Use these measures and the scale from Part A to make a completed scale drawing. Label your drawing with all the angle measures to the nearest whole degree and with the scale length of each side. What will be the actual dimensions of this flower bed?

 ACTIVITY

Lesson 8-6
Solve Problems Involving Area of a Circle

Go Online

I can...
solve problems involving the area of a circle.

© **Common Core Content Standards**
7.G.B.4, 7.EE.B.3, 7.EE.B.4a

Mathematical Practices
MP.2, MP.6, MP.7

Explore It!

Latoya cut a circle into 8 equal sections and arranged the pieces to form a shape resembling a parallelogram.

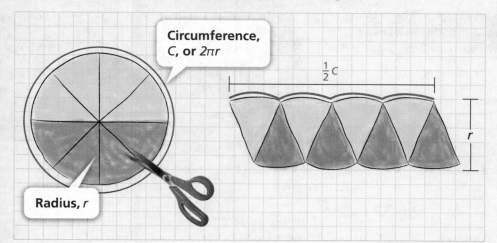

Circumference, C, or $2\pi r$

$\frac{1}{2}C$

r

Radius, r

A. How is the base length of the new shape related to the circumference of the circle?

B. How is the height of the new shape related to the radius of the circle?

C. Since this new shape was made from a circle, use the information from the diagram and the formula for the area of the parallelogram, $A = bh$, to discover the formula for the area of a circle.

Focus on math practices

Look for Relationships The formula $A = bh$ can be used to find a good estimate for the area of the cut-out diagram. What would happen to this estimate if the circle were cut into 100 sections? 1,000 sections?

465

VISUAL LEARNING   ASSES

EXAMPLE 1 **Solve Problems Involving the Area of a Circle**

Scan for Multimedia

The floor of a new butterfly conservatory will be a circle with an 18-foot radius. The material for the floor will cost $3.95 per square foot. About how much will the floor cost?

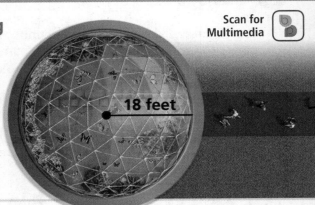

18 feet

STEP 1 Use the formula for the area of a circle to find the area of the floor.

> An approximation for π is 3.14.

$A = \pi r^2$

$A \approx (3.14)(18)^2$

$A = (3.14)(324)$

$A = 1,017.36$

18 ft
r

The area of the floor of the new conservatory is about 1,018 square feet.

> **Reasoning** Why round the area to the next whole foot?

STEP 2 Calculate the cost of the necessary floor material.

> Cost per square foot

$3.95 \times 1,018 = 4,021.10$

> Total square feet of floor   Total cost of the floor

The total cost of the floor will be about $4,021.

☑ Try It!

At a school play, there is a spotlight above the center of the floor that covers a lighted area with a radius of 7 feet. What is the area covered by the spotlight?

$A = \pi r^2$

$A \approx \left(\frac{22}{7}\right) \cdot \boxed{}^2$

> An approximation for π is $\frac{22}{7}$.

$A = \frac{22}{7} \cdot \boxed{}$

$A = \boxed{}$

The area covered by the spotlight is about $\boxed{}$ square feet.

$r = 7$ feet

Convince Me! If the diameter of a circle is given, how would you find the area?

EXAMPLE 2 Use Area to Find the Radius and Diameter

The athletic department wants to paint the school's mascot logo on the gym locker room wall. They start by painting a solid blue circle on the wall. What is the maximum diameter of the logo if only one quart of blue paint is used?

$A = \pi r^2$

> The radius is the unknown in the equation.

$78.5 \approx (3.14) \cdot r^2$

> An approximation for π is 3.14.

$\dfrac{78.5}{3.14} = \dfrac{(3.14) \cdot r^2}{3.14}$

$25 = r^2$

> What number times itself is equal to 25?

$5 = r$

1 quart of blue paint covers 78.5 ft².

The radius is 5 feet, so the diameter of the school's mascot logo can be up to 10 feet.

EXAMPLE 3 Use Circumference to Find the Area of a Circle

Ellie needs new grass in the circular pen for her chickens. What is the area of the pen?

> **Look for Relationships** How can you use the circumference to find the information needed to calculate the area?

176 feet of fencing

STEP 1 Find the radius, r, of the circular pen.

$C = 2\pi r$

$176 \approx 2 \cdot \left(\dfrac{22}{7}\right) \cdot r$

> An approximation for π is $\dfrac{22}{7}$.

$176 = \dfrac{44}{7} \cdot r$

$\dfrac{7}{44} \cdot 176 = \dfrac{7}{44} \cdot \left(\dfrac{44}{7}\right) \cdot r$

$28 = r$

The radius of the circular pen is about 28 feet.

STEP 2 Use the radius to find the area of the circular pen.

$A = \pi r^2$

$A \approx \dfrac{22}{7}(28)^2$

$A = 2{,}464$

The area of the circular pen is about 2,464 square feet.

☑ Try It!

a. How far away can a person live from a radio station and hear its broadcast if the signal covers a circular area of 40,000 square miles? Write your answer as a whole number.

b. What circular area is covered by the signal if the circumference is 754 miles?

KEY CONC

You can find the area, **A**, of a circle using the formula $A = \pi r^2$, where **r** is the radius.

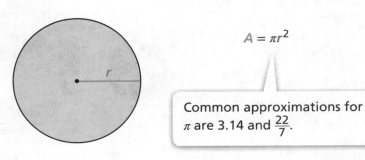

$$A = \pi r^2$$

Common approximations for π are 3.14 and $\frac{22}{7}$.

Do You Understand?

1. **? Essential Question** How can the area formula for a circle be used to solve problems?

2. **Be Precise** Is an area calculation exact when you use 3.14 or $\frac{22}{7}$ as a value for π? Explain.

3. **Use Structure** If you know the diameter of a circle, how can you find the area?

Do You Know How?

For 4–7, use 3.14 for π.

4. What is the area of a circle with a radius of 8 inches?

5. What is the radius of a circle with an area of 28.26 square feet?

6. What is the area of a circle with a circumference of 25.12 meters?

7. The diameter of a pizza is 12 inches. What is its area?

|← —————— 12 in. —————— →|

Practice & Problem Solving

8. Find the area of the circle. Use 3.14 for π.

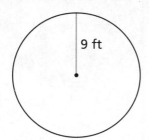

9 ft

9. Find the area of the circle. Use 3.14 for π.

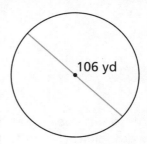

106 yd

10. Jaylon created this stained-glass window. The upper two corners are quarter circles, each with a radius of 4 inches. Find the area of the window. Use 3.14 for π.

4 in.   4 in.

26 in.

— 12 in. —

11. The circumference of a circle is 50.24 meters. What is the area of the circle? Use 3.14 for π.

12. Higher Order Thinking A circular flower bed is 20 meters in diameter and has a circular sidewalk around it that is 3 meters wide. Find the area of the sidewalk in square meters. Use 3.14 for π. Round to the nearest whole number.

13. A circular plate has a circumference of 16.3 inches. What is the area of this plate? Use 3.14 for π. Round to the nearest whole number.

14. A water sprinkler sends water out in a circular pattern. How many feet away from the sprinkler can it spread water if the area formed by the watering pattern is 379.94 square feet?

15. The circumference of a circular rug is 24.8 meters. What is the area of the rug? Use 3.1 for π. Round your answer to the nearest tenth.

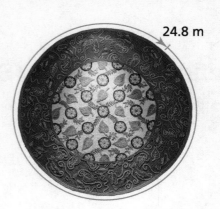
24.8 m

16. Frank wants to find the area enclosed by the figure at the right. The figure has semicircles on each side of a 40-meter-by-40-meter square. Find the area enclosed by the figure. Use 3.14 for π.

40 m
40 m

✅ Assessment Practice

17. Julia's bedroom is 10 feet by 10 feet. She wants to place a circular rug in the corner of her room.

PART A

She places a rug with a radius of 2 feet in her room. How much of her bedroom floor, in square feet, is not covered by the rug? Use 3.14 for π. Round to the nearest tenth.

PART B

Julia decides she wants a rug that covers about 50% of her floor. Which rug should she buy?

Ⓐ A rug with a radius of 5 feet

Ⓑ A rug with a diameter of 5 feet

Ⓒ A rug with a radius of 4 feet

Ⓓ A rug with a diameter of 4 feet

18. The circumference of a hubcap of a tire is 81.58 centimeters. Find the area, in square centimeters, of this hubcap. Use 3.14 as an approximation for π. Round your answer to the nearest whole centimeter.

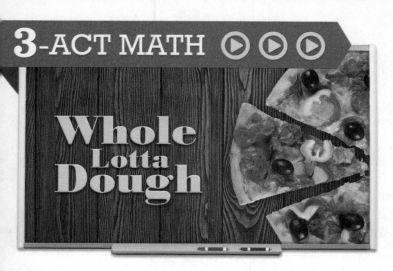

3-ACT MATH

3-Act Mathematical Modeling:
Whole Lotta Dough

Go Online

Common Core Content Standards
7.G.B.4

Mathematical Practices
MP.4, MP.1, MP.2, MP.3, MP.3, MP.5, MP.7, MP.8

ACT 1

1. After watching the video, what is the first question that comes to mind?

2. Write the Main Question you will answer.

3. Construct Arguments Predict an answer to this Main Question. Explain your prediction.

4. On the number line below, write a number that is too small to be the answer. Write a number that is too large.

Too small   Too large

←——|————————————————————|——→

5. Plot your prediction on the same number line.

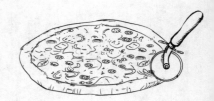

6. What information in this situation would be helpful to know?
How would you use that information?

7. Use Appropriate Tools What tools can you use to solve the problem?
Explain how you would use them strategically.

8. Model with Math Represent the situation using mathematics.
Use your representation to answer the Main Question.

9. What is your answer to the Main Question? Is it higher or lower than
your prediction? Explain why.

10. Write the answer you saw in the video.

11. Reasoning Does your answer match the answer in the video? If not, what are some reasons that would explain the difference?

12. Make Sense and Persevere Would you change your model now that you know the answer? Explain.

13. Model with Math Explain how you used a mathematical model to represent the situation. How did the model help you answer the Main Question?

14. Reasoning Explain why your answer to the Main Question does *not* involve the symbol π.

15. Use Structure If the regular pizza costs $8.99, how much do you think the big pizza costs?

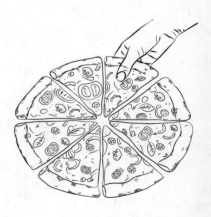

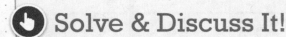 Solve & Discuss It!  ACTIVITY

How could Mrs. Mendoza divide the ream of paper equally between two art classes? She has a paper cutter to slice the paper, if needed. What will the dimensions for each sheet of paper be once she has divided the ream? How many sheets will each class receive?

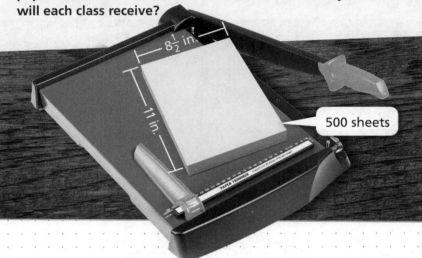

$8\frac{1}{2}$ in.

11 in.

500 sheets

I can...
determine what the cross section looks like when a 3D figure is sliced.

© **Common Core Content Standards**
7.G.A.3

Mathematical Practices
MP.1, MP.6, MP.7, MP.8

Focus on math practices

Use Structure How would the number of sheets of paper each class receives change if Mrs. Mendoza started with 300 sheets?

Essential Question How do the faces of a three-dimensional figure determine the two-dimensional shapes created by slicing the figure?

 VISUAL LEARNING   ASSESS

EXAMPLE 1   👁 **Describe Cross Sections of Right Rectangular Prisms**

Scan for Multimedia

Rachel and Francesca went to a restaurant that serves rectangular bread rolls. Each sliced her roll in a different way. What do the *cross sections* look like?

Use Structure What faces are parallel to the slice?

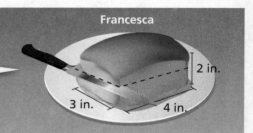

Rachel

A **cross section** is the two-dimensional shape that is exposed when a slice is made through a three-dimensional object.

Francesca

2 in.
3 in.   4 in.
2 in.
3 in.   4 in.

Rachel made a vertical slice that was parallel to the front and back faces of the roll.

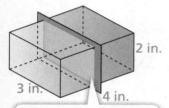

2 in.
3 in.
4 in.

3 in.
2 in.

The cross section is parallel to the front and back faces, so it is the same shape as those faces.

The cross section is a rectangle that is 3 inches by 2 inches.

Francesca made a horizontal slice that was perpendicular to the front and back faces of the roll.

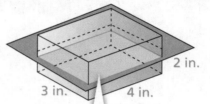

2 in.
3 in.   4 in.

4 in.
3 in.

The cross section is parallel to the top and bottom faces, so it is the same shape as those faces.

The cross section is a rectangle that is 4 inches by 3 inches.

✅ **Try It!**

Zachary made a vertical slice that was parallel to the left and right faces of a bread roll. What shape is the cross section, and what are its dimensions?

The shape of the cross section is a [   ]

that is [   ] inches by [   ] inches.

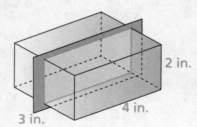

2 in.
4 in.
3 in.

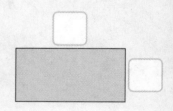

Convince Me! What are the shapes of horizontal and vertical cross sections of a rectangular prism, and how can you determine the dimensions of the cross sections?

EXAMPLE 2

Describe Cross Sections of Right Rectangular Pyramids

ACTIVITY   ASSESS

Kenya made a sand castle in the shape of a right rectangular pyramid with a height of 0.9 feet.

a. If Kenya sliced the castle horizontally, parallel to the base, what would the cross section look like?

> Horizontal cross sections are rectangles that are smaller than the base of the pyramid.

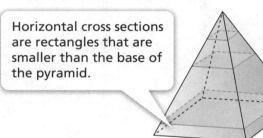

0.6 ft
0.75 ft

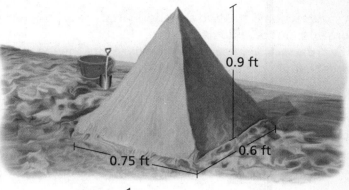

0.9 ft
0.6 ft
0.75 ft

b. If Kenya sliced the castle vertically, through the top vertex, perpendicular to the base, and intersecting the 0.75-foot edges, what would the cross section look like?

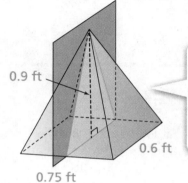

0.9 ft
0.6 ft
0.75 ft

> The cross section would be an isosceles triangle with a height of 0.9 feet and a base length of 0.6 foot.

EXAMPLE 3   Solve Problems Involving Cross Sections

A truck needs a metal divider that separates the refrigerated part of the truck from the dry goods. What should the divider look like, and how many square feet will the metal divider be?

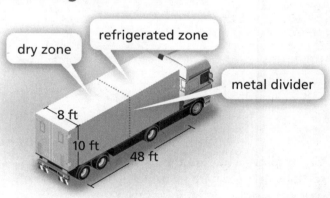

dry zone
refrigerated zone
metal divider
8 ft
10 ft
48 ft

STEP 1 Draw a picture of the cross section.

10 ft
8 ft

STEP 2 Find the area of the metal divider.

$A = \ell \times w$

$= 10(8) = 80 \text{ ft}^2$

The metal divider will be 80 square feet.

 **Try It!**

Draw the cross section that is created when a vertical plane intersects the top vertex and the shorter edge of the base of the pyramid shown. What is the area of the cross section?

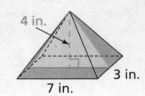

4 in.
3 in.
7 in.

KEY CONCEPT

A cross section is the two-dimensional shape exposed when a three-dimensional figure is sliced. The shape and dimensions of a cross section in a rectangular prism are the same as the faces that are parallel to the slice.

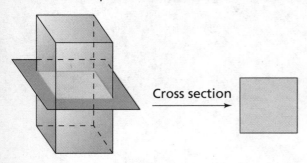

Cross section →

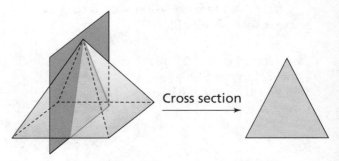

Cross section →

Do You Understand?

1. **❓ Essential Question** How do the faces of a three-dimensional figure determine the two-dimensional shapes created by slicing the figure?

2. **Generalize** What are the shapes of the cross sections that are parallel or perpendicular to the bases of a right rectangular prism?

3. **Generalize** What are the shapes of the horizontal cross sections of a right rectangular pyramid? What are the shapes of vertical cross sections through the vertex opposite the base?

Do You Know How?

4. The divider in a desk drawer is a cross section that is parallel to the front of the drawer. What is its shape, and what are its dimensions?

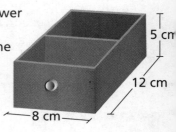

5. Use the diagram to answer the questions.

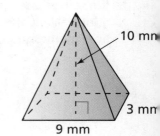

a. Draw the cross section that is formed when the pyramid is sliced vertically through its vertex and its right face, perpendicular to its base.

b. What is the area of this cross section?

Practice & Problem Solving

6. What are the dimensions of the vertical cross section shown on this right rectangular prism?

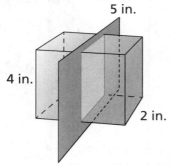

5 in.

4 in.

2 in.

7. Be Precise Describe the cross section that is formed by a vertical plane, perpendicular to the base of the pyramid, that intersects the 9-in. edge and the top vertex of the pyramid shown.

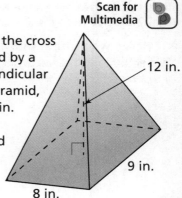

12 in.

9 in.

8 in.

8. Mason is slicing butter for the meal he is preparing. Describe the vertical cross section when the knife slices through the butter, parallel to its sides.

5 in. 3 in.

2.5 in.

9. a. Look for Relationships What are the dimensions of the vertical cross section?

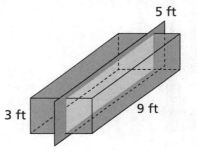

5 ft

3 ft   9 ft

b. What would be the dimensions of a horizontal cross section?

10. Use the figure to the right.

a. Describe the cross section shown.

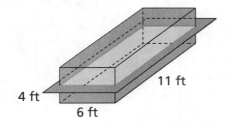

11 ft

4 ft

6 ft

b. Is it possible to have a horizontal cross section with different dimensions if you had the plane intersect the prism at another height? Explain.

11. Make Sense and Persevere The base of a right rectangular pyramid has a length of 12 centimeters, a width of 6 centimeters, and a height of 14 centimeters. Describe the cross section formed by a horizontal plane that intersects the faces of the pyramid above the base.

12. **Higher Order Thinking** Luis makes blocks from a painted piece of wood with dimensions of 27 inches × 24 inches × 1.5 inches. To make 72 blocks, the wood is cut into 3-inch squares.

Draw two pictures showing the horizontal cross section and the vertical cross section of each block.

13. **Make Sense and Persevere** The area of the cross section shown is 52 square yards. What is the length of the unknown side of the base of the pyramid?

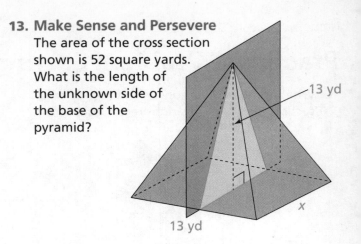

14. A waiter slices a cake shaped like a square pyramid vertically through the top point.

   a. **Make Sense and Persevere** Draw the cross section that is made by slicing the cake in this way.

   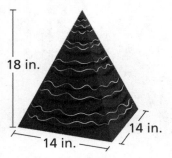

   18 in.
   14 in.
   14 in.

   b. What is the area of this cross section?

15. Miranda says that the triangle below represents the cross section of the rectangular pyramid shown.

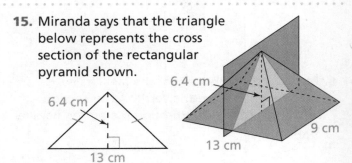

6.4 cm

13 cm

What mistake might Miranda have made?

16. Estimate, to the nearest whole number, the number of vertical cross sections needed to equal the area of the base of the figure to the right. Explain how you made your estimate, and decide whether your estimate is higher or lower than the actual number.

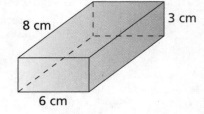

8 cm   3 cm

6 cm

👆 Solve & Discuss It!

📶 👆 ACTIVITY

Alaya will paint the outside of a box with three different colors. Decide how she could paint the box. What is the total area that each color will cover?

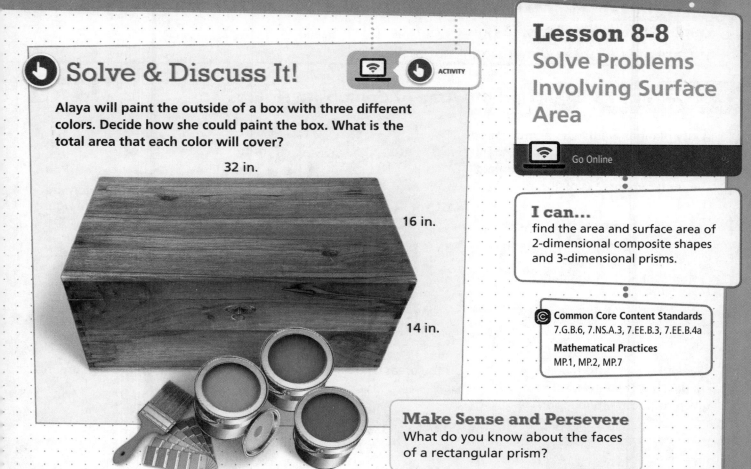

32 in.

16 in.

14 in.

I can...
find the area and surface area of 2-dimensional composite shapes and 3-dimensional prisms.

© **Common Core Content Standards**
7.G.B.6, 7.NS.A.3, 7.EE.B.3, 7.EE.B.4a
Mathematical Practices
MP.1, MP.2, MP.7

Make Sense and Persevere
What do you know about the faces of a rectangular prism?

Focus on math practices

Reasoning Trista paints each pair of opposite sides of the box with the same color. How many different areas does she need to find to determine the total area covered by each color? Explain.

? **Essential Question** How is finding the area of composite two-dimensional figures similar to finding the surface area of three-dimensional figures?

  VISUAL LEARNING ASSE

EXAMPLE 1 Find the Area of Composite Figures

Scan for Multimedia

A city planner wants all neighborhood parks to have more green space than non-green space. Does this park meet the requirements? Explain.

Look for Relationships
How are the areas of the green and non-green spaces related to the total area of the park?

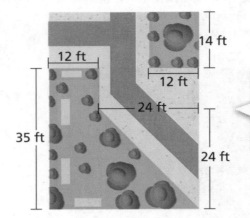

The shape of the non-green space is a *composite figure*. A **composite figure** is the combination of two or more geometric shapes.

Divide the park into familiar shapes. Use the information given to find the dimensions.

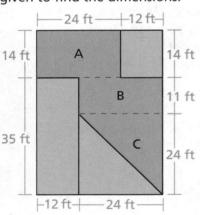

Add the areas of the non-green shapes.

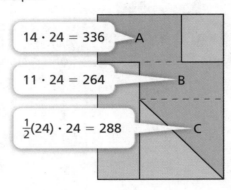

$14 \cdot 24 = 336$ A

$11 \cdot 24 = 264$ B

$\frac{1}{2}(24) \cdot 24 = 288$ C

$336 + 264 + 288 = 888$ ft^2
The total non-green area is 888 ft^2.

Find the area of the green space.

Area of entire park

$(49 \bullet 36) - 888$ Non-green area

$= 1,764 - 888$

$= 876$ ft^2

The park does not meet the requirements since the non-green area, 888 ft^2, is greater than the green area, 876 ft^2.

☑ Try It!

This diagram shows the area of a room to be carpeted. What will be the area of the new carpet?

A = [ ] = [ ] ft^2 B = [ ] = [ ] ft^2

Total area = [ ] + [ ]

The area of the new carpet is [ ] square feet.

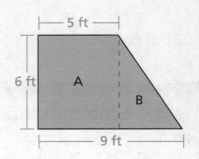

Convince Me! How does knowing the area of familiar shapes help find the total area of a composite shape?

EXAMPLE **2** **Solve Surface Area Problems** ACTIVITY ASSESS

Gavin constructed a model building and wants to cover the outside with paper. How much paper will he need to cover the entire model?

STEP 1 Find the area of each face of the model.

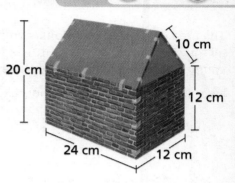

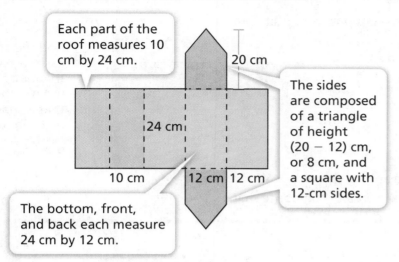

Each part of the roof measures 10 cm by 24 cm.

The sides are composed of a triangle of height (20 − 12) cm, or 8 cm, and a square with 12-cm sides.

The bottom, front, and back each measure 24 cm by 12 cm.

STEP 2 Find the total surface area of the model.

$(240 \cdot 2) + (288 \cdot 3) + (144 \cdot 2) + (48 \cdot 2) = 1{,}728$ cm²

EXAMPLE **3** **Solve Mathematical Problems Involving Surface Area**

What is the surface area of the composite figure shown?

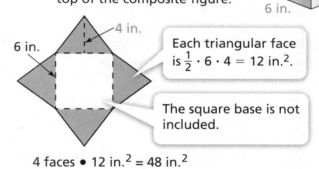

STEP 1 Find the surface area of the bottom of the composite figure.

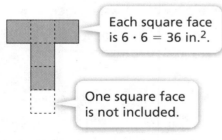

Each square face is 6 · 6 = 36 in.².

One square face is not included.

5 faces • 36 in.² = 180 in.²

STEP 2 Find the surface area of the top of the composite figure.

6 in.   4 in.

Each triangular face is $\frac{1}{2} \cdot 6 \cdot 4 = 12$ in.².

The square base is not included.

4 faces • 12 in.² = 48 in.²

The total surface area of the composite figure is 180 + 48 = 228 in.².

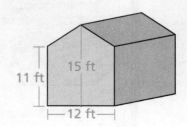

✓ **Try It!**

Hiromi is painting the front and back of a barn. Each can of paint covers 32 square feet. How many cans of paint does Hiromi need to cover the entire front and back of the barn?

The area of a two-dimensional composite figure is the sum of the areas of all the shapes that compose it. The surface area of a three-dimensional composite figure is the sum of the areas of all its faces.

Two-dimensional composite figure

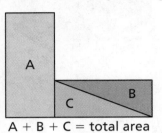

A + B + C = total area

Three-dimensional composite figure

Add the areas of each face of the rectangular prism, but not the face that is shared with Figure B.

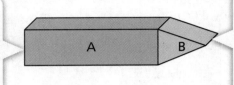

Add the areas of each face of the triangular prism but not the face that is shared with Figure A.

Surface area of shape A **+** Surface area of shape B
= Surface area of composite shape

Do You Understand?

1. **? Essential Question** How is finding the area of composite two-dimensional figures similar to finding the surface area of three-dimensional figures?

2. **Make Sense and Persevere** Laine wants to determine the amount of fabric needed to cover a triangular prism-shaped box. She begins by measuring the dimensions of the box. Explain her next steps.

3. **Use Structure** Explain how you would find the surface area of the figure below.

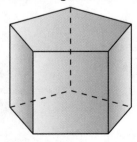

Do You Know How?

4. Paula is painting a henhouse. If a can of paint will cover 24 square feet, how many cans of paint does she need to buy? Explain the steps she might take to solve this problem.

5. Find the area of the composite figure. The two triangles have the same dimensions.

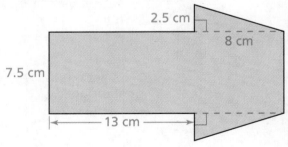

6. A stage block is being covered in carpet. The dimensions of the block are 2 feet by 3 feet by 6 feet. Every surface will need covering except for the surface touching the floor, which is 3 feet by 6 feet. How would you calculate the surface area that needs covering?

Practice & Problem Solving

Leveled Practice In 7, fill in the boxes to solve.

7. Jacob is putting tiles on the sections of his yard labeled A, B, and C. What is the area of the parts that need tiles?

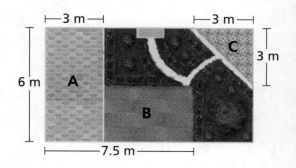

Part A = ☐ · ☐ = ☐ m²

Part B = ☐ · ☐ = ☐ m²

Part C = ½ · ☐ · ☐ = ☐ m²

Total area = ☐ + ☐ + ☐ = ☐ m²

---

8. What is the total area of the figure?

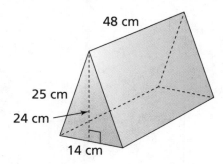

9. Find the surface area of the prism.

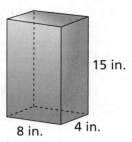

---

10. Find the surface area of the triangular prism. The base of the prism is an isosceles triangle.

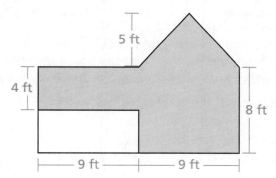

11. A block of wood has the shape of a triangular prism. The bases are right triangles. Find its surface area.

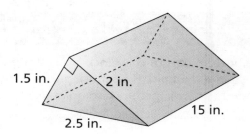

12. A box has the shape of a rectangular prism. How much wrapping paper do you need to cover the box?

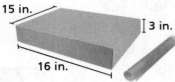

15 in.
3 in.
16 in.

13. Higher Order Thinking Find the surface area of the rectangular hexagonal prism. Show your work.

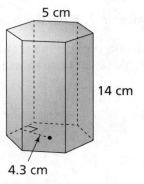

5 cm
14 cm
4.3 cm

14. A box has the shape of a rectangular prism with a height of 29 centimeters. If the height is increased by 0.7 centimeter, by how much does the surface area of the box increase?

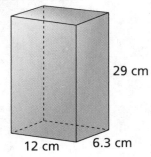

29 cm
12 cm
6.3 cm

15. The base of a prism is an equilateral triangle with an area of 73.2 square centimeters. The area of each lateral face is 104 square centimeters. Riley incorrectly claims that the surface area is 250.4 square centimeters.

a. What is the correct surface area?

b. What could have been Riley's error?

16. The bottom part of this block is a rectangular prism. The top part is a square pyramid. How much paper, in square centimeters, is needed to cover the block completely?

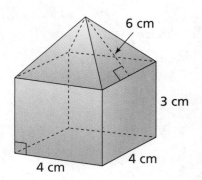

6 cm
3 cm
4 cm
4 cm

Solve & Discuss It!

ACTIVITY

Volunteers at a food pantry pack boxes of soup into crates. How many boxes of soup will fill each crate? Show your work.

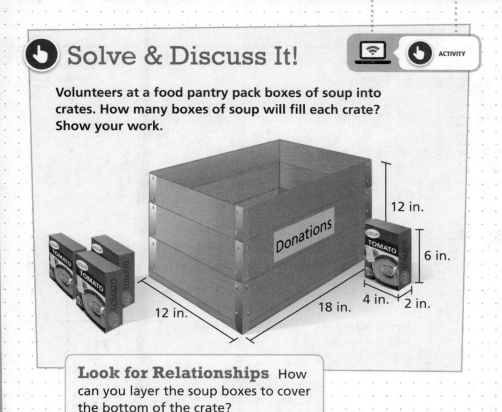

I can...
use the area of the base of a three-dimensional figure to find its volume.

© **Common Core Content Standards**
7.G.B.6, 7.NS.A.3, 7.EE.B.3, 7.EE.B.4a

Mathematical Practices
MP.1, MP.2, MP.4, MP.7

Look for Relationships How can you layer the soup boxes to cover the bottom of the crate?

Focus on math practices

Reasoning A supplier donated crates to the food pantry that are 15 inches long, instead of 18 inches long. All other dimensions are the same. What is the greatest number of boxes of soup that will fit in the donated crates? How will the volume of the soup vary from the total volume of the crate?

? **Essential Question** How does the formula for volume of a prism help you understand what volume of a prism means?

EXAMPLE 1 Find Volumes of Prisms

Scan for Multimedia

Cora has an aquarium with exotic fish. The tank is the size and shape of a trapezoidal prism. The distance from the front glass to the back is 2 feet. What is the volume of the aquarium tank?

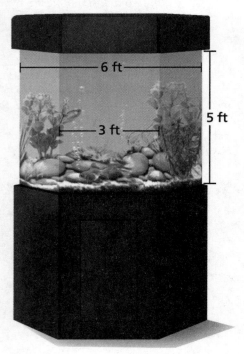

STEP 1 Identify the shape of the base.

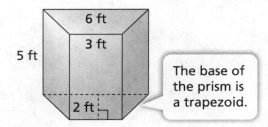

The base of the prism is a trapezoid.

STEP 2 Find the area of the base, B, of the prism.

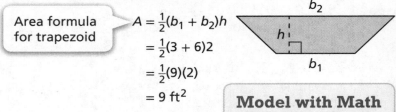

Area formula for trapezoid

$A = \frac{1}{2}(b_1 + b_2)h$

$= \frac{1}{2}(3 + 6)2$

$= \frac{1}{2}(9)(2)$

$= 9 \text{ ft}^2$

The area of the base is 9 ft^2.

Model with Math
Why does this formula work?

STEP 3 Find the volume of the prism.

Volume = Area of base of prism × height of the prism

$V = Bh$

$= 9(5)$

$= 45 \text{ ft}^3$ ← Volume is measured in cubic units.

The volume of the aquarium tank is 45 ft^3.

☑ Try It!

What is the volume of the triangular prism?

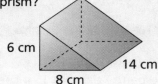

6 cm
14 cm
8 cm

The volume of the prism is ☐ cubic centimeters.

$V = B \cdot h$

$V = \left(\frac{1}{2} \cdot \boxed{} \cdot \boxed{}\right) \cdot h$

$V = \left(\boxed{}\right) \cdot \boxed{}$

$V = \boxed{}$

Convince Me! What is the shape of the base of the figure? What are its dimensions? Explain.

EXAMPLE **2** ▶ Solve Problems Involving Volume

 ACTIVITY ASSESS

Students are selling a souvenir basketball. Will the basketball fit inside the gift box that has a regular hexagonal base so that the lid fits on top?

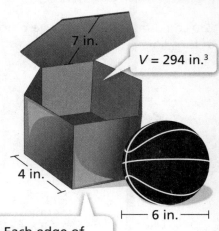

7 in.

V = 294 in.³

STEP 1 Find the area of the hexagonal base.

Area of base = 6 • (area of one triangle in base)

$A = 6 \cdot \left(\frac{1}{2}b \cdot h\right)$

$\approx 6 \cdot \frac{1}{2}(4) \cdot (3.5)$

$= 6 \cdot \frac{1}{2}(14)$

$= 42$

4

4   4

4   4

3.5   4

> You can decompose a regular hexagon into 6 equal triangles.

> The height of each triangle in the base is about 3.5 inches.

4 in.

⊢— 6 in. —⊣

> Each edge of the hexagon base is 4 inches.

The area of the base is about 42 square inches.

STEP 2 Use the volume formula to find the height.

$V = Bh$

$294 = (42)h$

$\frac{294}{42} = \frac{42h}{42}$

$7 = h$

The width of the box is given at 7 inches. The height of the box is 7 inches. Both the height and width are greater than the diameter of the basketball, so the basketball will fit with the lid on top of the box.

Look for Relationships
If you find the base area and the volume is given, can you find the height of the box?

EXAMPLE **3** ▶ Find Volumes of Composite Figures

Sequan has a shed for his athletic equipment. What is the total volume of the shed?

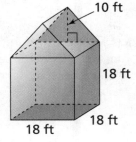

10 ft

18 ft

18 ft

18 ft

18 ft

STEP 1 Find the volume of the **bottom** section.

$V = Bh$

$= (18)(18) \cdot 18$

$= 324(18)$

$= 5,832$

18 ft

18 ft

18 ft

The volume of the bottom section is 5,832 cubic feet.

STEP 2 Find the volume of the **top** section.

$V = Bh$

$= \frac{1}{2}(18)(10) \cdot 18$

$= 90(18)$

$= 1,620$

10 ft

18 ft

The volume of the top section is 1,620 cubic feet.

STEP 3 Add the volumes together.

$5,832 + 1,620 = 7,452$

The total volume of the shed is 7,452 cubic feet.

☑ **Try It!**

Amber built a custom terrarium for her plants. What is the volume of the terrarium?

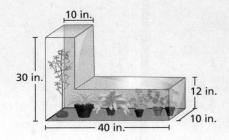

10 in.

30 in.

40 in.

12 in.

10 in.

You can use formulas to solve problems involving the volume of three-dimensional figures.

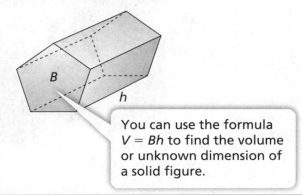

You can use the formula $V = Bh$ to find the volume or unknown dimension of a solid figure.

Find the volume of a composite figure by finding the sum of the volumes of each solid figure.

Do You Understand?

1. 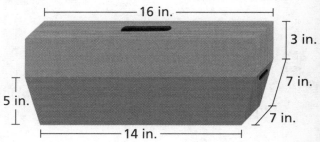 **Essential Question** How does the formula for volume of a prism help you understand what volume of a prism means?

2. Look for Relationships If you know the volume of a three-dimensional figure, how can you find a missing dimension of the figure?

3. Make Sense and Persevere How do you find the volume of a three-dimensional figure that can be decomposed into prisms?

Do You Know How?

4. An aquarium has a regular hexagonal base with side lengths of 15 centimeters. When the hexagon is divided into six equal triangles, the height of each triangle is about 13 centimeters. If the aquarium is 50 centimeters tall, what is its volume?

5. A cheese box is shaped like a right triangular prism. The box is 6 inches long, 4 inches tall, and has a volume of 24 cubic inches. Can a cube of cheese that is 2.5 inches on each side fit inside the box? Explain.

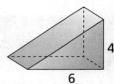

6. Ray made a toolbox with the dimensions shown to store garden tools. What is the volume of the toolbox?

16 in.

3 in.

7 in.

7 in.

5 in.

14 in.

Practice & Problem Solving ✏️ ⏻

Leveled Practice In 7–8, find the volume of each prism.

7.

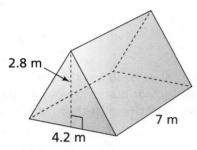

2.8 m

7 m

4.2 m

$V = Bh$

$= (0.5 \cdot \boxed{} \cdot \boxed{}) \cdot 7$

$= \boxed{}$ m³

8.

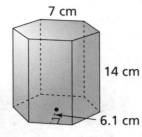

7 cm

14 cm

6.1 cm

$V = Bh$

$= (0.5 \cdot \boxed{} \cdot 7 \cdot 6) \cdot \boxed{}$

$= 128.1 \cdot \boxed{}$

$= \boxed{}$ cm³

---

9. A tunnel for an amusement park ride has the shape of a regular hexagonal prism with dimensions shown. The prism has a volume of 3,572.1 cubic meters. Can two 8-meter cars connected by a 3-meter connector pass through the tunnel at the same time? Explain.

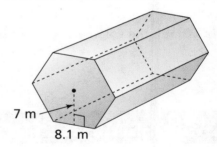

7 m

8.1 m

---

10. A volume of 185.5 cubic feet of concrete was used to make the section of a skateboard ramp shown. How long is the ramp?

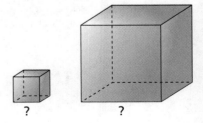

4 ft

7 ft

?

11. Make Sense and Persevere A small cube has a volume of 64 cubic feet. A larger cube has sides that are three times as long as the small cube. How long are the sides of each cube?

?   ?

12. What is the volume of the regular hexagonal prism, to the nearest cubic centimeter?

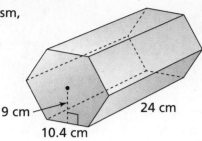

9 cm

10.4 cm

24 cm

13. A mailbox has the dimensions shown. What is the volume of the mailbox?

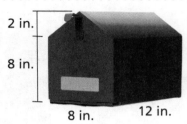

2 in.

8 in.

8 in.

12 in.

14. Use Structure A glass bead has the shape of a prism with a rectangular prism removed. What is the volume of the glass that forms the bead?

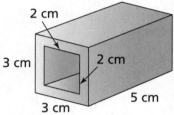

2 cm

3 cm

2 cm

3 cm

5 cm

15. Higher Order Thinking A cake has two layers. Each layer is a regular hexagonal prism. A slice removes one face of each prism, as shown.

a. What is the volume of the slice?

b. What is the volume of the remaining cake?

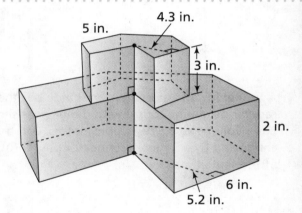

5 in.

4.3 in.

3 in.

2 in.

6 in.

5.2 in.

Assessment Practice

16. The area of the top of the box shown is 60 square centimeters. What is the volume, in cubic centimeters, of the box?

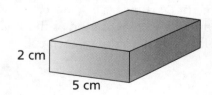

2 cm

5 cm

17. Which of the following freezers is the best buy in terms of dollars per cubic foot?

Ⓐ Freezer A has an interior of 1 foot by 1 foot by 5 feet and sells for $499.99.

Ⓑ Freezer B has two sections of 3 cubic feet each and sells for $629.99.

Ⓒ Freezer C has interior dimensions of 1.5 feet by 1.5 feet by 4 feet and sells for $849.99.

Ⓓ Freezer D has 3 sections of 1.5 cubic feet each and sells for $444.99.

? Topic Essential Question

How can geometry be used to solve problems?

Vocabulary Review

Complete each definition, and then provide an example of each vocabulary word.

Vocabulary
adjacent angles	circumference	complementary angles
composite figure	cross section	scale drawing
supplementary angles	vertical angles	

Definition	Example
1. The distance around a circle is the _____.	
2. _____ have a sum of 180 degrees.	
3. A(n) _____ is the combination of two or more geometric shapes.	
4. A(n) _____ is the two-dimensional shape that is exposed when a slice is made through a three-dimensional object.	

Use Vocabulary in Writing

Shawna drew this picture of three intersecting lines. Use vocabulary terms to explain how she could determine the value of x.

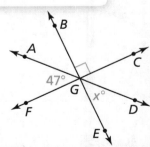

Concepts and Skills Review

Solve Problems Involving Scale Drawings

Quick Review

In a **scale drawing**, the scale is a ratio that relates each drawing length to the actual length it represents. To find unknown lengths, you can use the scale to write a proportion.

Example

A blueprint of a room is drawn to a scale of 2 inches = 7 feet. The actual length of one wall is 56 feet. What is the length of this wall on the blueprint?

Use the scale to write a proportion.

$$\frac{2 \text{ in.}}{7 \text{ ft}} = \frac{x \text{ in.}}{56 \text{ ft}}$$

56 feet = 7 feet × 8, so multiply 2 inches by 8

$x = 2$ inches × 8 = 16 inches

The length in the blueprint is 16 inches.

Practice

Use the scale drawing to answer the questions.

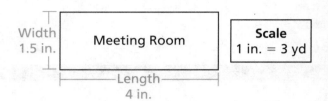

1. What is the actual area of the meeting room in square yards?

2. John decides to make a new scale drawing of the meeting room. He wants the length of the room in the new drawing to be 8 inches. What is the new scale for the drawing?

Draw Geometric Figures

Quick Review

You can classify a quadrilateral as a trapezoid, a rectangle, a square, or a parallelogram based on its side lengths, side relationships, and angle measures.

Example

Draw a quadrilateral with exactly two perpendicular sides and one angle measuring 120°. What is the name of the figure you drew?

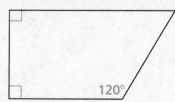

The figure has exactly one pair of parallel sides, so it is a trapezoid.

Practice

1. Draw a quadrilateral with two pairs of parallel sides, with one side measuring 5 centimeters, one side measuring 3 centimeters, and one angle measuring 45°. What is the name of the figure you drew?

2. What quadrilaterals can you draw that have two angles measuring 115° and two angles measuring 65°?

Draw Triangles with Given Conditions

Quick Review

When you are given certain conditions for a triangle, it may be possible to draw one triangle, more than one triangle, or no triangle.

Example

How many triangles can be drawn with side lengths of 3 inches, 5 inches, and 6 inches?

No matter how you position the sides, the triangle has the same shape and size. There is only one way to draw a triangle with these side lengths.

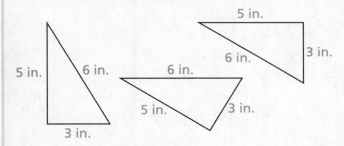

Practice

1. Can more than one triangle be drawn with side lengths of 4 centimeters and 2 centimeters and an included angle of 50°? Explain.

2. When given angle measures of 25°, 65°, and 90°, is it impossible to draw a triangle, possible to draw only one triangle, or possible to draw more than one triangle? Explain.

ESSON 8-4 Solve Problems Using Angle Relationships

Quick Review

Angles that have a common vertex and a common side but no common interior points are **adjacent angles**. **Supplementary angles** are angles with a sum of 180°. **Complementary angles** are angles with a sum of 90°. When two lines intersect, the angles that have no side in common are called **vertical angles**. Vertical angles are equal.

Example

List all pairs of vertical angles in this figure.

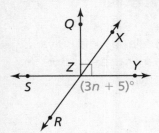

There are two pairs of vertical angles:

• ∠SZR and ∠XZY

• ∠SZX and ∠RZY

Practice

Use the figure from the example.

1. Name a pair of complementary angles.

2. The measure of ∠XZY is 55°. Which other angle has a measure of 55°? Explain.

3. Use the information from Problem 2. Find the value of n.

Solve Problems Involving Circumference of a Circle

Quick Review

The distance around a circle is called its circumference. The number π (pi) is the ratio of the circumference of any circle to its diameter. So when you know the diameter, *d*, of a circle, or its radius, *r*, you can determine its circumference, *C*, with the formula $C = \pi d$ or $C = 2\pi r$.

Example

What is the circumference of a circle with a radius of 6 meters? Use 3.14 for π.

$C = 2\pi r$

$C = 2\pi(6)$

$C \approx 2(3.14)(6)$

$C = 37.68$

The circumference is about 37.68 meters.

Practice

1. The length of the minute hand of a clock is 14 inches. What is the length of the path traced by the outer tip of the minute hand in one hour? Use $\frac{22}{7}$ for π.

2. The circumference of a bicycle tire is 126.5 centimeters. What is the diameter of the tire? Use 3.14 for π. Round to the nearest tenth as needed.

Solve Problems Involving Area of a Circle

Quick Review

The area, *A*, of a circle can be found using the formula $A = \pi r^2$, where *r* is the radius. You can use 3.14 or $\frac{22}{7}$ as an approximation for π.

Example

The diameter of the logo at the center of a basketball court is 10 feet. What is the area of the logo? Use 3.14 for π.

The radius of a circle is half the diameter. So the radius of the logo is half of 10 feet, or 5 feet. Substitute the radius into the circle area formula.

$A = \pi r^2$

$A = \pi(5)^2$

$A \approx 3.14(25)$

$A = 78.5$

The area of the logo is about 78.5 square feet.

Practice

1. Jessie wants to paint the top of the table shown. What is the approximate area that she will paint? Use 3.14 for π. Round to the nearest whole number of inches.

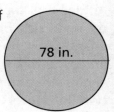

78 in.

2. What is the diameter of a circle with an area of 113.04 square centimeters. Use 3.14 for π.

3. The distance around a circular park is 88 yards. What is the area of the park? Use $\frac{22}{7}$ for π.

Quick Review

A **cross section** is the two-dimensional shape exposed when a three-dimensional figure is sliced. Recognizing the shape of a cross section can help in solving some problems.

Example

Muffins are packed in two layers in a box with a piece of cardboard placed between. What shape is the cardboard and what are its dimensions?

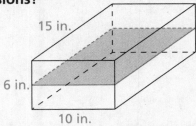

The cardboard lies on a cross section shaped like a rectangle that is 15 inches long and 10 inches wide.

Practice

1. The figure shows a vertical cross section of a right rectangular pyramid. What shape is the cross section and what is its area?

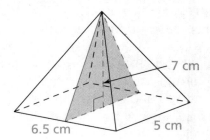

2. Zach wants to slice the pyramid along a horizontal plane that intersects the pyramid above its base. Describe the cross section that would be formed.

Quick Review

A **composite figure** is the combination of two or more geometric shapes. The surface area of a two- and a three-dimensional composite figure will be the sum of the areas of all the shapes, or faces.

Example

The figure shows the plan for a kitchen countertop. What is the area of the countertop?

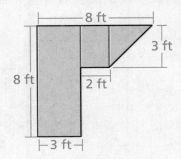

$(3 \cdot 8) + (3 \cdot 2) + \frac{1}{2}(3 \cdot 3) = 24 + 6 + 4.5 = 34.5$

The area of the countertop is 34.5 ft².

Practice

1. Kara wants to paint the four outside walls of her dog's house. She will not paint the roof or the door on the front of the house. What is the area of the surface that Kara needs to paint?

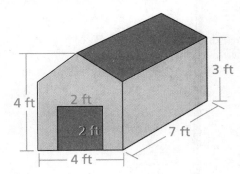

Quick Review

You can find the volume, *V*, of a prism using the formula $V = Bh$. In this formula, *B* represents the area of the base of the prism and *h* represents the height of the prism. Volume is measured in cubic units.

If the volume of a prism is known, you may be able to use this formula to find an unknown dimension of the prism. You also can use this formula to solve problems involving volumes of composite figures that are made up of two or more prisms.

Example

Rhonda received a package in a box shaped like a rectangular prism. What is the volume of the box?

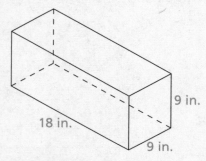

Find the area of the rectangular base.

$A = 9(18) = 162$ in.²

Find the volume of the prism.

$V = Bh$

$V = 162(9)$

$V = 1,458$ in.³

Practice

1. Holly has a gift box that is shaped like a regular hexagonal prism. What is the volume of the box?

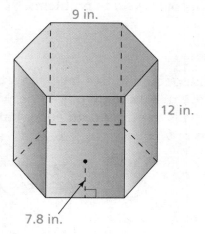

2. A designer is planning a trail mix box that is shaped like a rectangular prism. The front of the box must have the width and height shown. The volume of the box must be 162 cubic inches. What must be the depth, *d*, of the box?

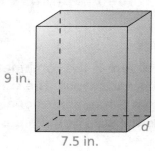

3. A building that is used for storage has the dimensions shown. What is the volume of the building?

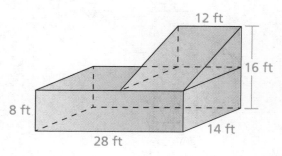

Pathfinder

Shade a path from START to FINISH. Follow the answers to the problems so that each answer is greater than the one before. You can only move up, down, right, or left.

I can...
use the percent equation to solve problems. © 7.RP.A.3

START

Amy deposits $360 in an account that pays 1.2% simple annual interest. How much interest will she earn in 6 years?

Nat opened an account that earns 1.4% simple annual interest. He will earn $21 total interest after 3 years. How much did he deposit when he opened the account?

An account is opened with an initial balance of $950 and a simple annual interest rate of 1.6%. What is the balance after 5 years?

Ilsa withdraws $300 from an account that had a balance of $1,000. How much interest will she earn on the remaining balance at a simple annual interest rate of 1.8% over 3 years?

Jacey gets a $500 loan at a simple annual interest rate of 5%. She will pay back the loan in equal monthly payments over one year. How much is each payment?

Travis has $1,500 in a savings account. He deposits $75. How much interest will he earn after 2 years at a simple annual interest rate of 1.3%?

Pablo saves $85 per month for 6 months. Then he deposits the money in an account that earns 2.1% simple annual interest. How much interest will he earn over 4 years?

Cam borrows $1,000 from her bank. She will pay back the loan at a simple annual interest rate of 4% over 4 years. How much will she pay back altogether?

Hank deposits money in an account that pays 1.5% simple annual interest. He earns $50.25 interest in the first year. How much money did he deposit?

FINISH

ACKNOWLEDGEMENTS

Photographs

CVR: GLYPHstock/Shutterstock, Akugasahagy/Shutterstock, Primopiano/Shutterstock, Smach2003/Shutterstock, AlexZaitsev/Shutterstock; **257:** bluebay214/Fotolia; **258** (BCR) Adam Stoltman/Corbis News/Corbis, (BR) yossarian6/Fotolia, (C) Reynold Mainse/Perspectives/Design Pics Inc/Alamy Stock Photo, (CL) mbongo/Fotolia, (L) rimglow/Fotolia, (TCL) photomelon/Fotolia, (TL) biosdi/Fotolia, (TR) lucian coman/123RF; **261** (T) Marina Rich/Shutterstock (B) Anna Jurkovska/Shutterstock; **262** (T) Markus Pfaff/Shutterstock (B) Digidreamgrafix/Shutterstock; **263** (Bkgrd) StarJumper/Fotolia, (C) kosmos111/Fotolia, (TC) shutswis/Fotolia, (TL) Chris Brignell/Fotolia, (TR) Eric Isselée/Fotolia; **264:** kosmos111/Fotolia; **271:** doomu/Fotolia; **274:** Ezume Images/Fotolia; **275:** Worachat Sodsri/Shutterstock; **283** (TC) michaeljung/Fotolia, (TCR) operafotografica/Fotolia, (TL) Brilt/Fotolia, (TR) blackzheep/Fotolia; **284:** Cherkas/Fotolia; **289:** Jenner/Fotolia; **293:** Don Farrall/DigitalVision/Getty Images; **299** (BCL) Gitusik/Fotolia, (BL) Lvonne Wierink/Fotolia, (TL) homydesign/Fotolia, (TR) Feng Yu/Fotolia; **300** (TCR) triling/Fotolia, (TR) Denys Rudyi/Fotolia; **305** (TC) Antonioguillem/Fotolia, (TL) lucadp/Fotolia; **306:** Michaeljung/Fotolia; **309:** littlestocker/Fotolia; **315:** RapidEye/iStock/Getty Images Plus/Getty Images; **317; 353:** Diane Keys/Fotolia; **318** (BCR) yossarian6/Fotolia, (BR) Pink Badger/Fotolia, (CL) Taras Livyy/Fotolia, (CR) Fotimmz/Fotolia, (TR) Aurielaki/Fotolia; **321** (T) Dragon Images/Shutterstock (B) Wanphen Chawarung/Shutterstock; **322** (T) Reisegraf.ch/Shutterstock (B) Stockphotofan1/Shutterstock; **323:** Michael Chamberlin/Fotolia; **325** (CR) Sergei Poromov/iStock/Getty Images, (TL) David_franklin/Fotolia; **326** (C) Africa Studio/Fotolia, (TC) Elisanth/Fotolia, (TR) Sorapop Udomsri/Shutterstock; **328** (BCR) Africa Studio/Fotolia, (BR) nikkytok/Fotolia; **330:** Denys Rudyi/Fotolia; **331:** Photoestelar/Fotolia; **332** (TCR) Marta Jonina/Fotolia, (TR) Pixelrobot/Fotolia; **336** (BCR) Guschenkova/Shutterstock, (BR) Jayzynism/Fotolia; **337:** niki2die4/Fotolia; **341** (CL) Neonshot/Fotolia, (TC) Marzanna Syncerz/Fotolia, (TCL) Blend Images/Shutterstock, (TL) Tolgatezcan/Fotolia, (TR) Monkey Business/Fotolia, CREATISTA/Shutterstock, Andy Dean Photography/Shutterstock, Atikinka/Shutterstock, Dean Drobot/Shutterstock; **343** (CR) Brian Jackson/Fotolia, (R) RedDaxLuma/Fotolia; **347:** Westend61/Getty Images; **348:** Auremar/Shutterstock; **349:** Monkey Business/Fotolia; **350** (C) Isantilli/Shutterstock, (CR) David_franklin/Fotolia; **351** (BR): MicroOne/Shutterstock; **363:** Anton Bryksin/Fotolia; **364** (BC) jo/Fotolia, (BCR) yossarian6/Fotolia, (BR) Photobank/Fotolia, (CR) flownaksala/Fotolia, (T) pomogayev/Fotolia, (TCR) booka/Fotolia, (TL) pomogayev/Fotolia; **367** (T) Christopher Boswell/Shutterstock (B) Nidvoray/Shutterstock; **368** (T) Shift Drive/Shutterstock (B) Khakimullin Aleksandr/Shutterstock; **369** (C) Montego6/Fotolia, (CL) Natalia Merzlyakova/Fotolia, (TL) freeskyline/Fotolia; **372** (CR) Alis Photo/Fotolia, (TC) Sam Spiro/Fotolia, (TL) Grum_l/Fotolia, (TR) Chris Hill/Fotolia; **375** (Bkgrd) Sergey Nivens/Shutterstock, (C) Sascha Burkard/Fotolia; **381** (TL): Fotokostic/Shutterstock; (BR) VectorTimes/Shutterstock; **383:** Jipen/Fotolia; **387:** Kozini/Fotolia; **399** (CL) Windu/Fotolia, (CR) Dmytro Sandratskyi/Fotolia, (TC) Indigolotos/Fotolia, (TL) Olga Kovalenko/Fotolia, (TR) BillionPhotos.com/Fotolia; **400** (TC) Konstantin Sutyagin/Fotolia, (TR) Lisa F. Young/Fotolia; **401** (C): Maddrat/Fotolia; **403** (CL) trinetuzun/Fotolia, (TCL) Sarawutk/Fotolia, (TCR) Jenifoto/Fotolia, (TR) Kimberly Reinick/Fotolia; **405:** Fotomek/Fotolia; **406** (TR): James Steidl/Shutterstock; **413:** James Peragine/Shutterstock, Iconic Bestiary/Shutterstock; **423:** Ryan Burke/DigitalVision Vectors/Getty Images; **426:** Images-USA/Alamy Stock Photo; **427:** Aboikis/Fotolia; **428** (BCR) yossarian6/Fotolia, (BR) connel_design/Fotolia, (CL) frenta/Fotolia, (CR) Gstudio Group/Fotolia, (TL) Andrew Kazmierski/Fotolia, (TR) lermannika/Fotolia; **429** (T) Darryl Brooks/Shutterstock (B) Luca Santilli/Shutterstock; **430** (T) Wes Lund/Shutterstock (B) Markus Gann/Shutterstock; **433** (TL) Dell/Fotolia, (TR) Travnikovstudio/Fotolia; **438:** Adisorn Chaisan/Shutterstock; **439** (C) Westend61/Getty Images, (CR) Lisa F. Young/Shutterstock; **447:** Sergii Moscaliuk/Fotolia; **445** (CR): Lucy Liu/Shutterstock; **446:** John Lund/Blend Images/Getty Images; **457:** Blueringmedia/Fotolia; **459** (CL) Yurakp/Fotolia, (TL) IuneWind/Fotolia; **460** (BR) Piai/Fotolia, (TR) Christian Mueller/Shutterstock; **462:** Konstantinos Moraiti/Fotolia; **463:** ifrpilot/Fotolia; **468** (B): SkyLine/Fotolia; **469** (CR) Denys Rudyi/Fotolia, (TCR) Cherezoff/Shutterstock, (TR) Kues/Shutterstock; **470:** Macrolink/Fotolia; **472:** Xijian/iStock/Getty Images; **477** (C) Miro Novak/Shutterstock, (CL) Soulart/Shutterstock, (TC) Axpitel/Fotolia; **481** (BCL) Nortongo/Fotolia, (CL) Pbnew/Fotolia; **483** (C) Rukanoga/Fotolia, (C) Rukanoga/Fotolia, (TL) Uros Petrovic/Fotolia; **488** (TCL) Darezare/Fotolia, (TL) Evdayan/Fotolia; **493** (BC) Galina Barskaya/Shutterstock, (BL) andersphoto/Fotolia; **494:** Joel_420/Shutterstock; Cunico/Fotolia; leungchopan/Shutterstock; donatas1205/Fotolia; Dule964/Fotolia; Elisanth/Fotolia; Ilya Akinshin/Fotolia; Mbruxelle/Fotolia; Th3fisa/Fotolia; yossarian6/Fotolia; Željko Radojko/Fotolia.